Guide to Madagascar

Chameleon

Guide to Madagascar

Hilary Bradt

BRADT PUBLICATIONS, UK
HUNTER PUBLISHING, USA

First published in 1988 by Bradt Publications, 41 Nortoft Road, Chalfont St.Peter, Bucks, SL9 0LA, England. Distributed in the U.S.A. by Hunter Publishing Inc., 300 Rariton Center Parkway, CN94, Edison, NJ 08818.

Second printing with corrections, November 1988

British Library Cataloguing in Publication Data
Guide to Madagascar.
　1.Madagascar – Visitors' guides
　916.9'1045

ISBN 0-946983-18-6

Maps by Hans van Well.
Photos and line drawings by the author, unless otherwise stated.
Cover photos. Front: female black lemur (Nosy Komba), Betsimisaraka girl, east coast. Back: Camoran wedding guest, Nosy Be.

Phototypeset from authors disk by Saxon Printing Ltd., Derby.
Printed and bound in Great Britain by
A. Wheaton and Company Ltd, Exeter, Devon.

THE AUTHOR

Hilary Bradt has visited Madagascar six times since 1976, both as an independent traveller and as a tour leader for an American company. Between times she runs Bradt Publications, writes articles, and leads trips in South America and East Africa.

THE CONTRIBUTORS

Sally Crook (*Village life in the South, the Sarimanok Expedition, Sambatra*).
The only woman on the 8-crew *Sarimanok* Expedition, Sally Crook is a nutritionist who has worked for the VSO in West Africa and travelled widely, and solo, in Madagascar. She took part in the Ankarana Expedition led by Jane Wilson.

Dick Byrne (*Nocturnal lemurs*, etc).
A lecturer at St Andrews University, Dick researches and teaches primate behaviour.

David Curl (Miscellaneous practical information and natural history).
A zoologist, writer and wildlife photographer, David's most recent visit to Madagascar was on behalf of the Jersey Wildlife Preservation Trust.

Gordon and Merlin Munday (*Flora, Man and Nature*).
A retired physicist/medical practioner team, the Mundays have a strong interest in conservation and botany, specialising in succulents and tropical vegetation.

Alison Richard (*Conservation*).A professor of Anthropology at Yale University, Alison Richard is one of Madagascar's leading conservationists. Her work in the field includes the new reserve of Beza Mahafaly in the south, and overseeing student studies in the east.

Damien Tunnacliffe (Highlands information).
A former resident of Madagascar, Damien has made several return trips as a tour leader. He is the publisher of Mervyn Brown's *Madagascar Rediscovered*.

Jane Wilson (Health)
A medical doctor with a degree in natural sciences, Jane Wilson has organised expeditions to many parts of the world. Her two expeditions to Madagascar (1981 and 1986) were to Ankarana. In addition to studies on the natural history of the reserve, Jane investigated Bilharzia in the surrounding villages.

ACKNOWLEDGEMENTS

No one person can thoroughly know a country as large and rich in interest as Madagascar, and I have made much use of information supplied by residents, naturalists and other specialists in their fields. For background information my grateful thanks go to Sir Mervyn Brown, former British Ambassador to Madagascar, whose book *Madagascar Rediscovered* was the source of the history sections. Alison Jolly's *A World Like our Own* gave inspiration and information on natural history, and John Mack, of the Musuem of Mankind, provided valuable help and corrections on the pages dealing with traditional practices (and ran a knowledgable eye over the history pieces). The author of *A Glance at Madagascar* (who wishes to remain anonymous) shared his wealth of miscellaneous knowledge acquired during 30-odd years of residence in Madagascar, and provided vital last-minute practical information.

Other travellers and naturalists were generous and thorough in their tips and comments on *The No Frills Guide to Madagascar* which preceded this book. Thank you to Dick Byrne, Sally Crook, David Curl, S. and E. Garnett, Bob Gillam, Oenone Hammersley, Olivier Langrand, Jytte Arnfred Larson, Patrick Marks, Shiela O'Connor, and Harry Sutherland-Hawes.

Major contributors of specialised sections are listed under *Contributors*.

For corrections incorporated into this updated edition (Nov. 1988) I am very grateful to Damien Tunnacliffe, Jean Marie de La Beaujardiers, the Rev. J.Hardiman, and Sir Mervyn Brown. The following readers provided new information: Damien Tunnacliffe, John R.Jones, Alan Hickling, Simon Hale, Ted Jackson, Julian Tennant, and Raniero Leto. Without their help I could not have kept abreast of the many changes in Madagascar. Heartfelt thanks to all.

Tantely tapa-bata ka ny foko no entiko mameno azy.
This is only half a pot of honey but my heart fills it up (used when a gift is deemed inadequate).

PERSPECTIVES ON MADAGASCAR

"[Madagascar is] the chiefest paradise this day upon earth."
Richard Boothby, 1630.

"I could not but endeavour to dissuade others from undergoing the miseries that will follow the persons of such as adventure themselves for Madagascar ... from which place, God divert the residence and adventures of all good men."
Powle Waldegrave, 1649.

Madagascar is my favourite country. My love affair has lasted over ten years and like any lover I am fulsome in my praise and intolerant of any criticism of my beloved. That this view is not shared by everyone is brought home to me from time to time as I lead parties of tourists round the island. It's been easy to dismiss such visitors as 'culturally unaware' or 'unsuitable' but a letter from a very experienced traveller has given me pause for thought. Bob writes: 'I find this difficult to say because I know Madagascar is your favourite country and it's not mine... I have been unhappy here and the good bits barely compensated..: I expected too much, I was wetting myself in anticipation which is a sure recipe for disappointment. I wanted to see everything and found it hard to accept the set-backs of ill-health and wonky transport... We looked forward to Madagascar's unique culture. I suppose it's not blatant enough for me. I need to be hit in the face with garish temples, outrageous costumes, bizarre practices. I agree toying with Grandad's bones is pretty bizarre but what chance has a tourist like me of seeing a *famadihana*?... My overriding impression of Malagasy society is of a people dragged into the 20th Century who are doing their best to drop out of it again. The air of decrepitude and decline was not quaint for me – it mingled with my own frustrations to make me sad or angry. Wasted potential; a people who deserved better.' Bob goes on to give some excellent (and enthusiastic) travel information (incorporated into the book) and rounds off with 'Whatever I say about Madagascar, I'll never forget a tiny Bourneville-and-lime tree frog, a Uroplatus gaping at me, and the Indris wailing'.

Bob's favourite country is India, and perhaps the fact that I haven't visited this sub-continent has made me over-impressed with the touch of Asia that is Madagascar. Perhaps my first rapture over Madagascar in 1976, coming as I did from two years in Africa, was also influenced by its contrast with the familiar African cultures. But no one can rationalise a love. For me it doesn't fade despite all the frustrations – and I should recall that the most ghastly travel experience of my life was in

Madagascar (see page 153).　　Here are some of the things that give me a thrill every time I return:

The natural history. I have seen spectacular wildlife in many parts of the world, but nothing to equal the surprises of Madagascar's small-scale marvels, such as the Uroplatus, the spiny tenrec, the spiders with their golden webs, the giant millipedes. Nor have I seen any mammals more endearing than lemurs. For the anthropomorphic, gooey brigade, they are winners!

The snorkelling. I have been told disdainfully that the snorkelling around Madagascar could not compare with Tahiti. I wouldn't know (nor did I respect that opinion from a tourist who never left her beach hut to sample the delights of the Indian Ocean). All I can say is that the underwater world around Nosy Tanikely (off Nosy Be) is so wonderful I have difficulty not gasping with delight and drowning.

The beauty of the Malagasy people. I remember last year sitting on a bus and gazing at the faces around me as though I were in an art gallery. I never get tired of their infinite variety. That it is combined with friendliness and courtesy is an added pleasure.

The tragic drama of Madagascar seen from the air. Erosion has caused great red fissures in the overgrazed hillsides. From a plane these terracotta fingers clawing the soft green landscape are beautiful, as are the emerald green rectangles of rice paddies in the valleys and stacked like tiles up the mountainsides.

Antananarivo. Surely the most attractive capital of any Third World country – a multicoloured tumble of buildings behind the white umbrellas of the *Zoma* or Friday market. And is there any better market anywhere? The colour, the variety of goods and the relative lack of sales-pressure make it very special.

The food. Not everyone agrees, but for me the abundance of sea food – oysters, lobster and shrimp – and the good French and Chinese cooking in the larger towns more than compensate for the mounds of sticky rice and tough meat that is normal rural fare. Nor does a wonderful meal have to be expensive: an old and grumbling Chinese proprietor of a ramshackle hotel on the east coast cooked the most memorable duck I have ever tasted. He turned it into three courses, which two of us shared, not being able to afford two times $5.

Now for the negative aspects, which irritate or depress all visitors, and are the last straw for some:

The towns. Apart from Antananarivo, there are no really attractive Malagasy towns. All are shabby, few have any buildings of note.

There are exceptions, of course, but even places like Antsirabe and Ambositra, which come as a pleasant surprise for those still coming to terms with the likes of Tulear, are only adequately agreeable.

Road transport. Trains are marvellous (I was tempted to put them in the first gushing list) but there are only two lines. For those who cannot afford to fly, or prefer not to, road transport is a constant trial. However, roads *are* being improved, surfaced even, so soon these trials may be a thing of the past. Maybe.

Shortages. Another thing that is changing. When I first came to Madagascar you couldn't get butter or cheese for love or money, and a bar of soap could be exchanged for an embroidered blouse representing a week's work. Although there are still shortages of basic items, it is now the lack of spare parts for motor vehicles that cause the biggest problem.

Whether Madagascar will work for you depends on your expectations and interests. Most of all, though, it depends on your sense of wonder. If that is intact, no hardship should prevent you falling in love.

You were quite right: we LOVED it! A fabulous country, I can't wait to get back there. (D.B.)

Houses in Ambositra

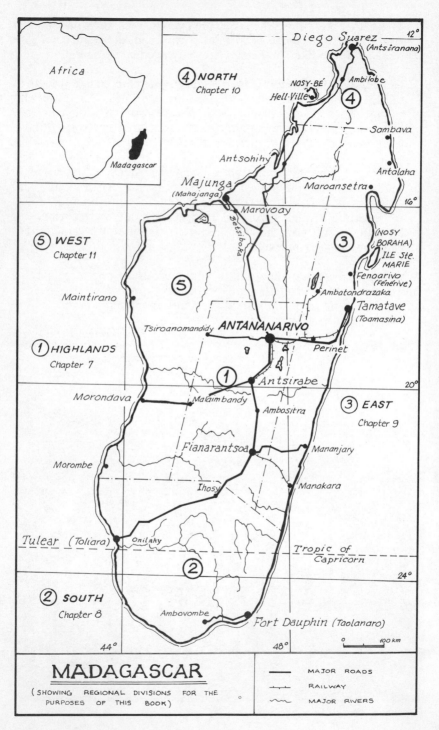

Africa

Madagascar

④ **NORTH**
Chapter 10

Diego Suarez
(Antsiranana)

12°

NOSY-BÉ
Hell-Ville
Ambilobe

④

Sambava

Antsohihy

Antalaha

Majunga
(Mahajanga)

Maroansetra

16°

Marovoay

Betsiboka

③

(NOSY BORAHA)
ILE Ste. MARIE

⑤ **WEST**
Chapter 11

Fenoarivo
(Fénérive)

⑤

Maintirano

Ambatondrazaka

Tamatave
(Toamasina)

Tsiroanomandidy

ANTANANARIVO

① **HIGHLANDS**
Chapter 7

Perinet

20°

①

Antsirabe

Morondava

Malaimbandy

Ambositra

③ **EAST**
Chapter 9

Fianarantsoa

Mananjary

Morombe

Ihosy

Manakara

Tulear (Toliara)

Onilahy

Tropic of Capricorn

24°

②

② **SOUTH**
Chapter 8

Ambovombe

Fort Dauphin (Taolanaro)

44°

48°

0   100 km

MADAGASCAR

(SHOWING REGIONAL DIVISIONS FOR THE PURPOSES OF THIS BOOK)

———— MAJOR ROADS

RAILWAY

MAJOR RIVERS

Contents

PART 1: BACKGROUND INFORMATION

PART 2: MADAGASCAR

Please note: this book was updated in November, 1988. See Addenda at the back.

Chapter 1

The Country

FACTS AND FIGURES

Location

Madagascar, also known as the Malagasy Republic, lies some 250 miles (400 km) off the east coast of Africa, south of the equator. It is crossed by the Tropic of Capricorn near the southern town of Tulear (Toliara). The incredible number of unique species of flora and fauna is due to the island's early separation from the mainland some 160 million years ago, and to the relatively recent arrival of man (around 500 AD).

Size

The world's fourth largest island (after Greenland, New Guinea and Borneo), 1000 miles (1580 km) long by 350 miles (570 km) at its widest point. Madagascar has an area of 227,760 square miles (590,000 square kilometres), two and a half times the size of Great Britain.

Topography

A chain of mountains runs like a spine down the east-centre of the island descending sharply to the Indian Ocean, leaving only a narrow coastal plain. These eastern mountain slopes bear the remains of the dense rain forest which once covered all of the eastern section of the island. The western plain is wider and the climate drier, supporting forests of deciduous trees and acres of savanna grassland. Madagascar's highest mountain is Tsaratanana (9450 ft – 2880 m), in the north of the island.In the south is the 'spiny desert'.

History

First sighted by Europeans, the Portuguese, in 1500, but there were Arab settlements from about the 9th century. The name Madagascar comes from Marco Polo, who described (from other travellers' imaginative accounts) a land where a giant bird, the Roc, picked up elephants with ease. United under one Malagasy monarch from the early 19th century, a time of British influence through the London Missionary Society. Became a French colony in 1896 and gained independence in 1960.

Government

A Democratic Republic practising its own brand of Christian-Marxism. President Didier Ratsiraka assumed power in 1975 and was re-elected in 1982 for a further seven year term. Early in 1988 the Prime Minister, Colonel Désiré Rakotoarijaona resigned for health reasons and was replaced by Lieutenant Colonel Victor Ramahatra.

Population

The people of Madagascar, the Malagasy, are of Afro-Indonesian origin, divided into 18 'tribes' or groups. Other races include Indian/Pakistani, Chinese, and European. The population numbers approximately eleven million, over 60% of whom are under the age of 20.

Language

The first language is Malagasy, which has strong Indonesian elements. French is widely spoken in towns, and is the language of business. Some English is spoken in the capital and major tourist areas.

Place names

Since independence some towns bearing Colonial names have been renamed. Although they bear their new names on maps and pamphlets most people – including Air Madagascar – call them by the old ones and so have I: (old name first) Fort Dauphin = Taolañaro, Tulear = Toliara, Perinet = Andasibe, Île Sainte Marie = Nosy Boraha, Diego Suarez = Antseranana. Antananarivo is often shortened to Tana.

Religion

Christianity is the dominant organised religion, with the Catholic church slightly stronger than other denominations. Islam and Hinduism are also practised, but to the majority of Malagasy their own unique form of ancestor worship is the most important influence in their lives.

Economy

Madagascar withdrew from the French Franc Zone in 1973 and set up its own central bank. It is a mainly agricultural country, exporting coffee, cloves and vanilla, along with some minerals. In the World Bank statistics of 1984, assessing poverty by Gross National Product per head of population, Madagascar came 183rd out of 203 countries.

Currency

The Malagasy Franc (FMG). In March, 1988, the rate of exchange was: US$1 = 1,400 FMG; £1 = 2,300 FMG.

Climate

A tropical climate with rain falling in the hottest season – coinciding with the northern hemisphere winter. The amount of rainfall varies greatly by region, falling almost daily on the east coast (averaging 140 inches – 355 cm – annually in the wettest area) but only on an average of 51 days of the year (12 inches or 30 cm) in the arid south. Hot and humid near the coast, temperatures can drop to freezing in Tana (4100ft, 1250 m) and close to freezing in the extreme south during the coldest month of June.

Flora and fauna

A naturalist's paradise, most of the island's plants and animals are unique. 80% of the native plants are endemic, all of the mammals (excluding those introduced recently), half of the birds, and well over 90% of the reptiles. Much of this 'living laboratory' has yet to be scientifically classified.

Scientific classification

Since many animals and plants in Madagascar have yet to be given English names, I have made much use of the Latin, or scientific name. For those not familiar with these and the associated terminology, here is a brief guide:

Having been separated into broad **classes** like mammals (mammalia), angiosperms (angiospermae) – flowering plants – etc., animals and plants are narrowed down into an **order**, such as Primates or Monocotyledons. The next division is **family**: Lemur (*Lemuridae*) and Orchid (*Orchidaceae*) continue the examples above. These are the general names that everyone knows, and you are quite safe to say 'in the lemur family' or 'a type of orchid'. There are also sub-families, such as the 'true lemurs' and 'the indri sub-family' which includes sifakas. Then come **genera** (**genus** in singular) followed by **species**, and the Latin names here will be less familiar-sounding. It is these two names that are combined in the scientific name precisely to identify the animal or plant. So *Lemur catta* and *Angraecum susquipedale* are recognisable whatever the nationality of the person you are talking to. We call them ring-tailed lemur and comet orchid, the French say maki and orchidée comète. With a scientific name up your sleeve there is no confusion.

King Andrianampoinimerina (1745-1810. From a contemporary painting).

A BRIEF HISTORY

Note: A more detailed regional history is given at the beginning of each chapter in Part 2.

The island was reached by the Portuguese in 1500, but hostility from the natives and disease prevented early attempts by Europeans to settle in Madagascar. Hence a remarkably homogeneous and united country was able to develop under its own rulers.

The first monarch to unite Madagascar was King Radama I who reigned from 1810 to 1828. Before then most regions had their own rulers, and empires rose and fell under monarchs with unpronounceable names such as Andrianalimbe, Andrianiveniarivo and Ratsimilaho (the son of an English pirate) who controlled much of the east coast. The powerful Merina kingdom was forged by Andrianampoinimerina (be thankful that this was a shortened version of his full name: Andrianampoinimerinandriantsimitoviaminandriampanjaka!) in 1794 when the various highland clans were conquered and united. It was his son who became Radama I and fulfilled his father's command to 'take the sea as frontier for your kingdom'. This king had a friendly relationship with the European powers, particularly Britain, and in 1817 and 1820 Britain signed treaties recognising Madagascar as an independent state.

To further strengthen ties between the two countries, the British Governor of Mauritius, which had recently been siezed from the French, encouraged King Radama I to invite the London Missionary Society to send teachers. They were later followed by a number of craftsmen and the LMS had a strong influence in Madagascar during this period, culminating in the development of a written language using the Roman alphabet.

The next monarch was Queen Ranavalona I who ruled for 33 years and is remembered for her rejection of European influences which included Christianity. The missionaries, who had done so much for the country, were driven out and many Christians massacred. This Queen initiated the first squabbles with England and France and during this time (1841) France took possession of the island of Nosy Be.

It was during Queen Ranavalona's reign that an extraordinary Frenchman arrived in Madagagascar: Jean Laborde, who single-handedly introduced the island to many aspects of Western technology (see Box).

After Queen Ranavalona came King Radama II, a peace-loving and pro-European monarch. He didn't last long, being assassinated after a two-year reign. The monarchy was now in decline and power shifted to the prime minister. This man, rather scandalously, married the Queen but was overthrown by a brother who continued the tradition by marrying three successive queens and exercising all the power. During this period (1863 – 1896) the monarchs (in title only) were Queen Rasoherina, Queen Ranavalona II, and – the last one – Queen

Ranavalona III.

In 1883 France (after some provocation) attacked Madagascar and proclaimed it a protectorate – but not without a struggle; the war lasted 30 months. Britain, which previously had had designs on Madagascar, settled for Zanzibar instead (the Convention of Zanzibar, 1890) and recognised the French protectorate. Inevitably France demanded more than the terms set out in the original treaty. War broke out in 1895 and by the end of the year power was fully in French hands. Madagascar became a colony in 1896, under the first Governor-General, Joseph Simon Galliéni. An able and relatively benign administrator, Galliéni set out to break the power of the Merina aristocracy and remove the British influence by banning the teaching of English. French became the official language. The monarchy continued, but with no power, and was finally abolished in 1897 when Queen Ranavalona III was exiled. There followed various insurrections, often put down very bloodily, and the spirit of nationalism grew. One French effort to quench the flames of independence was to eliminate references to the French revolution in school history books. The first world war saw 46,000 Malagasy recruited for the allies and over 2000 killed. Those that returned were now trained fighting men and resistance to Colonial rule took on a more organised aspect. Madagascar was occupied during the Second World War by British (and other allied) troops, and unrest increased, with rural populations losing their allegiance to their French District Officers. In 1947 came a major rebellion and an estimated 80,000 Malagasies were killed, many by Senegalese troops attached to the French Foreign Legion. The rebellion was finally suppressed a year later, after the bloodiest episode in Madagascar's history.

The Malagasy Republic was created in 1958, an autonomous but not independent state. Independence was granted by France in 1960.

The first president, Tsiranana, was pro-French and capitalist. In 1972 student and worker strikes, harshly suppressed, led to the assumption of power by General Ramanantsoa, head of the army, though Tsiranana remained President. However, after a referendum he stepped down.

In the rising tide of socialism Ramanantsoa resigned in January 1975, handing over to the Minister of the Interior, Richard Ratsimandrava, who was assassinated a week later. A military junta stepped in, quashed an uprising, and in June 1975 Didier Ratsiraka, a naval captain, assumed power. President Ratsiraka embarked on a Malagasy brand of socialism and was re-elected for a further seven year term in 1982.

CLIMATE

Madagascar has a tropical climate divided into rainy and dry seasons. South-east trade winds drop their moisture on the eastern mountain slopes and blow hot and dry in the west. North and northwest 'monsoon' air currents bring heavy rain in summer, decreasing southward so that the rainfall in Fort Dauphin is half that of Tamatave. There are also considerable variations of temperature dictated by altitude and latitude. On the solstice of December 22 the sun is directly over the Tropic of Capricorn, and the weather is warm. Conversely, June is the coolest month.

As was noted in *Facts and figures* rainfall varies enormously, but the rainy season is relatively consistent with some regional variations: the dry season is from April to October, and the rainy season from November to March.

The east of Madagascar frequently suffers from cyclones during February and March and these may hit other areas, particularly in the north. Majunga suffered severe damage when cyclone *Kamisy* struck in April 1984, as did Diego Suarez; Tamatave was flooded a metre deep and poor Île Sainte Marie, whose flimsy buildings bear the brunt of frequent cyclones, suffered devastating damage.

Average midday temperatures in the dry season are 77° F (25° C) on the *hauts plateaux* and 86° F (30° C) on the coast. These statistics are misleading, however, since in June the night-time temperature can drop to freezing in Tana and close to freezing in the southern desert, and the hot season is usually tempered by cool breezes on the coast.

The following chart and map give easy reference to the driest and wettest months and regions.

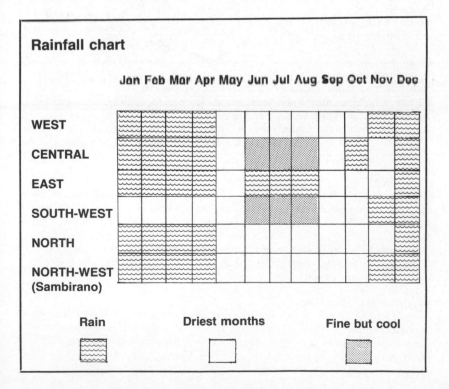

Climatic regions

West

Rainfall decreases from north to south.
Variation in day/night winter temperatures
increases from north to south.
Average number of dry months: 7 or 8.
Highest average annual rainfall within zone
(major town): Majunga, 152 cm.
Lowest: Tulear, 36 cm.

Central

Temperatures and rainfall
influenced by altitude. Day/
night temperatures in
Antananarivo vary 14° C. A
few days of rain in October are
known as *pluie des mangues* or
'mango rains' when that fruit is
ripening. The main rainy
season starts end of November.
Average number of dry
months: 7.
Highest average annual rainfall
within zone (major town):
Antsirabe, 140 cm.
Lowest recorded temperature:
− 8° C in Antsirabe

East

In the north and central areas there are no months (or weeks) entirely without
rain, but drier, more settled weather prevails in the south.
Reasonably dry months: May, September, October, November.
Possible months: April, December, January.
Impossible months (torrential rain and cyclones): February, March.
Highest average annual rainfall within zone (major town): Maroansetra 410 cm.
Lowest: Fort Dauphin, 152 cm.

Southwest

The driest part of Madagascar. The extreme west may receive only 5 cm of rain
in a year, with precipitation increasing to around 34 cm in the east.

North

This could be included with the East zone were it not for the dry climate of the
Diego Suarez region, which receives only 92 cm per year, during a long and
fairly reliable dry season.

North-west (Sambirano)

Dominated by the country's highest mountain, Tsaratanana, this region
includes the island of Nosy Be and has a micro-climate with frequent heavy rain
alternating with clear skies. Nosy Be gets an average of 203 cm a year on 175
days.

Chapter 2

The People

THE MALAGASY PEOPLE TODAY
Origins

Most accounts agree that the first people in Madagascar arrived about 1,500 years ago from Indonesia/Malaya and eventually settled in the highlands of the hitherto uninhabited island. The African races who later populated the lowlands had possibly already been colonized and absorbed by Indonesians in East Africa – a speculation based on the fact that their language is the same as the highlanders (derived from Indonesian) with only elements of Swahili and Bantu languages.

In *Madagascar, Island of the Ancestors* John Mack suggests that it is unlikely that a significant population could develop from such long-distance mariners – the journey is across at least 6,400 kilometres of open ocean – and gives credence to the East Africa colony theory. The Merina people of the highlands of Madagascar retain remarkably Indonesian characteristics and are thought to have arrived 500 – 600 years ago, but a 1985 Indian Ocean 'Kon-tiki' expedition set out to test the possibility that at least some Malagasy could have arrived much earlier, and by the direct route. The *Sarimanok*, a replica of the double-outrigger canoe used by the South-east Asians of the period the migrations may have taken place, reached Madagascar in 65 days after an eventful and dangerous voyage (see next page).

Beliefs and customs

The Afro-Asian origin of the Malagasy has produced a people with complicated and fascinating customs. Despite the various tribes or clans the country shares a common language and belief in the power of dead ancestors (*razana*). This cult of the dead, far from being a morbid preoccupation, is a celebration of life since the dead ancestors are considered to be potent forces that continue to share in family life. If they are remembered by the living, the Malagasy believe, they thrive in the spirit world and can be relied on to look after the living in a host of different ways.

The Malagasy believe in one God, *Andriamanitra* (which, interestingly, is also one of their words for silk, the material of shrouds) and Creator (*Zanahary*). This probably accounts for their ready acceptance of Christianity which is not at odds with their traditional

THE SARIMANOK EXPEDITION
By Sally Crook

The *Sarimanok* is a 60 foot double outrigger canoe constructed on the initiative and under the direction of Bob Hobman, a New Zealander, on the Philippine island of Tawi Tawi in the Sulu Sea, near to Borneo.

His intention was to construct a vessel of the kind that would have been used by the ancient island South-east Asians (linguistically closest to the people of modern Borneo) for their migrations to Madagascar, and to sail it directly across the Indian Ocean rather than following the coasts of India, Arabia and Africa. This safer coastal route is the one championed by most historians. Hobman, impressed by the courage and sailing prowess of modern day Indonesians, wanted to show that a traditional vessel made entirely of wood and bamboo, held together by rattan bindings with no contribution from metal nails, and propelled by wind in palm-weave sails, could weather the open ocean for long enough to reach Madagascar without other landfalls.

The food type, preservation techniques and cooking methods were also to be like those of 2500 years ago – the era in which he believes the migrations took place, though most consider the first millenium A.D. a more likely period – and the navigation was to be by readings of the positions of sun and stars.

The 'shakedown' voyage in 1984 from the Philippines to Bali was not performed with all the traditional elements, and an outboard motor had to be used to push against the wind. The voyage was eventful, however, with several stops on the coast of Sulawesi, Borneo and Java for repairs. Then Chico Hansen died of hepatitis shortly after the port town of Surabaya, Java, was reached. The loss was devastating to the crew, but preparations and improvements to the boat design continued the next year, and on 3rd June, 1985, the *Sarimanok*, now without motor, radio or sextant, set off across the Indian Ocean to be driven to Madagascar by the south-east trade winds.

Apart from a stop on the Cocos (Keeling) Islands to let off a sick member of the crew (eight men and one woman), the navigator, Bill McGrath, guided the vessel through high seas and unseasonal frequent rain directly to Diego Suarez on the northern tip of Madagascar. (An Argos satellite tracking device confirmed the accuracy of his calculation of the boat's position throughout the voyage to the tracking station in Toulouse, though the information was not accessible to the *Sarimanok* crew.)

Lack of help to land the unwieldy vessel resulted in the boat sailing on to Mayotte, the French island off the Comores where it was towed ashore. The *Sarimanok* finally landed at Nosy Be on 5th September 1985 to a warm welcome from the local people who were proud that their history had been relived by this seven week crossing of the Indian Ocean, and that the possibility that their revered ancestors had taken this more difficult and dangerous route had been vindicated. The *Sarimanok* is now installed at Andilana Beach, Nosy Be.

beliefs – the concept of resurrection is not so far from their veneration of ancestors. These ancestors wield enormous power, their 'wishes' dictating the behaviour of the family or community. Their property is respected, so great-grandfather's field may not be sold or changed to a different crop. Calamities are usually blamed on the anger of *razana*, and a zebu bull may be sacrificed in appeasement. Huge herds of zebu cattle are kept as a 'bank' of potential sacrificial offerings. As well as appeasing the ancestors, a sacrifice will do much to allay bad luck, as was demonstrated by the sacrifice of a zebu bull at the inaugural flight of Air Madagascar's first jumbo jet. The airline has an excellent safety record!

Fady

The dictates of the *razana* are obeyed in a complicated network of *fady* or taboos. These vary from family to family and community to community, and even from person to person. Perhaps the eating of pork is *fady*, or the killing of lemurs (most useful for conservation!). In Imerina it is *fady* to hand an egg directly to another person – it must first be put on the ground. Many villages have a *fady* against working in the rice-fields on Tuesdays and Thursdays, or consider it *fady* to dig a grave with a spade that does not have a loose handle since it is dangerous to have too firm a connection between the living and the dead. Other examples of regional *fady* are given in the *Ethnic groups* section.

Vintana

Along with *fady* goes an even more complex sense of destiny called *vintana*. Broadly speaking, *vintana* is to do with time – hours of the day, days of the week, etc, and *fady* involves actions or behaviour. Each day has its own *vintana* associated with a colour which makes it good or bad for certain festivals or activities.

The origin of *vintana* is the Arab-introduced lunar calendar, and this 'force of destiny' is believed to move round a house according to the phases of the moon. Houses are traditionally built north-south with their entrance on the west, and the first month of the year is the north east corner (sunrise). This is where special artifacts associated with the ancestors would be stored. People will be careful to move round their houses in the same direction as the *vintana* (clockwise) even if it means taking the long way round to enter the door.

In some respects *vintana* can be compared with astrology in that a person's destiny is tied up with the day and hour he or she was born; couples of opposing *vintana*, for instance, should not marry.

Healers and sorcerers

The Malagasy have a deep knowledge of herbal medicine and all markets display a variety of healing plants and artifacts. In large towns this is simply the 'chemist's shop' but in rural areas it will be presided over by the *ombiasy* or divine healer. As the name (*olona-be-hasina* –

person of much virtue) implies, their power is good. They do not just dispense herbal drugs but evoke the power of the ancestors to help effect a cure. In some areas they are also soothsayers. There are also witch doctors with an intimate knowledge of poison. These are the *mpamorika*.

Sorcerers are *mpisikidy* who use amulets, stones, and beads (*ody*) for their cures.

Mpanandro is an astrologer who has an intimate understanding of the vintana, and is thus a highly respected and sometimes feared member of a village. It is he who decrees the most auspicious day and time for family celebrations or major activities, such as *famadihana* (see below) or laying the foundations of a new house. He may also be at hand during a *tromba* – a trance-like state – to act as a medium for the ancestors.

After death
Burial, second burial, and 'bone turning' is an extremely important part of the Malagasy culture. Death is, after all, the most important part of a Malagasy's life, when he abandons his mortal form to become a much more powerful and significant ancestor. Burial practices among the different tribes are detailed in the *Ethnic groups* section and in regional chapters in Part 2.

Whatever method of burial is used, all tribes consider the fresh or decomposing body polluted, and must purify themselves with water after contact with it or its possessions. Objects laid on a tomb are there because they are polluted, and in some cases the house of the deceased is burnt down to prevent contamination. John Mack (*Madagascar: Island of the Ancestors*) reports one case of hospital patients burning all the bedding and medical equipment in the ward when someone died.

Bones, devoid of flesh, are the material presence of the ancestor, and the tomb his house. Exhumation is thus the logical way to collect these bones.

The southern tribes, who do not go in for second burial, carve commemorative wooden stelae, often depicting important scenes from the life of the deceased, and the tombs themselves are more elaborate and better built than any house in the area. A prodigous number of zebus will be killed for a rich man's funeral; 50 is not unusual.

In the highlands, among the Merina, *famadihana* (pronounced 'famad<u>ee</u>an') is still practised. The 'turning of the bones' ceremony is a time of great rejoicing, when the remains of a dead relative are wrapped in a fresh shroud (*lamba mena*) and paraded round the village before being returned to the family tomb. The corpse is treated as though it were alive – spoken to, shown new developments in the town and involved in the feasting.

The occasion for *famadihana* may be because an ancestor died elsewhere and his remains are being returned to the family tomb, or because a new tomb has been built, or because the *razana* decreed it was time for an outing (perhaps in a dream).

This is a family occasion in every way; the living relatives are gathered together (and will have contributed to the considerable cost of the *famadihana* feast) and the ancestors are grouped companionably together on their shelves in the tomb, thus increasing their power.

Famadihana is not just the custom of rural or more traditional Malagasy. Jane Wilson was lucky enough to be invited to a bone turning ceremony on the outskirts of Tana by a sophisticated and devoutly Christian family. She describes it below:

> When we arrived it looked as though the party had already been going on for some hours. We were given a drink and told to wait in the courtyard since the bones would soon be turned. There was a lot of activity in and around the tomb, and soon a group of six men came out carrying our hostess's great uncle. His bones, dusty and dry, were now held together in a polythene bag, the old *lamba mena* having disintegrated long ago. They brought him to a special shelter, wrapped him in a vastly expensive, beautifully embroidered new white *lamba mena* (*mena* means red, but the burial shroud is not always red) and laid him in the midst of the guests. Above his body hung a photograph of the man in his youth: with a waxed moustache and in the straw boater and fashionable clothes of the 1920s. The bones of his wife joined him on the little sheltered table and so did those of another relative.
>
> As a Catholic girls school choir began to sing, I studied the incongruous scene. There were around 200 guests, the men in their Sunday best and the women with their long, straight hair plaited into the traditional oval bun. They wore smart European clothes with fine embroidered *lambas* draped around their shoulders. A priest said some prayers and preached a short sermon before the Protestant girls choir took over, their faces glowing with pleasure as they harmonised.
>
> After the priest and choristers had dispersed our host showed us a room entirely filled with the butchered carcasses of perhaps 30 zebu cattle – there was going to be quite a feast! The bands were setting up their guitars and drums on the temporary stage and soon the room was throbbing with the sounds of rock music and everyone was disco dancing.
>
> Then I noticed that several more bodies were surreptitiously being taken out, quickly whisked around the tomb the required seven times (which makes it harder for death to re-emerge) and returned to their resting places. What was going on? The explanation was that the government taxes these *famadihana* parties according to the number of bodies turned. Our hosts were officially turning three ancestors and pulling a tax fiddle on the others. Or were they just pulling my leg!
>
> When we took our leave our hostess told us the party would continue for two or three days. 'But isn't it primitive?' she said.

Educated Malagasy may claim to be free of *fady* or other superstitions but it is quite likely that their lives are affected by these ancient traditions and beliefs, even if only by a sensitivity to the beliefs of older members of the family.

I have only touched on traditional Malagasy customs here. For more information you should read the entertaining and informative *Glance at Madagascar* and *Madagascar, Island of the Ancestors* (see *Bibliography*).

Ethnic groups

This section is mainly taken from 'A Glance at Madagascar' by kind permission of the author.

The Malagasy form one nation with one basic culture and language (though with many dialects), but there are eighteen different 'tribes' officially recognised by the government. This division is based more upon old 'kingdoms' than upon ethnic grouping. These tribes are listed individually below.

Antaifasy (People-of-the-sands)
Living in the south-east around Farafangana they cultivate rice, and fish in the lakes and rivers. Divided into three clans each with its own 'king' they generally have stricter moral codes than some tribes. They have large collective burial houses known as *kibory*, built of wood or stone and generally hidden in the forest away from the village.

Antaimoro (People-of-the-coast)
They are among the most recent arrivals and live in the south-east around Vohipeno and Manakara. They guard Islam tradition and Arab influence and still use a form of Arab writing known as *sorabe*. They use verses of the Koran as amulets. Their caste system includes 'untouchables'.

Antaisaka
Centred south of Farafangana on the south-east coast but now fairly widely spread throughout the island, they are an off-shoot of the Sakalava tribe. They cultivate coffee, bananas and rice – but only the women harvest the rice. There are strong marriage taboos amongst them. Often the houses may have a second door on the east side which is only used for taking out a corpse. They use the *kibory*, communal burial house, the corpse usually being dried out for two or three years before finally being put there.

Antankarana (Those-of-the-rocks)
Living in the north-west around Diego-Suarez they come from the Sakalava dynasty and are fishers or cattle raisers. Their houses are usually raised on stilts. Numerous *fady* exist amongst them governing relations between the sexes in the family, e.g. a girl may not wash her brother's clothes. The legs of a fowl are the father's portion, whereas amongst the Merina, for instance, they are given to the children.

Antambahoaka (Those-of-the-people)
The smallest tribe, of the same origin as the Antaimora, but with no caste system, and living around Mananjary on the south-east coast. They have some Arab traits and amulets are used. They bury in a *kibory*. Circumcision ceremonies are carried out every seven years (see page 161).

Antandroy (People-of-the-thorns)
They are mainly nomadic and live in the arid south around Ambovombe. A dark-skinned people, they wear little clothing and are frank and open, easily roused to either joy or anger. Their women occupy an inferior position. The villages are often surrounded by a hedge of cactus plants. They do not eat much rice but subsist mostly on millet, maize and cassava. They believe in the

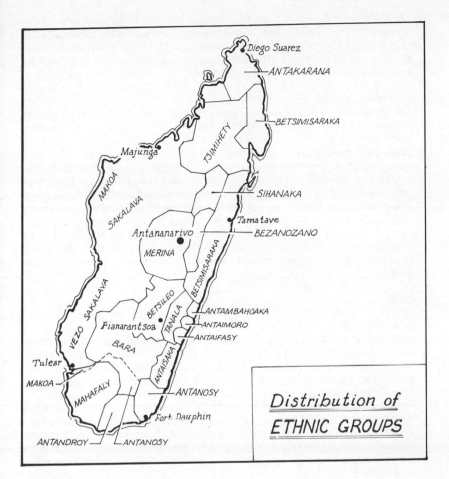

Distribution of ETHNIC GROUPS

THE VAZIMBA

Vazimba is the name given to the early or original occupants of Madagascar. There are two theories about the origin of these people: they made their way over from the east coast of Africa, or they were survivors of an earlier Malayo-Polynesian immigration before the waves of people that arrived after them.

Vazimba come into both legends and history of the Malagasy. Undoubtedly they existed, and were absorbed by subsequent groups rather than killed. Vazimba tombs are now places of pilgrimage where sacrifices are made for favours and cures. It is *fady* to step over such a tomb. Vazimba are also thought to haunt certain springs and rocks, and offerings may be made here. They are the ancestral guardians of the soil.

kokolampo – a spirit of either good or bad influence. Their tombs are similar to those of the Mahafaly tribe. Sometimes it is *fady* among them for a child to say his father's name, or to refer by name to parts of his father's body. Thus he may say *ni fandiany* (the-what-he-moves-with) for his feet; and *ny amboniny* (the-top-of-him) for his head.

Antanosy (People-of-the-island)

The island is a small one in the Fanjahira river. They live in the south-east and south-west principally around Fort-Dauphin. Their social structure is based on clans with a 'king' holding great authority over each clan. Many of them have emigrated to Rèunion and Mauritius. There are strict *fady* governing relationships in the family. For example, a brother may not sit on or step over his sister's mat. As with many other tribes there are numerous *fady* regarding pregnancy. A pregnant woman should not sit in the doorway of the house; she should not eat brains; she should not converse with men; people who have no children should not stay in her house overnight. Other *fady* are that relatives should not eat meat at a funeral and the diggers opening a tomb should not wear clothes. When digging holes for the corner posts of a new house it may be *fady* to stand up – and so one must sit down to do it.

Bara

Originally in the south-west near Tulear, they now live in the south central area around Ihosy and Betroka. Their name has no special meaning but it is reputed to derive from Bantu. They are nomadic and cattle raisers. They may be polygamous and women occupy an inferior position in their society. They attach importance to the *fatidra* or 'blood pact'. Cattle stealing is regarded as proof of manhood and courage, without which a man cannot expect to get a wife. So he must steal a few head of cattle before he can hope to get married! They are dancers and sculptors, a unique feature of their carved wooden figures being eyelashes of real hair set into the wood. They believe in the *helo* – a spirit that manifests itself at the foot of trees. Sometimes a whole village may move after somebody dies owing to the fear of ghosts. They use caves in the mountains for burial. It is the custom to shave the head on the death of a near relative.

Betsileo (The-many-invincible)

They are centred in the south of the High Plateau around Fianarantsoa but about 150,000 of them also live in the Betsiboka region. They are energetic and experts in the irrigation of terraced rice-fields. The soil is often prepared by chasing zebu cattle round and round to break the clods and soften it – a muddy, sticky job, but it is evidently great fun for the participants. The rice seedlings are planted by hand, the women being the experts at this work. The *famadihana* was introduced amongst them by the Merina at the time of Queen Ranavalona I. It is *fady* for the husband of a pregnant woman to wear a lamba thrown over his shoulder. It may be *fady* for the family to eat until the father is present or for anyone to pick up his fork until the most honourable person present has started to eat.

Betsimisaraka (The-many-inseparables)

They are the second largest tribe and live on the east coast in the Tamatave – Antalaha region. They have known some ancient European influence from pirates, etc. They cultivate rice and work on vanilla plantations. Their clothes are sometimes made from locally woven raffia. Originally their society included numerous local chiefs but they are not now important. The *Tangalamena* is the local official for religious rites and customs. They believe in *angatra* – ghosts; in *zazavavy an-drano* – mermaids; and in the *kalamoro* – which are little wild men of the woods, about 25 inches high with long flowing hair, who like to slip into houses and steal rice from the cooking pot. In the north coffins are generally placed under a shelter, in the south in tombs. Among the Betsimisaraka it may be *fady* for a brother to shake hands with his sister, or for a young man to wear shoes while his father is still living.

Bezanozano (Many-small-plaits)
The name refers to the way in which they do their hair. They were probably one of the first tribes to arrive, and live in an area between the Betsimisaraka lowlands and the Merina highlands. The *famadihana* is practised among them. As with most of the coastal tribes their funeral celebrations involve the consumption of considerable quantities of *toaka* – rum.

Mahafaly (Those-who-make-taboos or Those-who-make-happy)
The etymology of the word is sometimes disputed but the former meaning is generally regarded as being correct. One of the least known tribes, they probably arrived about the 12th Century, and live in the south west desert area around Ampanihy and Ejeda. They are farmers, with maize, sorgho and sweet potatoes as their chief crops; cattle rearing occupies a secondary place. They kept their independence under their own local chiefs until the French occupation and still keep the bones of some of their old chiefs – this is the *jiny* cult. Their villages usually have a sacrificial post, the *hazo manga*, on the east of the village where sacrifices are made on various occasions. Some of the blood is generally put on the foreheads of the people attending.

The tombs of the Mahafaly always attract a great deal of interest. They are big rectangular constructions of uncut stone rising some three feet above the ground and decorated with *aloalo* and the horns of the cattle slain at the funeral feast. The tomb of the Mahafaly king Tsiampody has the horns of 700 zebu on it. The *aloalo* are sculpted wooden posts set upright on the tomb, often depicting scenes from the person's life. The burial customs include waiting for the decomposition of the body before it is placed in the tomb. It is the practice for a person to be given a new name after death – generally beginning with 'Andria'.

The divorce rate is very high and it is not at all uncommon for a man to divorce and remarry six or seven times. It is very often *fady* for children to sleep in the same house as their parents. Their *rombo* (very similar to the *tromba* of other tribes) is the practice of contacting various spirits in order to obtain a cure for the sick. Amongst the spirits believed in are the *raza* who are not real ancestors and in some cases are even supposed to include *vazaha* (foreigners), and the *vorom-be* which is the spirit of a big bird.

Makoa
Spread along the north-west region many have moved south to the area of the Onilahy river. Descended from African slaves they are the most primitive tribe and the only true African negroid type in Madagascar.

Merina (People-of-the-Highlands)
They live on the High Plateau, which is the most developed area of the

Aloalo *on a Mahafaly tomb.*

country, the capital being 95% Merina population. Approximately 175,000 of them live outside the province of Antananarivo. They are of Malayo-Polynesian origin and vary in colour from ivory to very dark, the women usually having long straight hair. They used to be divided into three castes – the *Andriana* (nobles), the *Hova* (free-men) and the *Andevo* (serfs) – and these were again sub-divided. In law these castes and divisions no longer exist. Most Merina houses are built of brick or mud, some only one room affairs, but the better ones are two storey where the people live mostly upstairs. Most villages of any size have a church – probably two, Catholic and Protestant. There is much rice cultivation by irrigation. The Merina were the first tribe to have any skill in architecture and metallurgy. The *famadihana* is essentially a Merina custom.

Sakalava (People-of-the-long-valleys)
They live in the west between Tulear and Majunga and are dark skinned with Polynesian features and short curly hair. They were at one time the largest and most powerful tribe but could not unite properly amongst themselves. They were ruled by their own kings and queens and certain relics remain – sometimes being kept in the north-east corner of a house. They are cattle raisers, and riches are reckoned by the number of cattle owned. There is a record of human sacrifice amongst them up to the year 1850 at some special occasion such as the death of a king. The *tromba* (trance state) is quite common. It is *fady* for pregnant women to eat fish or to sit in a doorway. Women hold a more important place amongst them than in most other tribes.

Sihanaka (People-of-the-swamps)
They live in the north-east of the old kingdom of Imerina around Lake Alaotra and have much in common with the Merina. They are fishers, rice growers and poultry raisers. Swamps have been drained to make vast rice-fields cultivated with modern machinery and methods. They have a special rotation of *fady* days.

Tanala (People-of-the-forest)
They live in the forest inland from Manakara, and are rice and coffee growers. They immigrated about 250 years ago and are the most recent tribe to arrive. Their houses are usually built on stilts. They are divided into two groups – the Ikongo in the south and the Menabe in the north. The Ikongo are an independent people and never submitted to Merina domination in contrast to the Menabe. Burial customs include keeping the corpse for up to a month. Coffins are made from large trees to which sacrifices are sometimes made when they are cut down. The Ikongo usually bury in the forest and may mark a tree to show the spot.

Tsimihety (Those-who-do-not-cut-their-hair)
They refused to cut their hair to show mourning on the death of a Sakalava king in order to demonstrate their independence. They are an energetic and vigorous people in the north central area and are spreading west. Amongst them the eldest maternal uncle occupies an important position. The most famous member of the tribe is Philibert Tsiranana – the first President of the Malagasy Republic.

These are the eighteen officially recognised tribes. Other groups or clans include:

Vezo

They are not generally recognised as a separate tribe but as a clan of the Sakalava. They live on the coast in the region of Morondava in the west to Faux Cap in the south. They are not rice cultivators but fishers. They use little out-rigger canoes hollowed out from tree trunks and fitted with one outrigger pole and a small rectangular sail. In these frail but stable craft they go far out to sea. The Vezo are also noted for their tombs which are generally well-hidden, some good examples being near Belo and Morondava. They are graves dug into the ground surrounded by wooden palisades the main posts of which are crowned by wooden carved figures of the most erotic kind. No effort is made to keep them in repair as it is only when the palisades finally fall into decay and ruin that the soul of the dead is fully released.

Zafimaniry

A clan of about 15,000 distributed in about 100 villages between the Betsileo and Tanala south-east of Ambositra. It is a forest area and they are known for their wood carvings and sculpture. They are descendants of people from the High Plateau who went there early in the 19th Century and form an important historic group as they continue the forms of housing and decoration of past centuries. Their houses, which are made from vegetable fibres and wood with bamboo walls and roofs, have no nails and can be taken down and moved from one village to another.

St Marians

The population of Île St Marie (Nosy Boraha) is mixed. Although Indonesian in origin there has been influence from both Arabs and pirates of different nationalities.

The tribes may differ in various ways but, as usual, the Malagasy have suitable proverbs. *Tsihy be lambanana ny ambanilanitra* – 'All who live under the sun are plaited together like one big mat'; *Ny olombelona toy ny molo-bilany, ka iray mihodidina ihany* – 'Men are like the lip of the cooking-pot which forms just one circle.'

Village life

The Malagasy have a strong sense of community which influences their way of life. Just as the ancestors are laid in a communal tomb, so their descendants share a communal way of life, and even children are almost considered common property within their extended family (*fianakaviana*).

The village community is based on the traditional *fokonolona*, or council of elders, and it is they who make decisions on the day to day life of the village.

Rural Malagasy houses generally have only one room and the furniture is composed of mats (*tsihy*), often beautifully woven. These are used for sitting and sleeping.

Part of the Malagasy culture is the art of oratory, *Kabary*. Even rural leaders can speak for hours, using highly ornate language and many proverbs. In a society that reached a high degree of sophistication without a written language, *kabary* had an important communicative role to play and it was through *kabary* that the early Merina kings inspired and controlled their people.

The description below by Sally Crook, will give you further insights into life in a southern village.

VILLAGE LIFE IN THE SOUTH
by Sally Crook

I was warmly welcomed into the Tandroy (Antandroy) village and soon found that visiting all the houses in the family compound was the purpose of life. Children went from one house to another and ate, talked, played or crawled onto a mat to sleep. All houses are home to them and it was difficult to work out the complex family structure, multiple marriages and frequent divorces resulting in aunts playing with nephews and nieces older than them, and divorcees greeting their husband's current wives.

Children do not have a family name but belong to the father and even the shaven-headed widow who lived with her three young children would have to give them up to a brother-in-law as soon as she married elsewhere.

Most Malagasy men seem to be orators and my arrival and departure brought forth semi formal speeches from Tokoembelo, the head of the compound. Talking among the men also resolves disputes and resolves problems. The divorce of a 17 year old girl from an unworthy husband was a long standing difficulty, and the feud with a neighbouring village suspected of stealing their goats was another which occupied the older men of the compound.

My lack of the language did not exempt me from the visiting circuit and I began at the house of Imaria, the younger current wife of Tokoembelo, who had invited me to watch her weave a mat from start to finish. My presence in her mat-lined house for a couple of hours each day allowed me to sit in on the chats and arguments of women and children who visited her. My efforts at conversation elicited smiles of encouragement or gales of laughter. I soon learnt key words and could guess the gist of the question since everyone was curious on the same points. The key word method was not foolproof, however, and a stunned silence, then guffaws of laughter followed any glaring errors. The women loved to tease me over my frequent *vazaha*-style use of the word for thankyou, *misaotra*, which is unnecessary among family members.

The children played the universal games of children without toys, a boisterous game of wheelbarrows ending with a tangled heap of children giggling on the ground. They sat around me whenever I read on a mat outside, or crowded around my door to look in.

'*Aiza taratasy misy ombiasa, Shallee?*' This was a request for the book with the picture of the soothsayer on the front and they would turn over pages poring over the pictures of familiar things.

My *sarintany* ('earth picture', or map) was often requested too and the children, most of whom could not read, would point with arms or lips in the direction of the villages or rivers I named from the local map since they knew their area well from walking through it, in company or alone, from a very early age. Lack of schooling and TV left them alert and questioning and I could not look upon it as a misfortune.

Malagasy give directions using the points of the compass and do not talk of right or left. I found this easy enough to follow in the compound since the rectangular houses are aligned with one door on the west and two on the north; sitting one day in my hut with a young visitor looking for page numbers in a book he suddenly exclaimed, 'There they are, to the east!' and they were.

When Tokoembelo's first wife, Talilie, had been wooed back by gifts from her father's village where she had returned after an argument, I began to visit her too, as careful as the husband to treat each wife equally. He spent alternate nights with each wife. As in the other homes, I was given *abobo*, curdled milk, from a gourd where it had been left to sour. Custom does not demand that the bowl be emptied but I always finished it because it was so good, and did so quickly because of the vast numbers of flies landing on it, the bane of people living so closely with their livestock.

Cattle are kept as wealth that is hoarded, traded, used to pay dowries, or guarded until the day of their sacrifice for the master's internment when their horns are placed on the tomb. They are rarely eaten on other occasions by this clan, the lowly goat providing meat for our New Year's Eve celebration, which, being a recently embraced foreign festival, is not important. Sparse meals of maize, cassava or sweet potatoes are more usual than the rice-based meals of elsewhere, eaten with *traka* (potato or cassava leaves). It is considered rude to watch people eating and it is prudent to keep hold of your spoon until you've finished, since putting it down results in the dish being whisked away. Eggs are not usually eaten since raising the chicks to adulthood is more sensible.

Keeping cattle is the real work of a Tandroy, but cultivation is necessary for food. Work in the fields takes place in the morning after the cattle have been sorted out and assigned to the children to take out of the cactus-enclosed compound to graze. Wanting to try everything, I went out with the villagers one morning to their far and scattered fields. Tandroy people are proud of their liberty and he who takes the trouble to work a piece of land thereby lays claim to it.

My efforts at weeding – chopping horizontally at the unwanted plant roots with a hoe from a crouched position – were applauded but I was not allowed to do more than five minutes at a time before I was packed off to sit idly in the shade of a tree. I was not too sorry to be stopped since the accidental assassination of the legitimate inhabitants of the plots – maize, groundnut, melons, sweet potatoes and cassava – were too easy in fields planted with three different species together.

Barefoot teenagers and children came by with the cattle, lone herders sometimes singing to themselves at the top of their voices as they kept their charges away from unhedged fields. In the dry season the men set off with their spears (with hoe on one end for digging up roots) and take the zebu far afield for several months at a time to find enough grazing. They bivouac or build huts in a choice area, sometimes settling there permanently, happy to meet up with the Mahafaly to the west but not straying as far north as the Bara who are considered to be cattle thieves.

It was difficult for the family to understand what I considered interesting or unusual and I was called to look on only after a castration had been completed or a calf dropped which was already trying to get up on its weak legs for the first meal at the udder. I watched morning and evening milking in the cow pen. The cow's back legs were held loosely together with rope as she was milked by man and calf at the same time. Women are not allowed to milk into a container and men caught the twice daily half litre of milk in a calabash held in a hand.

Water is a problem even in the wet season. Most stream beds are dry and flow only occasionally when there is a heavy fall of rain on the hills feeding them. I was called down to the river one clear-skied evening to witness the torrent that the river had become from rain falling in the north, only to find next morning it had disappeared leaving newly contoured river banks and a muddy bed with pools of cloudy water stranded on the rocks. Holes are dug in the river bed for water and I was sent with a child who could choose the hole with the cleanest water that day or would dig a new one, the holes getting deeper and deeper until in the late dry season they would have to be several feet deep. My herding and farming companions did not carry water with them but dug a hole in the river bed when we reached it on the way home.

Pinde, cicadas, are caught for food by children in season while they are out herding or playing. These large bugs, whose stridulating makes the air ring in the heat of the day, are easy to locate and are pinned down by a thumb on a wing. I soon learnt to catch them too but did not play with them like the children who seem to have no concept of cruelty to non-human creatures. Divested of wings and legs, they are strung on a long piece of grass before cooking in a dry pot in the evening to make a crunchy, but tasty and nutritious snack. The ubiquitous termite hills are also broken open for chicks to feed on the insects. Creepy-crawlies are found all over the houses, many attracted in by the evening candlelight; and the sound of a large spider rattling its hurrying feet over the mat on which I was trying to sleep, ensured that I slept with a mosquito net each night, in spite of the puzzled enquiries as to why it was needed.

Visits to other compounds of this scattered village, as well as to other villages were also *de rigeur* and were always made with a precious bar of soap since whenever we came to running water in more secluded areas, we would take the opportunity for a proper bath. Honey was the ostensible object of one visit to a neighbouring compound. The split tree trunk hive was opened by an intrepid man brandishing burning grass, and puffing smoke from cigarettes to daze the insects. The owner of the hives claimed to be able to tell how much rain had fallen in his absence by the sweetness of the honey.

People are what matter in life and the old mother of the head man was treated kindly although it was clear she was senile. Mad people or those with epilepsy lived with their relatives and the blind young man from a nearby compound was often to be seen walking alone down the highway of the dry river bed, or picking his way down unknown paths apparently by the echo of his hand clapping from the obstacles in his path.

Old people are revered since they are closest to the ancestors. The most important man of the whole village was the *mpisoro* who makes the zebu sacrifices to the ancestors by the sacred posts in front of his house. I was taken to this man of 95-odd years to pay my respects. We entered his small wooden house through the north-west door, stooping and easing one shoulder in before the other through the tiny opening. The old man wore a traditional loin cloth with patterned edges which younger men sometimes wear over their western shorts. He was almost blind and I was invited to sit close as my visit was explained. He then took my right hand in his, putting his nose to it in a traditional greeting.

Our journey there took us over a scrubby landscape of hardy bushes and plants whose uses were explained to me. Tortoises making their pigeon-toed way over the thorn-strewn earth would suddenly retract into their shells or hiss if we touched them. The compound paths were strewn with ground nut shells as walking on these ensures a good harvest. A stroll across the river bed to another of the scattered village compounds took us to a young man who demonstrated the use of the leather sling that most herders carry over their shoulder, theoretically for self defence, soon gaining in accuracy and force as he sent stone after stone hurtling into a distant tree.

I was unfortunate that there none of the elaborate funerals or other ceremonies while I was there. Bodies left to rot in their former home are removed through a hole broken in the east wall and placed in a massive wall-enclosed tomb, filled with stones and adorned with the horns of sacrificed zebu.

I especially wanted to hear the unique music of the area and on New Year's Day a fiddler and his wife who walk from one ceremony to another to work, came to sing for us. So many people crowded into Talilie's wooden house to hear them that she had to squat outside in the drizzle as the singer sat cross legged on the floor to bow his warped-neck fiddle. His wife used flint and stone to light his cigarettes of tobacco and maize leaf paper or sang almost listlessly beside him. He sang too or provided a song rhythm by a strange rasping breathing like that of a man dying of thirst. I had not heard this harsh sound in the guise of singing before.

Teenagers spend evenings in the river bed when the moon sheds enough light. There the girls sing and drum, and the boys wrestle. I asked the children to sing for me one day and found their style more African than Asian (as are most characteristics of this tribe) consisting of a hard chant without vibrato, often in harmony with others and with drum beat accompaniment. Young children were, as elsewhere, pot-bellied with worms and some had scabies. Frequent hair inspections resulted in the killing of legions of lice.

On Friday nights, before market day in the town a 2 hour walk away, hair was washed and greased with cow fat. Ragged everyday clothes were discarded for the shared market best, and the distance was covered on foot, with a stop to wash feet at the flowing stream near the town. During the three market days of my visit, on only one was there any food to buy but the villagers undertaking the trip that week enjoyed the day chatting in the shade, seeing and being seen before trudging home in the rain.

We waded over a wide flowing river to another, country, market where the 'car park' was full of lounging zebu and the *sarety* (wagons) they had lately been hauling. People socialised under the shade of a large tree or bartered in the market square, and the young men leaned on their long staffs wearing straw hats with colourful knitted bands with small pom-poms dangling over the brim. They acted like men-of-the-world as they eyed the girls before chatting them up.

Morals among this clan of the tribe are what Europeans would call 'loose', and as I sat on the *taxi-brousse* to leave the nearby town for the north, one of the young men of 'my' compound made me a public proposition, which I took from the evident amusement of other passengers to be an 'improper' invitation. It showed how well I had been accepted.

MAN AND NATURE: THE HUMAN PROBLEMS OF CONSERVATION

By Gordon and Merlin Munday

Man must satisfy certain fundamental needs for survival. Most primitively these are fulfilled by hunting and gathering or crop growing for food and barter, pasturing of domesticated animals, fuel for warmth and cooking, materials for shelter, and remedies for alleviating ailments. Man is here interacting with nature and enforcing his demands on the environment; in Madagascar as elsewhere, this along with the population growth, has led to deterioration on a grand scale.

Destruction of habitat with the consequent extinction of animal and plant species is irreversible and we would all wish to see it halted, but a narrowly ecological solution is unacceptable to the hungry and impoverished. So, in looking at Madagascar's problem the outsider should bear in mind the following: it has a population of nearly 11 million with a low population density; 16 inhabitants per square kilometre (compare 25 for the USA and 228 for the UK, according to 1985 United Nations estimates); but a more significant figure is the high population growth rate with a doubling time of 25 years.

Crop Production

It was long believed that forest originally covered the whole island and man, in the fifteen hundred years or so of his presence, was entirely responsible for its destruction and the consequent erosion. More recently another possible cause appears to be that a general extension of a drier climate (cf Sahel in Africa) has adversely affected the already delicate balance of a fragile vegetation, leading to widespread erosion. However all agree that the advent of man practising a shifting agriculture with a slash-and-burn technique (*tavy*) has great responsibility for loss of primary forest. The age-old technique is simple and devastating, forest is cleared of trees, burnt after drying for a few months, then mixed subsistence agriculture undertaken. The land may be used for a year or two before being left fallow, a new area then being cut down and the process repeated. The fallow period is about 10 years but during that time the rains erode and leach the soil on which a degraded vegetation, initially forest (*savoka*) but ultimately grass takes over. It has been estimated that 10 to 15 clearances are possible before the land is spent agriculturally but this picture is over optimistic since the richest and most productive soil is known to be that of virgin land. But the people must be fed. The main crops produced for local use are rice (the dietary mainstay of the population), cassava, sugar cane and sweet potatoes: the most important cash crops are coffee, vanilla and cloves. The government, conscious of certain deficiencies in earlier plans, aims to make the island self sufficient in rice production this year, 1988. Rice yields are low compared with more developed countries, consequently attempts have been and are being made both to increase the yield and put larger areas under cultivation.

Livestock

A significant contributor to the problems of land use is the zebu cattle (ten million; roughly the same as the population). They play a determinant role in most Malagasy lives, even in cultures that are not cattle-based, representing wealth for rural families and an outward sign of well-conducted lives; in short symbolising duty done towards ancestors and much that gives a meaning to existence. Even for rice-based cultures (Merina and Betsileo in the centre, Betsimisaraka, east coast) the zebu is at hand to prepare the paddies, pull carts etc. but its prime function is for sacrifice at the funeral.

In the cattle-based cultures, Mahafaly and Antandroy and much of the western region, where the zebu form the very basis not only of material wealth but aesthetic interest, spiritual beliefs, social structure such as family and kinship ties, and even language, the zebu unites them with ancestors and the hereafter. Large numbers of selected cattle become feast and sacrifice; afterwards the horns are placed on the tomb. Meat is rarely eaten apart from such symbolic meals.

Whilst it is true that zebu are well adapted to the climate, it is a beast that grows and matures slowly (edible yield 330-420 kg after 6-8 years); calf loss is about 32% and average milk yield only one litre per day; a general performance worse than that of other cattle developed in tropical areas. To maintain the cattle requires one hectare per head of pasture and in the dry season they suffer considerably despite great efforts to tide them over. Dry remains of grass are finally fired to hasten regrowth of young sprouts at the first rains; firing which is uncontrolled and often attacks forest edges.

Wood

In the cooler parts of the island people, at least part of the time, need fuel for warmth; everywhere fires are required for cooking (estimated at a little more than one kg of wood per person day). In a country with reputedly very little coal and without foreign currency to buy and equip itself with the products of the modern oil industry, wood is the only practical source of fuel. Should it cause surprise that forests have been cut down to provide wood for fuel? Put into numbers, 80% (1.2 million tonnes of fuel oil equivalent per year) of the total energy consumption in Madagascar goes in firewood: a problem preoccupying governments since the colonial era. Many of the local tree species grow slowly or very slowly, replacement has therefore been by faster growing foreign species, including *Acacia dealbata* and various species of pine and eucalyptus.

Medical

All countries and peoples have over the ages developed remedies from locally available materials for their ailments and disabilities. The study of plants for this purpose is known as ethnobotany. Although the pharmaceutical industry may have refined them, the origin of many useful drugs is the tropical forest rather than laboratory synthesis. It is estimated that one product in four in the pharmaceutical market is derived from wild plants and in 1985 the annual value of these medicines was worth at least £35 billion. The Madagascan Rosy Periwinkle (*Catharanthus roseus*) is the source of many alkaloids two of which are used with success to treat leukaemia: retail worldwide sales of these drugs was worth about $100 million in 1980. As the periwinkles are grown commercially in countries other than Madagascar the Malagasy have made no financial profit. Another species of *Catharanthus* (*C.coriaceus*) is included in the IUCN Plant Red Data Book (1978) as endangered as it is only known in a few localities where the forests in which is grows are threatened with fire; the genus, apart from its botanical interest is of pharmacological importance. Madagascar has a long record of ethnobotanical investigation as is shown by the number of publications in existence; a preliminary database has been compiled by WWF/IUCN. In 1977 the World Health Organisation adopted a resolution at its Assembly urging governments to promote research and interest in traditional medical systems; subsequently a Department of Ethnobotany was established at the National Pharmaceutical Research Centre (Antananarivo). It is hoped that these moves will accelerate the process of finding other plants without depletion of wild sources by over-collection, but lead rather to their being cultivated under supervision.

'People must eat'. Mahafaly children with coucal bird.

The people of Madagascar are known as the Malagasy. Some English-speakers pronounce this as in the French *Malgâche* – Malgash. The French, however, have occasionally allowed the pun of *Malgâche* and *Mal gâché* – badly spoiled – to bring a derogatory slant to the name, so it is better to stick to the English pronunciation.

LANGUAGE

The Indonesian origin of the Malagasy people shows strongly in their language which is spoken, with regional variations of dialect, throughout the island. (Words for domestic animals, however, are derived from Kiswahili, indicating that the early settlers, sensibly enough, did not bring animals with them in their outrigger canoes.) Malagasy is a rich language, full of images and metaphors, and the art of oratory, *kabary*, is an important part of the culture. Literal translations of Malagasy words and phrases are often very poetic. Dusk is *Maizim-bava vilany*, 'Darken the mouth of the cooking pot'; two or three in the morning is *Misafo helika ny kary* – 'When the wild cat washes itself'.

Learning, or even using, the Malagasy language may seem a challenging prospect to the first time visitor. Place names may be fourteen or fifteen characters long (because they usually have a literal meaning, such as Ambohibao, The New Village), with erratic syllables stress. However, it is well worth taking the time to learn a few Malagasy words and phrases. English-speakers should remember that their noble efforts at communicating in French are not much use in villages where it is an equally alien language. If Malagasy seems difficult, thank the London Missionary Society that at least it is not still in Arabic script!

Some basic rules
Pronunciation
The Malagasy alphabet is made up of 21 letters. C, Q, U, W, and X are ommitted. Individual letters are pronounced as follows:

a: as in Father.
e: as in the a in Late.
g: as in Get.
h: almost silent.
i: as ee in Seen.
j: pronounced dz.
o: oo as in Too.
s: usually midway between sh and s but varies according to region.
z: as in Zoo.

Combinations of letters needing different pronunciations are:

ai: like y in My.
ao: like ow in Cow.
eo: pronounced ay-oo.

When k or g are preceded by i or y this vowel is also sounded *after* the consonant. For example *Alika* (dog) is pronounced *Aleekya*, and *Ary koa* (and also) is pronounced *ahreekewa*.

Stressed syllables.

Some syllables are stressed, others almost eliminated. This causes great problems with visitors trying to pronounce place names, and unfortunately – like English – the basic rules are frequently broken. Generally, the stress is on the penultimate syllable except in words ending in na, ka, and tra when it is generally on the last syllable but two. Words ending in e stress that vowel. Occasionally a word with the same spelling changes its meaning according to the stressed syllable, but in this case it is written with an accent. For example, *Tánana* means Hand, and *Tanána* means Town.

When a word ends in a vowel, this final syllable is pronounced so lightly it is often just a stressed last consonant. For instance the Sifaka lemur is pronounced – rudely, but memorably – as 'She-fuck'. Words derived from English, like *Hotely* and *Banky* are pronounced much the same as in English.

Vocabulary

The following basic travellers' vocabulary has kindly been provided by the author of *A Glance at Madagascar* (see *Bibliography*). He has also written an excellent *English – Malagasy Vocabulary* which is available in Antananarivo at the Lutheran Bookshop. This is much better than *An elementary English – Malagasy Dictionary* which is aimed at the Malagasy student of English and gives definitions of English words rather than single-word translations.

A Malagasy phrase book is due to be published by Damien Tunnacliffe (a contributor to this book) in 1988. It will be available from Bradt Publications.

Stressed letters or syllables are underlined.

English	**Malagasy**
Hello/How are you?	*Man__g__o ah__o__ana, T__o__mpoko**.
or,(on the coast)	*Sal__a__ma, T__o__mpoko.*
How is your health?	*Fahasalaman__o__, T__o__mpoko?*

* It is polite with many Malagasy expressions to add the word *Tompoko*, a form of address meaning roughly 'Sir' or 'Madam' but not so formal. A Malagasy will not reply just 'yes' or 'no' but will always add *Tompoko*.

I'm well	*Salama tsara aho.*
Good-bye	*Veloma, Tompoko.*
See you again	*Mandra pihaona.*
Yes	*Eny, Tompoko.*
No	*Tsia, Tompoko.*
Very good	*Tsara tokoa.*
Bad	*Ratsy.*
Thankyou	*Misaotra, Tompoko*
Excuse me	*Aza fady, Tompoko*
I don't understand	*Tsy azoko, Tompoko*
Give me...	*Mba omeo ... aho.*
I want...	*Mila ... aho.*
I'm looking for...	*Mitady ... aho.*
How much?...	*Hoatrinona?.*
Is there a place to sleep?	*Misy ve toerana hatoriana?*
I would like to buy some food/a meal	*Te hividy hanina/sakafo aho.*
Where is ...?	*Aiza ...?*
Is it far?	*Lavitra ve izany?*
Is there any ...?	*Misy ve ...?*
Please help me!	*Mba ampio aho!*
What's your name?	*Iza no anaranao.*
I'm hungry	*Noana aho.*
I'm thirsty	*Mangetaheta aho.*
I'm tired	*Vizaka aho.*
Village	*Vohitra.*
Countryside/Out in the country	*Ambanivohitra.*
House	*Trano.*
Food	*Hanina (Safako – meal)*
Water	*Rano.*
Rice	*Vary.*
Eggs	*Atody.*
Chicken	*Akoho.*
Bread	*Mofo*
(European-type bread	*Mofo-dipaina).*
Milk	*Ronono*
(Tinned milk	*Nestle).*
Road	*Lalana.*
Town	*Tanana.*
Newspaper	*Gazety*
Paper	*Taratasy.*
Hill	*Tendrombohitra.*
Valley	*Lohasaha.*
River (large)	*Ony.*
Stream	*Riaka.*
Ox/cow	*Omby/Omby vavy.*
Child/baby	*Ankizy/zaza kely.*
Man/woman	*Lehilahy/Vehivavy.*

Chapter 3

Natural History

INTRODUCTION

For many people it is the flora and fauna of Madagascar that make this island continent so fascinating. Unlike other parts of the world with unique wildlife, Madagascar has hitherto received little exposure from the media so its weird and wonderful creatures are all the more astonishing.

The reason so many unique species evolved in Madagascar goes back to the dawn of history. It is thought that in the early Cretaceous era a huge land mass known as Gondwanaland began to break up and form the present continents of Africa and Madagascar, Asia, South America, and Australasia. The phenomenon of continental drift explains why some Malagasy plants and animals are found in South America and Asia but not Africa. The boa constrictor, for instance, occurs only in South America and Madagascar, and the urania moth and six plant families are also limited to these two places.

Madagascar broke away from Africa as much as 160 million years ago, when mammals were at a very early stage of evolution, so it is probable that the early lemurs, fossas and tenrecs were carried across the then narrower Mozambique channel on uprooted trees or rafts of vegetation. Once the channel widened, they had little need for evolutionary change since there were no large carnivores to threaten their existence and the thickly forested island provided food without competition. Thus the term 'living fossil' is appropriate here.

Man, however, arrived somewhere around the fifth century (although there is some speculation that it may have been considerably earlier) and quickly exterminated the largest animals. Up to that time eleven giant species of lemur swung through the branches or browsed on the forest floor; some were the size of gorillas. There were giant tortoises bigger than any today, and – largest of all – the *aepyornis*, or elephant bird, which stood ten feet high. Man was probably responsible for the extinction of all these animals, either by direct hunting or – more likely – by destroying their habitat.

Conservation has now become a government priority to halt the destruction of forests (reduced by half since 1950) which threatens Madagascar's amazing percentages of unique species: of the flora, 90% of all forest species are endemic (found only here); there are six unique families of plants. The eastern hardwood forests have 97 varieties of

The rukh (roc), as visualised by an artist in 1595.

Elephant bird (Aepiornis) egg (in comparison with a hen's egg), Berenty museum. (Photo: Olivier Langrand.)

ebony; six species of baobab flourish (there's only one in Africa); all but two of the 130 palm species are unique. Eight genera of fish are found only here; Madagascar contains two-thirds of the world's chameleons, and 225 of the 235 reptile species are endemic. There are 155 species of frog; apart from a few recently introduced animals all the land mammals are endemic: 34 genera and 66 species.

Geology

The main geological features of Madagascar are a precambrian basement (eastern two thirds of the island), overlaid with laterite, a sedimentary region along the west coast, and volcanic (mainly upper Cretaceous) outcrops.

There are no active volcanoes in Madagascar, but the Itasy region of the highlands shows craters and ashcones, and many hot springs.

Minerals mined include mica and titanium, but not in commercial quantities. Madagascar has an amazingly large number of mineral deposits, but none are large enough to add to the national wealth. The crystaline rock basement produces a fine variety of gemstones, sold in the market and near the places of origin. They include: petrified wood, rhodonite, agate, marble, labradorite (moonstone), amazonite and ammonite. There are many kinds of crystals (sometimes available in block or geode form) including quartz: smoky, rose, citrine, along with haematite, amethyst, celestite, and tourmaline. A beryl unique to Madagascar is the pink morganite.

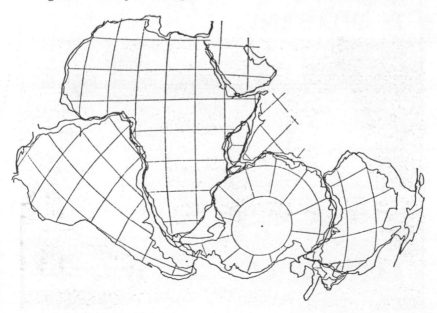

GONDWANALAND AND THE FIT OF THE SOUTHERN CONTINENTS

THE DRONGO

One of the most recognisable birds in Madagascar is the drongo. Unmistakable in silhouette, with its deeply forked tail and silly crest, it is ubiquitous and fearless, and is said to be an excellent mimic. For the villagers near Maroansetra it is *fady* to kill a drongo. Here's why:

Centuries ago the pirates who raided the east coast made incursions into the hills to pillage and take captives. At the warning that a pirate band was on its way the villagers would flee into the jungle.

One day in Ambinanetelo word came that a pirate band was approaching. The people scattered, but the women with young children could not keep up with the others and hid in a thicket. Just as the pirates were passing them a baby wailed. The pirates spun around and approached the source of the cry. They heard the baby again, but this time the cry came from the top of a tree. It was a drongo. Believing themselves duped by a bird, the pirates gave up and returned to their boats. And the drongo has been honoured in this valley ever since.

FLORA

The account below is extracted from a more detailed survey of the island's flora, kindly written by Gordon and Merlin Munday. Botanists may order a full copy from Bradt Publications.

Introduction

You may be surprised to discover that you already know a few Madagascan plants – many house or florists plants come from Madagascar. These include 'Crown of Thorns' (*Euphorbia millii*), with its bright red flowers and sharp spines, 'Flaming Katy' (*Kalanchoe blossfeldiana*) with brilliant red and long lasting flowers, 'Panda Plant' (*Kalachoe tomentosa*), 'Madagascan Dragon Tree' (*Dracaena marginata*), 'Madagascan Jasmine' (*Stephanotis floribunda*) – the bridal bouquet with waxy, white, heavily scented flowers, the 'Polka dot' plant (*Hypoestis phyllostachya*), and 'Velvet Leaf' (*Kalanchoe beharensis*).

Few of Madagascar's many unique species have been given English names, but one Malagasy plant name has made its way into English: raffia. The palm *raphia ruffia* grows in swampy ground to the west and has been a mainstay for craft workers and gardeners all over the world.

Estimates of the number of species of flora in Madagascar range from 7,370 to 12,000, making it one one of the richest botanical areas in the world. Of about 400 flowering plant families worldwide almost 200 are known to occur in Madagascar. There are eight endemic families and 18% of the genera and nearly 80% of the species are also endemic.

FLORA OF MADAGASCAR (Vascular Plants)

(After F.White, 1983: The Vegetation of Africa (UNESCO/AETFAT/UNSO)

	Species (endemic %)	Genera (endemic %)	Families (endemic)	Species in common
Eastern region	6100 (4800:79%)	1000 (160: 16%)		
Western region	2400 (1900:79%)	700 (140: 20%)		600
Madagascar (total)	8500 (6700:79%)	1700 (300: 18%)	190 (8)	
Comparable figures for the British Isles (including casuals)				
Britain	1750	611	133	

Evidence suggests that primitive flowering plants (Angiosperms) originated in the western part of Gondwanaland, probably in the early Cretaceous period, and that subsequently they spread north while diversifying, leading to the establishment of flora in the two large supercontinents. Africa has many genera in common with Madagascar, but individual species are quite distinct. For example, of the 300 African aloe species, not one is identical to the 60 found in Madagascar, and the

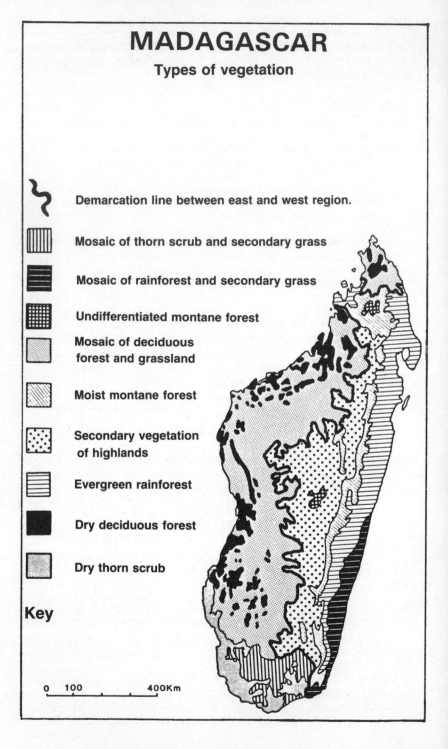

MADAGASCAR
Types of vegetation

Key

Demarcation line between east and west region.

Mosaic of thorn scrub and secondary grass

Mosaic of rainforest and secondary grass

Undifferentiated montane forest

Mosaic of deciduous forest and grassland

Moist montane forest

Secondary vegetation of highlands

Evergreen rainforest

Dry deciduous forest

Dry thorn scrub

0   100   400Km

'succulent' euphorbias are here more woody than succulent. Africa has only a few hundred species of orchid, whilst Madagascar claims around a thousand. Nevertheless, many plants such as the African violet (*Viola abyssinica*) and *Cardamine africana* are widely distributed and identical in both places. Mangroves, as one would expect of water disseminated plants, are all identical with those found on the East African coast, whereas Madagascar's endemic palms – 13 genera – almost all show affinities with those of Asia and South America.

Regional flora and vegetation

The island's vegetation falls naturally into two regions: east and west (see map). These are further divided into domains, giving a broad classification in terms of geography, climate and vegetation.

Eastern region

This coincides with the climatic eastern region but includes the Sambirano domain and Nosy Be. The central domain is also included; this is the backbone of the region with erosion creating deep gullies, or *lavaka*. Heavy storms carry away the soil – thin clay over friable sedimentary layers – made vulnerable by tree clearance. Vegetation of the region is classified as evergreen forest, mosaic of rainforest and secondary grass, moist montane forest, secondary vegetation of the highlands, and montane bushland and scrub.

Evergreen forest   Occurs below 800 m. The rainfall is generally over 2,000 mm and in some places up to 3,500 mm. The vegetation is stratified in canopies, and the competition for light resulting in no undergrowth. Many trees have buttress roots or stilt-like aerial roots. Epiphytes, including orchids and ferns, are abundant.

The Madagascan rainforest is distinct from corresponding forests in Africa in having a higher species diversity, a lower main canopy and an absence of large emergent trees. Tree density is also three times greater than comparable rainforests in other continents. Families that form part of the upper canopy include Euphorbiaceae (nearly all with the milky latex sap), Sapindaceae (woody lianas), Rubiaceaae (including wild coffee), Ebenaceae, including the genus *Diospyros* (with 97 species, one of which is the true ebony), and palms.

Tourist-accessible evergreen forest can be seen in Lokobe (Nosy Be), the area round Maroansetra, and Nosy Mangabe.

Île Ste Marie is botanically rewarding. Here you can see the spectacular comet orchid, *Angraecum sesquipedale*. The tubular nectary of this creamy-white flower is 38 cm (15 inches) long. When Charles Darwin was shown the orchid he predicted that a hawkmoth with a 15 inch tongue must exist in Madagascar to fertilise it. Sure enough; the moth is named *praedicta*, and the flower sometimes called Darwin's Orchid. Features of the coastal landscape on the island are large Barringtonia trees on the shoreline, with 'bishop's hat' fruits, and coconut palms leaning into the sea which disseminates their fruit.

Mosaic of rainforest and secondary grass   An outstanding example of a successful indigenous secondary forest tree is the Traveller's Palm (*Ravenala madagascariensis*) the symbol of Madagascar and the logo of Air Madagascar. It gets its name from the relief it affords a thirsty traveller:

water is stored in the base of its leaves and can be released with a panga blow. The fan arrangement of the leaves is extremely decorative. The Ravenala is, in fact, not a palm but is related to the *Strelitzia* or Bird of Paradise flower. It often occurs in combination with Pandanus (screw pine), which is somewhat like a palm, and Typhonodorum, which grows in or by water and has huge spinach-like leaves.

Other indigenous vegetation does less well in competition with introduced grasses, ferns and shrubs which take over after fire. Indigenous forest species able to colonise the edges of cut forests include some useful to man such as *Canarium*, a valuable all-purpose wood and a source of essential oils, *Croton*, from which drugs are derived, and two guavas, *Psiadia altissima* and *Haronga madagascariensis* which is also the source of a valuable drug, Harunganin, used for stomach disorders.

This type of vegetation (unfortunately) can be seen anywhere near inhabited places by the east coast, where the landscape is degraded as a result of fire, and dominated by grass. There are few trees.

Moist montane forest   Generally occurs between 800 m and 1,300 m but can go as high as 2,000 m if the conditions are right. The canopy is about 5 m lower than the lowland forest, and there is more undergrowth, including some temperate genera such as *Labiatae* and *Impatiens*. There are abundant epiphytes, ferns and mosses, and large lianas and bamboo. As the altitude increases, so the height of the canopy decreases, letting in more light and permitting the growth of epiphytes and shrubby, herbaceous undergrowth with an abundance of moss. Leaves become tougher, with a thicker cuticle to help retain water.

Trees at this altitude include *Dalbergia*, rosewood, and *Weinmannia*, a useful light timber; species of palm and tree fern grow in lower areas.

The most accessible example of medium altitude moist montane forest is Perinet (see p. 157). The upland variety can best be seen in Montagne d'Ambre National Park (p. 174). This is an ideal location for aspiring botanists since many of the trees are labelled. High altitude moist montane forest is best shown on the lower slopes of the Maronjejy massif (see p. 153).

Highland vegetation (the central domain)   The forest that formerly covered the *hauts plateaux* has been replaced by grassland. These are relieved by granite outcrops which harbour succulents (Route National 7, between Ambalavao and Ihosy give you good views of such rock formations). These hills are called 'Inselbergs'. *Pachypodium* occur in this environment, with, among others, aloes and euphorbia.

High altitude montane forest   Beginning at 1,300 m and extending to 2,300 m, the vegetation here is shaped by lower, more varied temperatures, wind, sun and rain. The forest resembles tall scrub with small, tough leaves. Moss and lichens clothe branches and cover the ground up to 30 cm, and provide anchorage for epiphytic ferns and orchids. Ericaceous species predominate in the undergrowth.

The massif of Maronjejy provides the best example, along with the botanical reserve of Ambohitantely, 80 km north of Antananarivo.

Tapia forest   This is the local name for the dominant species *Uapaca bojeri*, a tree with a thick, crevassed bark which is very fire resistant. The forest is on the western slopes of the central highlands, with a drier climate than eastern domains. The impenetrable vegetation appears similar to Mediterranean cork oak forests. There are few epiphytes or ground mosses.

Isalo National Park has Tapia groves and also various succulents on its sandstone outcrops.

Montane bushland and thicket   Characterised by a single stratum, up to six metres, of impenetrable branching evergreen woody plants growing above 2,000 m, and interesting for trees belonging to the daisy family (*Compositae*).

None of Madagascar's high mountains are easily accessible. Probably Andringitra (page 119) offers the best possibility.

The western region

Dry deciduous forest   The flora is extensive and varied but of lower density and less rich than in the moister eastern forests. The deciduous trees grow to a height of 12 to 15 m with some emergent trees up to 25 m. There are abundant lianas, and shrubby undergrowth, but no ferns, palms or mosses covering the forest floor, and few orchids.

Dry deciduous forest grow on clay or sandy soil. The latter includes the luxuriant gallery forests along rivers where tamarind trees predominate. Away from water, it is the baobabs that take precedence. A third environment, calcareous plateaux, produces a lower forest canopy with fewer lianas and evergreens. Trees and shrubs with swollen trunks or stems (pachycauly) are much in evidence.

The Forestry Station of Ampijoroa (p.173) is an easily accessible area of dry deciduous forest. Harder to reach, but rewarding when you get there is the reserve of Tsingy de Namorka, which has a dense combination of dry forest, savanna, and plants specially adapted to the pinnacles, or calcareous karst (*tsingy*, which gives the reserve its name.

Deciduous thicket ('spiny desert')   Madagascar's most strikingly unique landscape comes into this category, where Didiereaceae, an endemic family are associated with tree Euphorbias. There are some evergreens here, probably because of sea mists bathing the plants. Heavy morning dews are a boon to the local people who collect the precious water with 'dew ladles'. Thickets vary in height from three to six metres, and with their thorns are impenetrable. Emergent trees are mostly baobab.

Didiereaceae show some resemblance to the Boojum cactus (Fouquieriaceae) of the south-west USA and Mexico. There are four genera, exclusive to the west and south of Madagascar: *Alluaudia* (six species), *Alluaudiopsis* (two species), Didierea (two species), and Decaryia (one species). Examples of the tree Euphorbia of the thicket are *E.stenoclada* (thorny, the latex used for caulking pirogues), *E. enterophora* (thornless, up to 20 metres), and *E. plagiantha*, also thornless, and characterised by peeling yellowish-brown bark.

Very conspicuous are the 'barrel' and 'bottle' trees with their massive trunks adapted for water storage. *Adansonia* (three species), *Moringa* (two species), and *Pachypodium* are the genera.

Leaf succulents are well represented, with several species of tall (3 − 4 metre) aloes. The shrivelled redundant leaves wrap the stem and give some resistance to fire. Look also for the genus *Kalanchoe*. One of the most interesting species, *K. beauverdii* (two to three metres long) forms buds around the leaf margins, each of which then becomes a tiny daughter plant, thus giving it great survival powers.

These are only a few examples of from well over a thousand species belonging to genera of widely different plant families, which nevertheless show much resemblance to one another in their methods of circumventing drought. After rain, leaves and flowers form fast and in some species the flowers even form before rain, thus giving maximum time for fruit formation and dispersal before the next drought.

The best place to view the spiny desert is near Tulear, along the Fort Dauphin – Ambovombe road, and in Berenty reserve (page). Berenty is also an excellent example of gallery forest. Another nature reserve, but not as accessible, is Tsimanampetsotsa (partly a brackish lake) 100 km south of Tulear (page 127).

Secondary grassland   After the excitement of the spiny desert this is inevitably a let down, but inescapable as about 80% of the western region is covered with secondary or wooded grassland, burnt yearly. Two species of palm, *Medemia nobilis* and *Borassus madagascariensis* (both riverside species) have settled in this habitat.

Mangrove   This is an environment of shrubs or small trees growing in muddy lagoons, river deltas, bays or shores, their roots washed by salt or brackish water. Mangroves are found mainly on the west coast and are characterised by stilt-like roots, some of which emerge above the water to take in oxygen. Some have another advantage because their seeds germinate in the fruit while remaining on the tree (vivipary), the fruit then dropping into the mud with its plantlet well on the way to independence. There are three families (nine species) in Madagascar. In the Tulear region the contrast of spiny vegetation in land and a bright green band of mangroves is particularly striking. They are economically important to the people for various aspects of fish or shellfish farming. The wood is hard and very dense but not very durable, and is used for poles and planks and also firewood. The bark is good for tanning leather.

Apart from the Tulear region, there is a population of *Avicennia marina* in the Betsiboka estuary (Majunga) and Nosy Bé has the same species in a much smaller area.

FAUNA

Mammals

There are five orders of land mammals in the island: Primates (lemurs), Insectivora (tenrecs and shrews), Chiroptera (bats), Carnivora (carnivores, including the fossa), and Rodentia (rodents, such as the giant jumping rat). Of these it is the three families of lemur that get the most attention so it is worth describing them in some detail.

Once upon a time there were lemur-type animals all over the world, including North America. Known as prosimians, these creatures had evolved from the ancestral primate, father of all primates including ourselves. They had some monkey-like characteristics but retained the foxy face of their insectivorous forebears, the long nose being needed for a highly developed sense of smell. Lemurs have changed little since the Eocene period 58 − 36 million years ago. Other descendants of the ancestral primate evolved into monkeys; faced with competition from other mammals these developed a greater intelligence and better eyesight. Their sense of smell became less important so their noses lost their physical prominence.

Lemurs are the only surviving prosimians in the world apart from the bushbabies of Africa and lorises of Asia. From their faces it's hard to believe they are our relatives, but quoting from *Defenders of Wildlife* magazine (April 1975) 'One needn't be a scientist to look at a lemur's hand...and feel the thrill of recognition across a gap of 60 million years".

Of the 29 species of lemur only a handful are diurnal so easily seen. Dedicated lemur-watchers, however, can look for nocturnal species at night (see Box) with the help of a headlamp. The diurnal lemurs that are common in certain nature reserves are described in those sections: ring-tails and sifakas in *Berenty*, indri in *Perinet* and black lemurs in *Nosy Be* but there are some generalities which are interesting.

Lemurs have a very low metabolism, and need to sunbathe in the morning to raise their body temperature enough to start the day's activities. Unlike most other primates the two sexes are the same size – with this low metabolism it would be inefficient for males to be larger and more aggressive purely for the purpose of fighting and other macho behaviour. With no difference in size, the females are dominant because their needs are greater – to feed and care for their young.

One lemur that you are very unlikely to see is the aye-aye, but its strangeness symbolises the uniqueness of Madagascar so it deserves a description. It took a while for scientists to decide that the aye-aye *is* a type of lemur, and it has a family of its own, *Daubentonia madagascariensis*.

The aye-aye has been described as appearing to be assembled from the leftover parts of a variety of animals. It has the teeth of a rodent (they never stop growing), the ears of a bat, the tail of a fox, and the hands of no living creature since the middle finger is like that of a skeleton. It's this finger which so intrigues scientists as it shows the aye-aye's adaptation to its environment. In Madagascar it fills the

IDENTIFYING NOCTURNAL LEMURS. ———————
By R.W.Byrne

Seeing nocturnal lemurs isn't hard at all. They are far less shy than the often-hunted diurnal species and let you walk right underneath them in the trees, and their eyes have a silvery tapetum behind the retina which reflects the light, so 'eyeshine' is easily picked out with a torch. To see eyeshine, the axis of the torchlight has to be close to your own eyes so a strong headtorch is best. Then you can see a smallish, brown lemur... but what is it? Most illustrations are pretty confusing, but it's not hard to work out what genus it is. Notice if it sits upright, or along branches like a squirrel; whether the face is flattened or pointed; any markings or colour contrasts; the size; the tail. Then, assuming it's smaller than a brown lemur and brown or grey, use this key:

1.   (a)   Face flattened, owl-like; body usually held upright, see 2.
     (b)   Face pointed, body usually held horizontally, see 3.
     (c)   Face blunt but not flat; body usually held horizontally; big, thick tail; short legs. Chiefly diurnal, no prominent dark marks (e.g. on face), no white marks = HAPALEMUR. *H. griseus*: rabbit sized, eating bamboo, greyish. *H. simus*: much bigger – size of brown lemur, greyish, nearly extinct. *H. aureus*: much bigger, size of brown lemur, orange-brown, nearly extinct, newly discovered in the forests of Ranomafana.

2.   (a)   Tail invisible or curled up in front of body; pale underside or hind limbs show no stripe on thigh; ears tiny; yellowish and reddish colour. Sluggish, strictly nocturnal = AVAHI (*A. Laniger*).
     (b)   Tail quite easily seen; animal smaller (size of rabbit or less); no clear contrasts in colour, ears small or tiny. Nocturnal, may sleep in visible position, especially Nosy Be. = LEPILEMUR. (The best way of telling the seven species apart is by range).

3.   (a)   Tiny, rapid running and leaping in branches; tail thin. Nocturnal = MICROCEBUS (mouse lemur. Either *M. murinus* or *M. rufus* – very hard to separate, range different).
     (a)   Medium small, contrasting pale underparts; black 'spectacles' and black ears and nose; long thick tail. Nocturnal = CHEIROGALEUS (dwarf lemur). *C. medius*: relatively small but tail very fat, greyish. *C. major*: relatively large, tail untapered and not flattened, brownish.

This key doesn't include *Microcebus coquereli*, which is very local and I suspect would look like a big edition of *M. rufus* and act like one, nor *Allocebus trichotis* which hasn't been seen for years, nor *Phaner furcifer* which is conspicuously marked and anyway very localised.
    If what you've seen still doesn't fit, could it be a 'diurnal' lemur like brown lemur, which forages much of the night? And if it's hefty, has big bat-like ears, a bushy tail and sparse grey fur.... you hit the jackpot, it's an aye-aye!

ecological niche left empty by the absence of woodpeckers. The aye-aye uses its skeletal finger to hook grubs out of trees, having detected their movement with its bat-like ears and gnawed through the bark with its rodent's teeth. Its fingers are unique among lemurs in another way – it has claws not fingernails (except on the big toe).

This fascinating animal was long considered to be on the verge of extinction, but recently there have been encouraging signs that it is more widespread than previously supposed. Although destruction of habitat is the chief threat to its survival, it is also endangered because of its supposedly evil powers. Rural people believe it is the heralder of death. If one is seen near a settlement it must be killed, and even then the only salvation may be to burn down the village. A sorcerer can gain great powers if he has the courage to bite the aye-aye's skeleton finger from the living animal. The aye-aye is protected on the island reserve of Nosy Mangabe to which it was introduced in 1966.

Aye-aye

'Nature seems to have retreated there into a private sanctuary, where she could work on different models from any she has used elsewhere. There, you meet bizarre and marvellous forms at every step.'

Philibert Commerson, 1771. French Naturalist.

Almost as strange as the aye-aye are the 21 species of tenrec. These insectivores are considered by some zoologists to be the most primitive of all mammals, and the most prolific. A female may give birth to 32 young! Many tenrec species have prickles and resemble miniature European hedgehogs, and the tiny striped tenrec (*Hemicentetes*) has rows of specialised spines which it can vibrate and strike together, producing a sound (inaudible to humans) which is used to call the young when they scatter to feed. Not all tenrecs have prickles. Some are furry, resembling mice or shrews, and the largest species, known as the tail-less tenrec, is the size of a rabbit. Spines seem to be the favoured form of defence, however, and even the furry species often have a few prickles hidden in the fur.

Some species of tenrec gestivate (i.e. go into a torpor) during the dry season when food is scarce.

Not all the 26 bat species in Madagascar are endemic (evidently they could fly across the Mozambique Channel), but 13 live only here. Very few studies have been done on them. The most visible are the 'flying foxes' (*Pteropus rufus*), an endemic species closely related to those of Asia and seen in Berenty. They are much sought after for food.

The seven species of Malagasy carnivore all belong to the family Viverridae, and are related to the mongoose, civet and genet of Africa. The largest is the puma-like fossa, (also spelt fosa to avoid confusion with the smaller nocturnal *fossa fossana* or fanaloka). The fossa's scientific name is *Cryptoprocta ferox* and although rarely seen it is not uncommon. The fossa is an expert tree climber, and the only serious predator (apart from hawks) of lemurs. It has reddish fur, short strong jaws, retractable claws, a long tail, and is roughly the size of a labrador. More often seen are the four species of mongoose-like *Galidia*. Quite common is *G. elegans* which is chestnut brown with a stripy tail and frequents the east and northern rain forest.

None of the rodents are the same as ours (although mice and rats have been introduced and the latter seem very at home in cheaper hotels). There are seven genera of which the giant jumping rat is the most interesting: it leaps like a rodent wallaby amongst the baobabs near Morondava, where it now has a reserve.

Amphibians and reptiles
Madagascar is particularly rich in this group of fauna – there are 144 species of frogs (the only amphibians here – there are no toads, newts or salamanders) most of which are treefrogs, and 257 reptiles. Many species have only recently been discovered so the number will almost certainly be increased as more studies are made.
Of the many types of lizards in Madagascar, chameleons deserve special mention because they are easily seen and handled. Most people think they know one thing about chameleons – that they change colour to

match their surroundings. In fact this is not really true: chameleons do have a remarkable ability to change colour but emotional factors play a much more important part than environment. A green chameleon crossing a brown road remains green, but when confronted with another chameleon it will break out into spots and stripes of rage. Chameleons turn darker in the sun and lighter during the night. They can and do vary their normal colour to blend with their surroundings, but rely more on slow movements and concealment behind branches to render them inconspicuous.

Chameleons are only found in the Old World, and 'chameleons' sold as pets in the U.S.A. are actually anolis lizards. Although they share the true chameleon's colour-changing abilities, there are many important differences: chameleons can move their eyes independently, looking forward and back at the same time; their feet are adapted for grasping branches, and their tongues can shoot out to a length exceeding their body to catch insects or even small birds. Madagascar is the home of two thirds (59 species) of the world's chameleons, including the smallest and the largest.

Chameleons may be good at camouflage, but the real masters of the art are the fringed gekkos (also called leaf-tailed lizard) of the *Uroplatus* genus. These reptiles blend so perfectly into the bark of the trees on which they spend the day, that when I pointed one out on Nosy Mangabe (particularly rewarding for *Uroplatus*) my companions failed to see it until I had encouraged it to gape in self defence. Not only does the lizard's skin perfectly match the bark, but its sides are fringed so no shadow appears on the tree; even its eye is flecked like bark. It is truly almost invisible.

None of Madagascar's snakes are venomous; or to be accurate, since they are all rear-fanged they cannot inflict a venomous bite. There are plenty of different kinds, the most common of which is the *do*, or boa constrictor, whose nearest relative is in South America.

There are several species of tortoise, of which the radiated and plow-share tortoise are the most attractive, and also in danger of extinction.

Butterflies
Madagascar has over 300 species of butterfly and moth, of which 233 are endemic. Since Madagascar probably became separated from Africa before the evolution of butterflies, the forefathers of these butterflies probably flew – or were blown – over from East Africa, where they show most affinity. However, there is a swallowtail, *Atrophaneura antenor*, whose nearest relative is in India, and the Urania moth, *Chrysiridea madagascariensis*, is very similar to the one found in South America.

The most spectacular moth is the comet, *Argema mittrei*, one of the largest in the world, with a beautiful silver cocoon. They are still relatively common but large numbers are collected for the tourist trade.

Birds

The avifauna of Madagascar is characterised by a poor number of species, by the high degree of endemism and by the important number of bird species occurring in the forests. There are 256 species, of which 201 are resident and 105 endemic. There are three endemic families: Mesites (Mesitornithidae, 3 species), Ground Roller (Brachypteraciidae, 5 species), and Asitys (Philepittidae, 4 species, including 2 species of false-sunbird). Two other families occur only in Madagascar and the Comores: Cuckoo-roller (Leptosomatidae, 1 species) and Vanga (Vangidae, 14 species, with just one also present in the Comoros). There is one endemic sub-family, (Couinae, 10 species, 1 considered extinct).

The above information was supplied by Olivier Langrand.

Perhaps the most striking group are the couas, which, with their long broad tails, resemble the African touraco. The insect-eating vanga family is also conspicuous, particularly the spectacular helmet bird with its oversized blue beak, and the aptly-named sickle bill. More details of birds are provided in descriptions of nature reserves in Part 2.

Helmet vanga

Sicklebilled vanga

Books

There are now some good books on the natural history and nature reserves of Madagascar (see *Bibliography*). The best news is that the long-awaited *Field Guide to the Birds of Madagascar* by Olivier Langrand is due to be published by Yale University Press (publishers of the marvellous *A World like our Own* by Alison Jolly) in 1988. Having been privileged to see a proof copy I can assure ornithologists that it is everything they could wish for. Yale is also publishing a song guide to the birds of Madagascar.

Also in preparation is the *Field Guide to the Mammals of Madagascar* by Martin Nicoll and Russell Mittermeier. With luck this will be available in 1989.

CONSERVATION IN MADAGASCAR: THE PAST AND THE FUTURE

By Alison Richard

Introduction

In the eastern rain forests of Madagascar it is told how once upon a time there lived an animal called the *babakoto* who ate the leaves and fruit of the trees and led an easy, carefree existence. The *babakoto* had four children. Two grew up and lived off the fruit and leaves of the forest as their ancestors had done. Two left the forest and set to work cultivating the land. These were the first ancestors of the Malagasy people, and this is why today it is forbidden, or *fady*, to hunt or kill the *babakoto* or *Indri indri*.

This traditional tale is but one of many still to be heard throughout rural Madagascar, each one explaining why a particular animal or plant should be protected or, at least, left unharmed. At what point in Madagascar's history *fady* became widely applied, particularly to the island's species, we do not know. There is mounting evidence that hunting by the first settlers contributed to the extinction of the largest animals and it would be misleading to suggest that Madagascar's remaining animals are all protected by this belief system today. To the contrary, as traditional beliefs break down, as people become hungrier, as migrant labourers move into areas containing species unknown to them and to which their own *fady* do not apply, the protection afforded by the system of *fady* is incomplete and perilous. Even so, the national government's recent and mounting concern with the conservation of the island's natural heritage finds echoes in the tradional beliefs of people living alongside and, sometimes, quite literally in the midst of this natural heritage. This fact alone provides some hope that the government's efforts, coupled with increasing assistance from the international community, will have a chance of succeeding.

Reserves and Parks

In 1929 a network of ten natural reserves was established, and an eleventh was added in 1934. Together, these reserves represent a total surface area of about 570,000 ha. and they encompass a cross-section of most of the main types of environment on the island. The reserves are completely protected in principle, with access to them regulated by a system of permits. In addition, there are two national parks and 23 smaller special reserves under direct government administration, and two privately owned reserves. The parks and special reserves are regulated by a confusing assortment of laws but without exception their protection under the law is less complete than that of the natural reserves. But whatever the legal status of the various protected areas may be in principle, in practice Madagascar lacks the resources to enforce their status. Moreover, many are quite inaccessible, making it difficult even to know if there are problems.

Integrating conservation and development.

By establishing a national strategy for conservation and sustainable development in 1984, the government of Madagascar became one of the first in the world to give formal recognition to the importance of integrating these activities. Searching for ways of implementing the strategy, late in 1985 the government hosted a major international conference on conservation for development and many collaborative efforts, large and small, are now underway as a result. The Ministry of Animal Production (Fisheries, Husbandry), Waters and Forests – abbreviated as MPAEF – which administers the reserve system, has entered into a series of partnerships with international organisations ranging from the World Bank to the World Wildlife Fund. Diverse as these organisations may be in their scale and mode of operation, they share with the MPAEF a commitment to slow down and eventually halt encroachment into and exploitation of the reserves, by protecting them better and, in particular, by providing people living around them with economically viable alternatives. The MPAEF's activities with the World Wildlife Fund are a good example of these efforts.

The first step in the joint MPAEF/WWF programme which began in 1986 was to do a thorough evaluation of all protected areas in the country to find out which were the most severely threatened and to formulate preliminary proposals for their future management. Now these efforts have focused on Andringitra (Reserve No.5) in the south-east, Andohahela (Reserve No.11) in the south, Marojejy (Reserve No.12) in the north-east, and the Montagne d'Ambre National Park in the north. In the conventional conservationist tradition, staffs in these reserves are being increased in size and provided with uniforms and the transportation needed to patrol effectively. Scholarships enable the heads of reserves to seek further training in natural resource management. Reserve boundaries are themselves gradually being delineated better and posted with signs. These are all essential activities that the government of Madagascar has been unable to undertake in the past for want of funds and perhaps also because only recently has a real sense of urgency set in. What is particularly exciting and just as essential as these traditional measures, however, is the new effort being made to coordinate them with activities initiated by organisations concerned with economic development. In this context, the emphasis is upon enhancing agricultural practices or techniques of livestock management, increasing fuelwood production, instituting or improving soil conservation measures, and so on. The specific activity varies according to local needs but the goal is the same: to ensure that conservation efforts focusing on the reserves go hand in hand with, rather than at the expense of, economic development in the areas surrounding them.

The success of this programme, and others like it, will ultimately depend on the support and participation of the people most immediately affected. Accordingly, a serious effort is being made to find out what people living around the reserves consider to be their greatest problems and needs, and to include these people in the planning process rather than simply to impose conservation measures and development schemes upon them. Public awareness and education are also important components of the overall effort, and a mobile unit equipped with audio-visual aids and a trained staff is now travelling to villages around the reserves to explain the magnitude of the environmental problems and to discuss ways of alleviating or solving them.

At the Special Reserve of Beza Mahafaly in the southwest, another level of education is also being promoted. With the enthusiastic support of people living in the area, Beza Mahafaly was established as a university reserve in 1977 by the University of Madagascar and two American universities (Washington University and Yale). Financial support was provided by the World Wildlife Fund. Remote, relatively inaccessible and just 600 ha. in area, the Beza Mahafaly reserve helps protect what satellite images suggest is the only significant patch of riverine forest left in southwest Madagascar, as well as the ecological gradient from this habitat type to the dry, spiny forest characteristic of much of the south. Ring-tailed lemurs (*lemur catta*) and sifakas (*Propithecus verreauxi*) are abundant and approachable in the reserve, and at night the mouse lemur (*Microcebus murinus*) and sportive lemur (*Lepilemur mustelinus*) can be seen. Among the other wildlife forms present are more than 65 species of birds, and a large population of the highly endangered radiated tortoise (*Geochelone radiata*).

The Beza Mahafaly reserve was founded to promote conservation in the south-west and to serve as a testing ground for ideas about ways of making the survival of Madagascar's natural heritage compatible with the economic needs of its people. Activities connected with these goals are in full swing today. But it was also intended to serve as a training ground for students at the University of Madagascar's School of Agronomy: from the ranks of these students will come the next generation of managers and administrators in whose hands the future of the island's natural resources will lie. A field school, held twice yearly at Beza Mahafaly, has gradually been developed to expose these students to the practical aspects of conservation biology, to 'get their feet wet', as it were, and simply enhance their knowledge of the unique and diverse plants and animals for which they will soon be responsible. Each year Beza Mahafaly also accommodates a small number of students for longer periods to do research on the vegetation, wildlife and socio-economic problems of the area.

If the possibility of drawing upon traditional beliefs protecting some plants and animals provides grounds for cautious optimism about the future survival of Madagascar's natural riches, so too do the developments of the last few years. For instance, when the Beza Mahafaly project began in 1977, small in scale as it was, it was nonetheless the only project of its kind in Madagascar. Ten years later, it is but one of a growing number of efforts to transform the ideal of conservation into a practical reality. The threats are real, and great. But so too, increasingly, are the resolve and wherewithal with which to combat them.

VISITING THE NATIONAL PARKS AND RESERVES

There are five categories of protected area:
1. Réserves Naturelles Integrales (Strict Nature Reserve).
2. Parcs Nationaux (National Parks).
3. Réserves Speciales (Special Reserves).
4. Forêts Classées (Classified Forests).
5. Perimètres de Reboisement et de Restauration (Reafforestation Zones)

1.   There are eleven reserves in this category, four of which are described in this book: Andringitra, (p. 119), Tsimanampetsotsa (p. 127), Marojejy (p. 153), and Lokobe (p. 181). Strictly speaking, these nature reserves may only be visited by scientists.

2.   As in other countries, National Parks are to encourage the

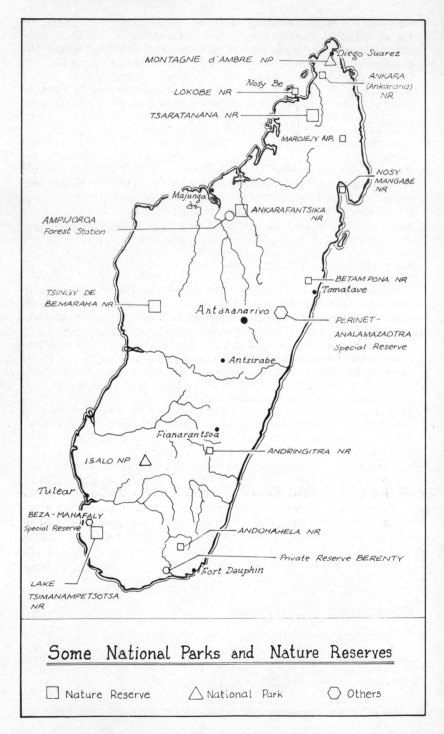

MONTAGNE d'AMBRE NP — Diego Suarez

ANKARA (Ankarana) NR

LOKOBE NR — Nosy Be

TSARATANANA NR

MAROJEJY NR

NOSY MANGABE NR

Majunga

AMPIJOROA Forest Station

ANKARAFANTSIKA NR

BETAMPONA NR

Tamatave

TSINGY DE BEMARAHA NR

Antananarivo

PERINET-ANALAMAZAOTRA Special Reserve

Antsirabe

Fianarantsoa

ANDRINGITRA NR

ISALO NP

Tulear

BEZA-MAHAFALY Special Reserve

ANDOHAHELA NR

Private Reserve BERENTY

Fort Dauphin

LAKE TSIMANAMPETSOTSA NR

Some National Parks and Nature Reserves

☐ Nature Reserve   △ National Park   ⬡ Others

Malagasy to enjoy their national heritage. There are only two national parks, Montagne d'Ambre (p. 174), which is popular, and Isolo (p. 123) which receives few visitors. A permit is easily obtained, in Antananarivo or locally.

3. There are 23 Special Reserves, of which Beza Mahafaly (p. 60), Perinet-Analamazoatra (p. 157), Nosy Mangabe (p. 149), and Ankara (Ankarana, p. 174) are described here. These reserves are for the protection of certain plant or animal species. Not all are supervised.

4. and 5. The 158 Classified Forests and 77 Reafforestation areas conserve forests and watersheds using accepted forestry principles. The Forestry Station of Ampijoroa (p. 194) is one of them.

Permits to visit the reserves and parks are available from the Department d'Eaux et Forêts in Antananarivo. The office is in the Nanasana district, best reached by taxi although buses numbered 1,2 and 3 take you in the general direction. It is open from 8.00 to 12.00, and 14.00 to 18.00. At the time of writing, authorisation is given by Mr Ratsirarson, assistant to the head of the Service de la Protection de la Nature. An 'autorisation d'acces' is often available on the spot, but it is safer to apply in the morning with a view to returning in the afternoon. If you are planning to stay overnight in any of the reserves make sure you mention it since a separate permit may be needed. Have your itinerary worked out – you will need to give approximate dates.

   If you are visiting reserves as part of an organised tour the permits will be arranged for you along with a local guide. Local Eaux et Forêts staff (Chefs de Station) usually know their reserves well, and may be willing to act as guides.

Note: I have not included names and descriptions of all reserves since many are extremely difficult to visit without your own transport. Serious naturalists are advised to buy a copy of the IUCN book *Madagascar – an environmental profile* which gives information on all protected areas including lists of fauna and flora. The same book has descriptions of all the lemur species – with their English names – and some other fauna including the more endangered species of bird. It is available for £17 from the Publications Department, IUCN Conservation Monitoring Centre, 219c Huntingdon Rd, Cambridge CB3 0DL.

When to go (naturalists)

By David Curl

Timing a natural history trip is very important: you will be less concerned than ordinary tourists about rainy and dry seasons, and more interested in the best months for viewing the flora and fauna.

January/February Can be very wet wherever you are, though the extreme south could never truly be described as wet. Very good for mosses, and not bad for some species of orchid.

April   The end of the wet season, and difficult to get around in out-of-the-way places. However the country is still green, animals still active, and some orchids still in flower.

July/August   The European summer sees much of Madagascar (eastern rainforest excluded) drying out. Great if you're in search of sun and sea but the western forests, for instance, seem pretty dead. Nonetheless, lack of leaves in the deciduous forests can actually make lemurs much easier to see at this time of year, and some species will already have young.

September/October   In anticipation of the wet season, life returns to the forests. In the eastern rainforest there is also a slight respite from almost incessant downpours. Many animals, lemurs included, have young. A good time to visit.

November/December   Beginning to get a bit wet – and hot – but good for wildlife.

CONSERVATION ORGANISATIONS

Madagascar needs all the financial help it can get. If you can spare some money to help save the rain forests and improve the lot of the Malagasy themselves, the following agencies will welcome donations:

World Wide Fund for Nature (UK)
Panda House
Weyside Park
Godalming
Surrey GU7 IXR

Friends of the Earth
377 City Rd
London EC1V INA

Money for Madagascar
29 Queen's Rd
Sketty
Swansea SA2 O5B
(A church-based organisation working with small communities and funding village agricultural projects.)

Those wishing to visit Madagascar in a useful capacity should contact **Earthwatch** who sometimes organise one of their working holidays there. Trip members pay for the privilege of working in the field with a renowned zoologist/conservationist.
Earthwatch
Box 403
Watertown
MA 02272
USA
Tel: (617) 926 8200

Chapter 4

Planning and preparations

RED TAPE
Visas

A visa is required by everyone except citizens of Malawi and Lesotho and is valid for a stay of one month, within six months of the date of issue. Applications from some professions, such as journalists, may have to be referred to Head Office before a visa will be granted. Forms must be completed in quintuplicate but most embassies have a photocopier. You will need five photos. You may be asked to show evidence of a return ticket; a letter from the travel agent dealing with your flights is sufficient.

Embassy and consulate addresses (Democratic Republic of Madagascar)

GREAT BRITAIN
Honorary Consulate. 69/70 Mark Lane, London EC3R 7JA. Tel: 01 481 3899. Hours 9.30 – 1.00. Visas supplied immediately; very helpful. £30.

CONTINENTAL EUROPE
France
Embassy. 4 Ave Raphael, 75016 Paris. Tel: 45 046211. Apply a.m., collect your visa p.m. Price FF 200.

Italy
Embassy. Via Riccardo Zandonai 84/A, Roma. Tel: 327 7797 & 327 5183.

Belgium
Embassy. 276 Ave de Tervueren, 1150 Bruxelles. Tel: 770 1726 & 770 1774.

West Germany
Consulate. Rolandstrasse 48, 5300 Bonn Bad Godesberg (Postfach 188). Tel: 228 331057/58.

Austria
Consulate. Potzleindorferstr. 94-96, A-1184 Wien. Tel: 47 41 92 & 47 12 73.

Switzerland
Birkenstr. 5, 6000 Lucerne. Tel: 01 211 2721.

THE UNITED STATES
Embassy. 2374 Massachusetts Ave N.W., Washington D.C. 20008. Tel: (202) 265 5525.
(Visas also available from the Permanent Mission of Madagascar to the United Nations, 801 Second Ave, Room 404, New York, N.Y. 10017. Tel: (212) 986 9491.)

Honorary Consulate. 19th floor Fidelity, 123 South Broad St, Philadelphia, PA 19109. Tel: (215) 893 3067.

Honorary Consulate. 867 Garland Drive, Palo Alto, CA 94303. Tel: (415) 323 7113. Extremely helpful; good information. Visas $22.50.

CANADA
Honorary Consulate. C X Tranchemontagne Cie Lte, 459 St Sulpice, Montreal 125, Quebec. Tel: (514) 844 4427.

Honorary Consul. 335 Watson Ave., Oakville B.P. L6J 3V5 Toronto. Tel: (418) 845 8914.

AUSTRALIA
Consulate. Suite 2, 4th Floor, 92 Pitt St, Sydney, NSW 2000. Tel: 221 3007. Hours 9.00 to 12.00, 14.00 to 15.00. Helpful.

AFRICA AND INDIAN OCEAN
Tanzania
Embassy. Magoret St 135, Dar es Salaam. (P.O. Box 5254.) Tel: 29 442.

Kenya
Consulate. Nairobi Hilton. (P.O. Box 41723.) Tel: 25206/26494.

Mauritius
Embassy. Ave Queen Mary Floreal, Port Louis. Tel: 6 50 15 & 6 50 16.

Réunion
Consulate. 39 Angle Rues Mac Aulife et Juliette Dodu, 97461 Saint Denis. Tel: 21 05 21.

Extending your visa
It is not difficult to extend your visa in Madagascar for one month. If you plan to stay more than two months you must make your arrangements

before you leave home, or briefly leave the country by flying to Réunion. (But see Addenda for recent information.)

Applications for visa extensions (*prolongation*) must be made at the Ministry of the Interior, near the Hilton Hotel in Antananarivo. You will need: three photos, a photocopy of your currency declaration, a typewritten declaration (best done at home) of why you want to stay longer, and your passport. Your money will be checked and will influence whether you will be granted an extension. Four working days are needed for the permit to come through, and during that time they will keep your passport.

Other entry requirements

Vaccination certificate: although cholera and yellow fever are only required if arriving from an infected area, you are advised to have the recommended shots (see *Health*) and the relevant certificate.

GETTING THERE

From Europe

The cheapest way of getting to Madagascar from Britain is via Aeroflot. It's 3 hours to Moscow where you have a 3 hour stop ('dinner' pass provided) then another dawn stop in Aden. There are all sorts of disadvantages: they are notorious for changing their flight dates at the last minute, losing luggage, and being booked up months in advance. That said, the fare of £410 return (1987) is half that of Air France/Air Madagascar so for those on a tight budget there is no choice.

The plane leaves London on Sundays, around 12.00 noon, and arrives in Antananarivo at 12.00 noon local time (3 hours later than GMT). Don't try to book direct through Aeroflot, but use their agent **Sam Travel** (tel: 01 636 2521). (See also addenda.)

Harry Sutherland-Hawes claims that happy travel on Aeroflot is all a question of being prepared: 'The first five rows of seats to the right of the door have more room than most airlines' business class (behind those they have less room than most charter flights). You have to push and shove to get those (no numbered boarding passes!) but it's well worth it. Take plenty to drink (2 litres per person) and eat. The 'mineral water' on board is chlorine, the food ... well, find out! 'Dinner' at Moscow airport was three bottles of sticky, sweet fizzy drink between four of us, and anchovies and bread.'

The alternative to Aeroflot is the much more comfortable and gourmet Air Madagascar. Arrangements in Britain are made through Air France (whose planes may be used) or Air Mauritius (01 434 4379), who can also book internal flights. It is worth buying some of your internal flights before arriving in Antananarivo because a 40% discount is sometimes available off certain flights. And for very popular destinations such as Île Sainte Marie and the south, flights are heavily booked in the peak

season. If you are travelling on Air Madagascar/Air France you can buy the FF2000 Air Tourist Pass, giving you unlimited internal travel (see Chapter 6, *Transport*).

Air Madagascar's return fares (1988) are as follows:
High season (June 15 – Oct 15) excursion (19 – 60 days): FF 10,350 (approximately £1000). Low season (Sept 15 – June 15) excursion FF 7,025 (approx. £700). 'Tarif jeunes' (young person's fare – under 28 yrs old or students under 31), valid all year, 14 – 75 days, FF 7,395 (approx. £740).

These prices are from the Air Madagascar's Paris office, Agence Air Madagascar, 7 Avenue de l'Opera, Paris 75001. Tel: 42 60 30 51. If you have difficulty getting the pass or discounted tickets in London, try phoning them (in French!). They are unlikely to answer letters. Other Europe agencies for Air Madagascar are:

Air Madagascar, c/o ATASH Sa, 34, Neumuhlequai, 8006 Zurich, Switzerland, tel: (0)1 362 72 40 (English spoken); and Air Madagascar, Herzog-Rudolf-Strasse 3, 8000 München 22, West Germany. Tel: 089 2318 0113. Very efficient and English-speaking. However, they can only sell full fare tickets to customers. Discounted tickets must be purchased through a tour operator.

Two excellent British companies do discounted flights (through Air France) to Madagascar: Wexas International (01 584 8116), and Trailfinders (01 938 3366). Their prices are in the £770 range from London via Paris to Antananarivo. Wexas also do Aeroflot for £468. The disadvantage of flying via Paris is that you must cross town from Charles de Gaulle airport to Orly. If possible, go from Zurich.

Flights depart (1988 schedule) Mondays (leaving Orly at 17.15, via Jeddah, arriving Antananarivo 07.40), Wednesdays (leaving Orly 13.40, via Marseille and Djibouti, arriving 05.40), and Saturdays (leaving Orly 16.05, via Zurich and Nairobi, arriving 08.00).

For those willing to be creative over flights, there are alternative ways of getting to Madagascar. Perhaps the best bet is to get a cheap charter to Nairobi then buy a 21 day excursion for £186 (1986 prices) to Antananarivo (more than 21 days is £309). Air Madagascar planes leave Nairobi three times a week, Sunday (05.00), Tuesday (13.30) and Friday (12.15). It's best to avoid the Sunday flight which is a 747 originating in Paris; there are more passengers to be processed on arrival and they are often overbooked so tend to 'bump' those joining the plane in Nairobi. Other flights tend to be full but I have successfully gone standby.

You can also get a charter flight to Reunion with the French companies Le Point – tel: 89 42 4451 (Mulhouse) or 42 96 6363 (Paris) – or Nouvelle Frontière – tel: 42 73 1064 (Paris). From Reunion there are flights five times a week to Antananarivo.

There are also regular flights from Mauritius but no cheap charter flights to that island.

From North America

Americans have no good alternative to getting a cheap flight to Europe and making their arrangements from there. For those on the west coast it *may* work out cheaper to fly west to Nairobi. But I doubt it.

From Australia

Air Madagascar have an office in the same building as the Sydney Consulate, but they do not sell airline tickets. The nearest Air Madagascar gateway to Australia is Mauritius.

WHAT TO BRING

There are two main factors to bear in mind: the varied climate and the shortage of 'luxury' goods.

Give some thought to luggage. A sturdy canvas duffle bag or backpack with internal frame are more practical than suit-cases. Bring a light folding nylon bag for taking purchases home.

Clothes

You will be meeting every temperature, from cool/cold in the highlands to very hot by the coast. Layers of clothing – tee shirt, sweatshirt, light sweater – are warm and versatile, and take less room than a heavy sweater. You will need a long-sleeved shirt against mosquitoes. A showerproof jacket and rain cape and perhaps a small umbrella will also be needed, and if you are planning to spend much time in the rainforests, take good waterproof clothing (including rain-trousers) and light rubber boots. The highlands (and also Perinet) get very cold on winter evenings, as does the southern desert; a fibre-pile jacket or bodywarmer are practical. A light cotton jacket is always useful for breezy evenings by the coast.

The most versatile footwear are trainers (running shoes) and sandals. Hiking boots will be needed if you are planning a lot of walking, and off the road excursions in the south, but are not necessary for the main tourist circuits.

Give some thought to beachwear if you enjoy snorkelling. In addition to a swim suit you'll need an old pair of sneakers (or similar) to protect your feet from the coral (or buy a pair of plastic sandals in the market) and teeshirt and shorts or even long trousers to wear while in the water. The underwater world is so absorbing it is very easy to get badly sunburnt, especially on the shoulders and back of thighs.

The major beach resorts usually have snorkelling equipment available, but of course it's safer to bring your own.

Toiletries

I once forgot to take a toothbrush to Madagascar. Although I bought a Chinese one in the market it was more like a paint-brush and my teeth were grey by the end of a month! Good quality soap, toothpaste, shampoo, moisturiser, handcream, etc. are still almost impossible to find, as is decent toilet paper. Good hotels do provide it, but it is the sort favoured by the rural French – more like tree-bark than anything you want to bring in repeated contact with your skin. This is awkward for those planning a long stay; one traveller, pointing out that you can't bring enough toilet paper to last the trip, recommends wetting the local stuff to make it less abrasive – and cooler. If you normally blow your nose on loo paper you'd better bring a handkerchief...

Women should bring enough tampons to last the trip. The brands without an applicator take up less luggage space.

Some toilet articles have several uses: dental floss is excellent for repairs as well as for teeth, and a nail brush gets clothes clean as well.

Don't take up valuable space with a bath towel – a hand towel is perfectly adequate.

Rough travel equipment

Basic camping gear gives you the freedom to travel adventurously and can add a considerable degree of comfort to overland journeys.

The most important item is your backpack: this should *not* have an external frame which is antisocial on the very crowded vehicles that serve as public transport, and anyway will get stomped on and broken. Invest in a good pack with an internal frame and plenty of pockets. Protect it from oil, dirt, and the effluent of young or furry/feathered passengers with a canvas sack or similar adapted covering.

A light sleeping bag (or blanket, which you can buy in the market) will keep you warm in cheap hotels with inadequate bedding, and on night stops on – or off – 'buses'. Add a sheet sleeping bag for hot nights, and when the hotel linen is missing or grubby.

An air-mattress or pillow pads your bum on hard seats as well as your hips when sleeping out. One of those horseshoe-shaped travel pillows which allow you to sleep sitting up.

A mosquito net will add greatly to your comfort as well as protecting you from malaria-carrying mosquitoes. The free-standing type is the most practical (see advertisements on pages 46 and 208). You can also buy mosquito nets from MASTA (page 81).

A lightweight tent allows you to strike out on your own and stay in nature reserves, on deserted beaches and so on. It will need to have a separate rain fly and be well-ventilated.

To complete your independence you will need a stove. Camping Gaz cylinders are sometimes available, but you would be safer to bring a meths burning stove. This fuel is called *alcohol à brûler* and is bought in general stores (*épicerie*).

Miscellaneous

Assume that you can buy nothing (factory manufactured) in Madagascar. Although imported goods are beginning to reach the shops, even the most basic items like writing paper are safer brought from home. Here is a suggested checklist:

Small torch (flashlight) with spare batteries and bulb, or headlamp for nocturnal animal spotting, travel alarm clock (or alarm wristwatch), penknife, sewing kit, scissors, tweezers, safety pins, sellotape (Scotchtape), Magic Marker or felt-tipped pen, ballpoint pens, a small notebook, a large notebook for diary and letters home, plastic bags (all sizes, sturdy; Zip-loc are particularly useful), universal plug for baths and sinks, elastic clothes line or cord and pegs, concentrated detergent (available in tubes in camping stores), ear plugs (a godsend in noisy hotels), insect repellent, sunscreen, lipsalve, spare glasses or contact lenses, sunglasses, medicine kit (see *Health*). A good 2-litre water bottle and water-purifying tablets or a filter, are essential.

Compact binoculars, camera, plenty of film (twice as much as you think you'll need), books, miniature cards, Scrabble and/or a pocket chess set.

Goods for presents, sale or trade

Before giving presents please read *Village etiquette* on p.92. In remote areas it's much better not to give gifts at all; show-and-tell items such as photos of your family, postcards of your home country, etc, will give you a chance to inter-relate with the people. Games and things like cats cradles or origami, which can be done with easily-available materials, are ideal. Not in this category, but a good gift because of the fun it affords is a frisbee (it makes a useful plate, too!). Acceptable small gifts are matches, soap, shampoo, hairslides or other ornaments, hand mirrors, and so on. But always consider what you are introducing into the culture and be very wary of giving an appetite for hitherto unwanted consumer goods.

In urban areas or with the more sophisticated Malagasy people, presents are a very good way of showing your appreciation for kindness or extra good service. Good quality toiletries such as shampoo, after-shave lotion, cologne, cosmetics, etc. are in great demand, as are batteries, particularly long-life AA size; these can also be sold or traded for local handicrafts. The same applies to alcohol (it's always worth bringing in your allowance of duty-free whisky) and cigarettes. Clothes, especially jeans, are often requested by those with an appetite for the 'western' look, and you will always find a home for running shoes.

Import restrictions mean that cameras are extremely expensive in Madagascar, and it is easy to sell photographic equipment for a good price. If you are willing to part with your camera towards the end of a trip, ask at photographic shops or even ordinary stores (particularly those run by Asians) in smaller towns.

Money

How much money to take is covered in Chapter 6, but give some thought to *how* to take it.

Bring your money in French francs or American dollars. It is not easy to change pounds outside Antananarivo. If using dollars, American Express travellers cheques are best – some banks don't accept less known brands, and American Express are the most efficient at replacing stolen cheques (although there is no Am Ex office in Madagascar).

In addition to travellers cheques bring cash. This is easier to change in smaller towns and you do not always need your passport (useful if you have had to surrender it for visa extension).

The large hotels and Air Madagascar accept credit cards; American Express is the best.

WHEN TO GO

Read the section on climate before deciding when to travel. Broadly speaking, the dry months are between April to September, but rainfall varies enormously in different areas. The months to avoid are August, when popular places are crowded with holiday makers from Reunion and France, and January, February and March (the cyclone season) when it will rain. However, if you stick to the west and south this off-peak season can be rewarding, with cheaper international airfares and very few other tourists.

My favourite months are October and November, when the weather is usually fine, the lemurs have babies, and the markets are offering endless varieties of fruit.

PACKAGE TOUR OR INDEPENDENT TRAVEL?

Even the most diehard independent travellers should consider a package tour in Madagascar, at least for part of their trip. Unless you have plenty of time and a good command of French, it is difficult to see the most interesting parts of the country on your own. The great advantage of a tour is that you get ground transport laid on, so can stop and look at scenery, tombs, birds, villagers... Public transport tends to be so crowded that even looking out of the window (if there *is* a window) may be impossible. Special interest groups (botany, ornithology) would be particularly advised to go with a group organised in their own country, to be sure of having an expert guide as well as the necessary transport to reach remote areas.

Package tours

The tour operators below do trips to Madagascar.

Britain   Twickers World (01-892 7606), Hann Overland (01-834 7337), Guerba Expeditions (0373 826689), Silk Cut Travel (0730 65211), Swan Hellenic (01-831 1515); Ornitholidays (0243 821230) – birdwatching,

David Sayers Travel (01-995 3642) – botany, and Alfred Gregory (0742 29428) – photographic.

U.S.A. Wilderness Travel (California – 415 548-0420 or 800 247-6700), Questers (New York – 212 673-3120).

Tour operators in Madagascar

Madagascar Airtours, Hilton Hotel, Antananarivo. B.P. 3874. Tel: 341-92. Telex: 222-32 AIR MAD MG, or 222-61 HILTEL MG.

By far the most experienced agency, running a wide variety of tours including natural history, ornithology, speleology, trekking, minerology, river trips, sailing, etc. Such specialised tours would be set up for groups, rather than individuals, but whatever your requirements it's worth talking to the helpful and sometimes English-speaking staff in the Hilton office.

Other tour operators, who may be just as good but I haven't used them, are:

Transcontinents, 10 Ave de l'Indépendance, Antananarivo. B.P. 541, Tel: 223-98. Telex 22259 ZODIAC.

Voyages Bourdon, 15 Rue P.Lumumba, Antananarivo. Tel: 296-96. Telex 22557 YOYDON MG.

Trans 7, 11 Ave de l'Indépendance, Antananarivo. B.P. 7117. Tel: 248-38. Telex 22381.

Touring Fima, 41 Rue Ratsimilaho, Antananarivo. B.P. 6073. Tel: 222-30. Telex: 22464.

Liounis Voyages, Immeuble COROI, Antsahavola, Antananarivo. B.P. 425. Tel: 238-26. Telex: 22214 COROI MG.

Julia Voyage, 7 Rue P.Lumumba, Antananarivo. B.P. 3178. Tel: 268-74.

Tourisma, 15 Ave de l'Indépendance, Antananarivo. B.P. 3997. Tel: 287-57 & 289-11.

Independent travel – suggested circuits

One of the hardest decisions facing the first-time visitor to a country as diverse as Madagascar is where to go. Even a month is not long enough to see everything so itineraries must be planned according to interests. Here are some suggestions for tours lasting three to four weeks.

The comfort circuit

This includes all the most interesting places which have comfortable accommodation (categories A and B) and are accessible by air. Most organised tours cover the same ground.

Antananarivo – Fort Dauphin and Berenty – Antananarivo – Perinet (by train or road) – Tamatave – Diego Suarez – Nosy Be – Antananarivo.

The rough explorer

For those on a limited budget, their own sleeping bag, etc., and a willingness to exchange comfort for Amazing Experiences. (A month would be needed for each full circuit here.)

Antananarivo – Antsirabe (by train) – Fianarantsoa (by road) – side trip to Ranomafana (road) – Manakara (by train) and back – Fianarantsoa – Fort Dauphin (by road) – Tulear (by road or plane) – Antananarivo.

Alternatively or in addition (if no time limit):

Antananarivo – Majunga (by road or plane) – Nosy Be (by road or plane) – Diego Suarez (by road) – Sambava or Maroansetra (plane) – Tamatave (plane) – Île Ste Marie – Antananarivo. Or Île Ste Marie – Tamatave – Perinet (train) – Antananarivo.

The naturalist

A three to four week tour could take in the following:

Antananarivo – Fort Dauphin and Berenty – Antananarivo – Majunga (Ampijoroa) – Nosy Be (Lokobe) – Diego Suarez (Montagne d'Ambre) – Maroansetra (Nosy Mangabe) – Tamatave – Perinet – Antananarivo.

Ethno-tour (tombs and things)

Antananarivo and area (for Merina tombs) – Fianarantsoa (with excursions to Ambositra and Ambalavao) – Tulear (excursion through Mahafaly country) – Fort Dauphin (Berenty and visit to Antanosy tombs) – Antananarivo – Tamatave and east coast (Betsimisaraka graves) – Antananarivo.

History

Antananarivo – Ambohimanga – Fort Dauphin – Antananarivo – Île Ste Marie – Tamatave – Mahavelona (fort) – Tamatave – Antananarivo.

Remember: The east coast should be excluded from these tours in the rainy season (December to March). If you want to avoid other travellers there are plenty of interesting places mentioned in this book and not on the circuits above. And hundreds of other places not mentioned in the book!

Chapter 5

Health and safety

HEALTH

By Dr Jane Wilson

Staying healthy in Madagascar, as in other developing countries, is a matter of good preparation and common sense.

Before you go

Malaria

Madagascar boasts three species of malaria and drug (chloroquine) resistance is now becoming a problem. Since one form of the disease, cerebral malaria, is dangerous it is worth getting up to date advice on malaria prophylaxis. This is available from the Malaria Reference Laboratory in London, tel: 01 636 7921 (a continuous loop tape giving general information) or 01 636 3924 from 9.30 – 10.30 and 14.00 – 15.00, Mondays to Fridays, for specific advice.

At the time of writing two chloroquine (Nivaquine) weekly and two proguanil (Paludrine) daily was recommended. These drugs are best absorbed after food and when taken after a meal are less likely to cause the side effect of nausea which troubles some people. You should start taking malaria phrophylaxis one week before leaving for Madagascar and continue six weeks after returning home. It is inadvisable to take anti-malarials if you are pregnant because of possible damage to the foetus, and pregnancy apparently increases your susceptibility to the disease.

Even if you have been taking your malaria prophylaxis carefully there is a slight chance of contracting malaria. You should therefore consult a doctor (mentioning that you have been abroad) if you get a flu-like illness within a month or so of getting home.

Immunisations

Disease patterns and international health regulations change so it is worth taking special advice. It would be sensible to have up-to-date immunisations for polio, tetanus, typhoid and cholera and probably gamma globulin against hepatitis. It is also worth having a Schick Test to check that your childhood immunisation for diphtheria is still protective. An 'ordinary' intramuscular shot against rabies is now available and may be worth arranging if you think you are at risk. The disease is a problem in Madagascar because of the quantity of semi-feral dogs in many parts of the island.

Yellow Fever does not exist in Madagascar but you may be required to show an International Vaccination Certificate if you have come from a Yellow Fever area. The immunisation lasts for 10 years.

Remember that 'live' vaccines cannot be taken within a fortnight of each other, so plan well ahead. There is a list of vaccination centres at the end of this section.

Teeth
Have a dental check-up before you go.

Insurance
Make sure you have insurance covering the cost of treatment in Madagascar and a flight home or to Reunion or Nairobi which offer more sophisticated medical facilities than are available in Madagascar.

In Madagascar
Local medical facilities
The local medical services are excellent considering the constraints imposed by poor communications, lack of drugs and facilities. Malagasy doctors are knowledgeable and well trained (often in Moscow) and all I met seemed reliable, trustworthy and friendly. Many of the younger doctors speak English.

Insects and insect-borne diseases
The one known Trypanosome organism (sleeping sickness) which exists in Madagascar affects only chameleons! The African forms of sleeping sickness do not exist in Madagascar as there is no tsetse vector to spread it. However, there are plenty of mosquitoes which spread malaria, elephantiasis and viral diseases. It is worth avoiding being bitten to prevent contracting these diseases but also to avoid the itching bites which so easily become infected later. So cover up. In the evening in the forest and low-lying areas wear trousers, socks and shoes and it may be worthwhile tucking your trousers into your socks. In Madagascar mosquitoes seem to favour ankle-biting but in other countries I have found it most comfortable to put on a long sleeved shirt in the evening and prevent the beasts flying inside by sealing the neck with a cotton handkerchief. That leaves only the hands and face readily accessible to mosquitoes and these can be covered in mosquito repellent. [Repellent should contain at least 40% Diethyl toluamide (popularly known as Deet) or ethoheadiol, a newer, less smelly ingredient.]

Locally available mosquito coils are excellent and very effective if you are sleeping inside, and mosquito nets (self-standing) are a good investment for cheap, unscreened hotels. Some hotels provide mosquito nets, others have fans which baffle the mosquitoes; they are unable to fly in turbulent air.

Once bitten, calamine lotion or calamine-based creams seem best to stop the itching.

Other nasty animals

Malagasy land-snakes are back-fanged so are effectively non-venomous. Sea-snakes however are dangerous but being brightly coloured are easy to see and the few I met were unaggressive.

Particularly when in the forest it is wise to be wary of scorpions and centipedes. Neither are fatal but are very unpleasant. Scorpions are nocturnal but often come out after rain; they like hiding in small crevices during the day. If you are camping in the forest it is not unusual to find they have crept into the pocket of a rucksack – even if you have taken the sensible precaution of suspending it from a tree. Scorpion stings are very painful for about 24 hours but are not life-threatening. After a sting on the finger I had an excruciatingly painful hand and arm for several days, which was only eased with morphine, and an anaesthetic finger for a month.

Centipedes are probably the best fighting machine ever designed. They bite at one end, sting at the other and each leg is capable of inflicting a small wound. Madagascar has some very large (15 cm) species which are best avoided. The large spiders can be dangerous and the (over-rated!) black widow occurs in Madagascar. The large navy digger wasps have an unpleasant sting. In my experience, however, it is only the scorpions which cause problems because they can be very common in the forest and because they favour hiding in places where one might plunge a hand without looking.

If you wish to sleep on the ground, in forest areas, it would be prudent to isolate yourself from these creatures – mat, hammock or tent with sewn-in ground sheet.

Leeches can be a nuisance in the rainforest but they are only revolting, not dangerous. These are best avoided by covering up, again tucking trousers into socks and applying insect repellent (even under the socks). Once leeches have become attached they should not be forcibly removed. Either wait until they have finished feeding (when they will fall off) or encourage them to let go by applying a lit cigarette or salt. In Nepal people carry muslin bags of salt to dab on leeches' tails – a film canister is a convenient container. The wound left by a leech bleeds a great deal and may become secondarily infected if not kept clean.

Plants

Madagascar has quite a few plants which cause local skin irritation. The worst one I have encountered is a climbing legume which has pea-pod like fruits which look furry. This 'fur' penetrates the skin as thousands of tiny needles which must be painstakingly extracted with tweezers. Relief from secretions of other irritating plants is often obtained by bathing. Sometimes it is best to wash your clothes as well and immersion fully clothed may be the last resort!

Some travellers' diseases

Traveller's diarrhoea, etc. Most people suffer gastro-intestinal upsets at some stage, and this is more likely if you are new to tropical travel. The best foods to eat to ensure illness are, in descending order of danger: ice cream, ice, water, salads, uncooked foods, cooked food which has been hanging around or has been inadequately reheated. Street sellers' foods may be safe if they are sizzling hot. There is a high prevalence of tapeworm in cattle, so I would recommend eating your steaks (which are usually excellent in Madagascar) well done.

The best treatment for traveller's diarrhoea is 24-48 hours starvation: no solid food but plenty of clear fluids. Only resort to antidiarrhoeal drugs if you really must (e.g. when travelling) since they delay recovery by slowing the natural expulsion of toxic products. Should the diarrhoea be associated with passing blood, treatment may be advisable but as long as you drink plenty no harm will be done by waiting a couple of days. I would try Metronidazole (Flagyl) first. This is also a useful antibiotic if the upset is associated with production of *a lot* of sulphurous wind. If in doubt starve for 48 hours and in most cases you'll start feeling better.

Sometimes the gut alternates between mild diarrhoea and constipation. Constipation is made worse by dehydration (a problem in the heat) and bananas. Other fruits will help relieve it.

Some people believe in having a stool check-up when they return home. Personally I would only bother if I had symptoms.

Bilharzia Sometimes called 'Swimmer's Itch', this is a problem in much of Madagascar (mainly from swimming/paddling in still water, not fast-flowing rivers) but is easily cured with a single dose of Praziquantel.

Sexually transmitted diseases There are plenty in Madagascar, and although the country was still reportedly Aids-free in early 1988, it is probably only a matter of time. If you enjoy nightlife, condoms will make encounters less risky.

Medical kit

You can't take all the medicants you may need when you are travelling, and apart from personal medication taken on a regular basis it is unnecessary to weigh yourself down with a comprehensive medical kit as many of your requirements will be met by the pharmacies.

The list below is for the 'ordinary' tourist/traveller. Expeditions or very adventurous travellers should contact MASTA (Useful addresses, below).

Malaria tablets, lots of plasters (Band-aids) to cover broken skin, infected insect bites, etc. Antiseptic such as Dettol (salt in boiled water is also excellent), small pieces of sterile gauze (Melonin dressing) and sticky plaster, soluble aspirin – good for fevers, aches, and for gargling when you have a sore throat. Lanosil or some kind of soothing cream for sore anus (post diarrhoea), Canestan for thrush and athletes foot. A course of Flagyl, a course of Amoxyl or similar antibiotic – good for chest infections, skin infections and cystitis, Cicatrin antibiotic powder for infected bites, etc., antibiotic eye drops, anti-histamine cream or tablets.

Useful addresses

Thomas Cook Vaccination Centre, 45 Berkeley Square, London W.1. (near Green Park tube station). Tel: 01 499 4000.

British Airways Medical Department (vaccination service), 75, Regent St, London W.1. Tel: 01 439 9584.

The Ross Institute of Tropical Hygiene, London School of Hygiene and Tropical Medicine, Gower Street, London, WC1E 7HT. Tel: 01 636 8636. The Malarial Reference Laboratory is located here.

An excellent service for travellers is MASTA (Medical Advisory Service for Travellers). For £9.50 they will provide an individually tailored Concise Health Brief. This gives up to date information on how to stay healthy in Madagascar (or any country you specify) and includes malaria, inoculations, and what to bring. For expeditions they offer a Comprehensive Health Brief for £25.00. Forms for ordering your Health Brief are available from Boots or other chemists, or ring 01 631 4408. MASTA also sells basic tropical supplies such as mosquito nets, insect repellent (neat deet), and a Medical Equipment Pack with sterile syringes, etc. The latter is available by mail (cash with order) for £9.80 from MASTA, Keppel St, London WC1E 7HT.

SAFETY

Only in the capital, Antananarivo, are you in real danger of being robbed. Thursday evening and Friday (market day) are particularly bad, and the area around the station is the worst. It pays to be paranoid. Tamatave is also said to be popular with thieves.

There are bandits and cattle thieves in the south, but I have yet to hear of tourists being involved. Sadly though, increasing tourism is almost bound to bring an increase of thieves in all popular areas, so be sensible. Here are some ways of protecting your valuables:

Carry your cash in a money belt or neck pouch and divide up travellers cheques so they are not all in one place. Keep a note of the numbers of your travellers cheques, passport, credit cards, plane ticket, insurance, etc. in your money belt. Keep a copy in your luggage.

Keep a photocopy of the first page of your passport and of your

Madagascar visa. Guard your currency declaration as carefully as your passport.

Bring a combination lock that can be used on your hotel door (in cheap hotels in cities).

In posh hotels leave your valuables in a security box.

Be very careful of handbag slashers in the market or on crowded buses. They use a razor and are very skilful (I was thoroughly and competently robbed this way in the local bus to Ivato airport; I was sure that my handbag was out of harm's way, but the side was accessible to the thief and his accomplice who had helped me into the bus and companionably got in beside me).

Do not wear gold chains or jewellery of any sort.

Avoid leaving your clothes on the beach while you go swimming (in areas where they are used to tourists).

If you are robbed, go to the police. They will write down all the details then send you to the chief of police for a signature. It takes hours, but you will need the certificate for your insurance.

Women travellers

In my experience, and in that of the women contributors to this book (all of whom travelled very adventurously), Madagascar is one of the safest and most enjoyable countries in the world for a lone woman traveller. Of course, in a country where there are many prostitutes it is sensible to dress modestly and make it clear through your general demeanor that you are not soliciting custom.

My only experience that comes remotely close to what one has come to expect in more 'hot-blooded' countries was when a small man sidled up to me in Hell-ville harbour and asked – in English – 'Have you ever tasted Malagasy man?'.

Useful books

Travellers' Health Dr Richard Dawood.
O.U.P., £6.95. Detailed and up to date.

The Traveller's Health Guide Dr Anthony Turner.
Roger Lascelles, £4.95. Clearly written and straightforward.

Travel Safety Uniquest Publications, USA.
(Available from Bradt Publications). £4.95. Geared to more dangerous countries than Madagascar, this little book nevertheless gives numerous very helpful tips for travellers.

Chapter 6

In Madagascar

COST OF LIVING/TRAVELLING

Is Madagascar a cheap country for foreigners? Well, it depends. For years the exchange rate was highly unfavourable (Dervla Murphy talks about a large bottle of Coke costing £4 in 1982, and in 1984 I saw an advertisement for a second-hand colour television for the equivalent of £1,800). When I travelled in 1986 I kept to a budget of £10 a day, but only by staying in the cheapest hotels and rationing the good meals. In late 1987 there was a fifty percent devaluation and recent travellers reported spending a daily $24 (£14) for a couple, including internal airfares and some slap up meals. Then, in February 1988, a new law came into practice: tourists must pay for 3, 4, or 5 star hotels in hard currency, on which a 15% tourist tax is added. Domestic airfares must also be paid for in hard currency as well as first class train fares. Comfortable travel is thus back to European prices, but there is no tax or hard currency requirement on restaurant meals so you can eat well whatever your budget.

In Madagascar a couple can travel almost as cheaply as one person, since most rooms have double beds and are charged as such. Those watching their budgets will need to cut down on imported alcohol, and internal air travel. A reader travelling in September 1988 reports that he spent £10 a day, staying in B hotels, eating well, and travelling by road and rail.

Malagasy Francs

Since 1973, when Madagascar broke from the French Franc Zone, it has had its own currency, the Franc Malgache (FMG). Apart from notes, there are coins of 1, 2, 5, 10, and 20 francs. To thoroughly confuse you, there are also large silver coins which look, at face value, to be for 10 and 20 francs. Closer inspection show that they are *ariary*, which is 5 francs, so they are worth 50 and 100 francs respectively. (The other coins also give the ariary value, but in Malagasy not figures so it is not confusing.)

The September 1988 rate of exchange was 2,600 FMG to the pound (1,700 FMG to the dollar) but it is sure to change.

Note: I give prices in FMG (mostly 1986 rates). New price information is given with the date beside it. You should soon learn what multiplying factor is needed to bring the old prices to current levels.

TRANSPORT

There are three ways of getting around Madagascar: rail, road and air. Railways (highly recommended) are described in the *East* chapter, which leaves road and air.

Road

I would normally head this section 'bus' but in Madagascar public transport is anything on wheels, even zebu carts and rickshaws!
Taxi-brousse, **car-brousse** and **Taxi-be.** All are varieties of 'Bush taxis' and run between major towns. I doubt if there is any country offering more crowded transport. If you think you're a well-seasoned traveller, wait until you try Madagascar! Taxi-brousses are generally Citroen vans, with seats facing each other so no good view out of the window. More comfortable are the Peugeot 404s (known as taxi-be or taxi-brousse) designed to take 9 people, but often packed with 14. A car-brousse is any sort of vehicle sturdy enough to cope with bad roads. Being sturdy it is usually excessively uncomfortable. There are also, occasionally, buses. Madagascar has a problem with its public transport because there is so little hard currency to pay for spare parts. If this situation improves the vehicles will also improve.

Vehicles leave from a *gare routière* on the outskirts of town by the road leading to their destination. You should try to go there a day or two ahead of your planned departure and buy a ticket in advance (there is always some sort of kiosk selling tickets). It is also wise to arrive early to claim your seat, since they are usually allocated on a first come first served basis. But be prepared for the vehicle to leave hours later than

Digging out a taxi-brousse. (Photo: Sally Crook.)

scheduled. On short journeys vehicles simply leave as soon as they fill up.

There is no set rate per kilometre; fares are calculated on the roughness of the road and the time the journey takes. The five day (approx) journey from Antananarivo to Fort Dauphin cost 19,000 FMG (about £20) in 1986 – roughly half the airfare. Now airfares are subjected to the tourist tariff, overland transport will be a fraction of the cost.

Drivers stop to eat and sleep. Most passengers spend the night in the vehicle or on the road outside, but there is often a hotel – of sorts – nearby.

There is much that a committed overland traveller can do to soften his/her experiences on taxi- or car-brousses – see *What to bring* on page 70. In addition to basic camping equipment, bring a good book, cards, Scrabble, etc, as well as snacks and drink, to pass the time during inevitable breakdowns and delays. If you're prepared for the realities, an overland journey can be very enjoyable (one traveller told me that the trip to Fort Dauphin was one of his best memories of Madagascar) and gives you a unique chance to get to know the Malagasy. Oh, and bring a knowledge of French – you won't get very far without it!

Car hire

Unless you are an expert mechanic, you are not advised to hire a self-drive car in Madagascar. (If you insist, Aventour has been recommended.) Various agencies have chauffeur-driven cars available. Madagascar Airtours is one, and you can also try the other agencies listed on page 75, or Société Auto Express, Route Circulaire Ampahibe. Tel: 210 60. Car hire must be paid for in hard currency.

Transport within cities

There are **taxis** in all cities. Their rates are reasonable – usually a fixed price for the centre of town – and they will pick up other passengers. They have no meters (bargaining recommended). The fare is approximately 800 FMG (1988) Some major cities (Majunga, Diego Suarez) have good **buses**.

from the time they operated in the capital and needed one man behind to push up the steep hills), are a Madagascar speciality and provide transport in Antsirabe, Majunga, and Tamatave. Occasionally you see them in Antananarivo, but they are mostly used for transporting goods.

Many western visitors are reluctant to sit in comfort behind a running, ragged, bare-foot man and no-one with a heart can fail to feel compassion for the *pousse-pousse* drivers. However, this is another case of needing to abandon our own cultural hang-ups. These men want work. Most rickshaws are owned by Indians to whom the 'drivers' must pay a daily fee. If they take no passengers they will be out of pocket – and there's precious little *in* their pockets. I square my conscience by taking a *pousse-pousse* whenever possible, bargaining them down to the

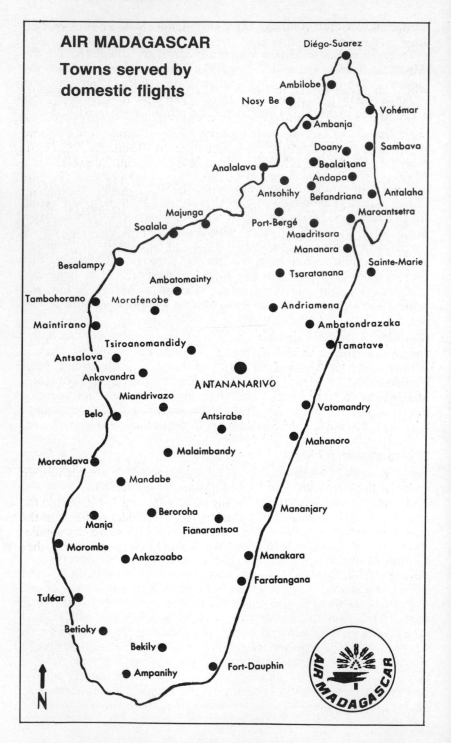

AIR MADAGASCAR

Towns served by domestic flights

Diégo-Suarez

Ambilobe

Nosy Be

Vohémar

Ambanja

Doany

Sambava

Analalava

Bealaizana

Andapa

Antsohihy

Befandriana

Antalaha

Majunga

Maroantsetra

Soalala

Port-Bergé

Mandritsara

Besalampy

Mananara

Sainte-Marie

Ambatomainty

Tsaratanana

Tambohorano

Morafenobe

Andriamena

Maintirano

Ambatondrazaka

Tsiroanomandidy

Tamatave

Antsalova

Ankavandra

ANTANANARIVO

Miandrivazo

Vatomandry

Belo

Antsirabe

Mahanoro

Malaimbandy

Morondava

Mandabe

Beroroha

Mananjary

Manja

Fianarantsoa

Morombe

Ankazoabo

Manakara

Tuléar

Farafangana

Betioky

Bekily

Ampanihy

Fort-Dauphin

N

normal 500 FMG (25p) or so, then giving them a good – and unexpected – tip at the end of the ride.

Air

Air Madagascar started its life in 1962 as Madair but understandably changed its name after a few years of jokes. It now serves 59 destinations, making it by far the best way – and for some people the only way – of seeing the country. Some sample prices from Antananarivo (Tana) with the new fare structure: Tamatave, £32 ($50); Nosy Be, £80 ($160); others are given in the relevant chapters.

An **Air Tourist Pass** gives you unlimited flights for a month. The pass costs 2,000 French Francs (about £200) in 1987 – but the price may go up in conjuction with the new fares – and is supposedly only available outside Madagascar when an Air Madagascar international ticket is also being purchased. However, if you have found it impossible to buy in your own country and can show that you flew with Air Madagascar, you may still be able to purchase a pass in Tana (try Madagascar Airtours for help). In addition to the unlimited flying, pass holders are supposed to get priority on crowded planes.

If you are arranging your flights once you arrive in Antananarivo be warned of the crush of passengers trying to do the same thing. You are advised to get to the office when it opens at 8.00. Often flights which are said to be fully booked in Tana are found to have seats when you reapply at the town of departure. In any case, you should reconfirm your next flight as soon as you arrive at your destination (at the Air Mad office in town). You can very often get on fully booked flights if you go standby, but do not expect to buy a ticket at the last minute, at a small airport, with a credit card; fares must be paid for in hard currency.

There are no numbered seats or refreshments on internal flights.

It is useful to know that *Enregistrement Bagages* is the check-in counter, and *Livraison Bagages* is luggage arrival.

Since January 1988, prices have increased by over 400%.

Air Madagascar have the following planes: Boeing 737 (flying to the larger cities and Nosy Bé), the smaller Hawker Siddeley 748, and the very small and erratic Twin Otter and Piper which serve the smaller towns. Inevitably planes get delayed or occasionally cancelled, but they are basically safe and reliable.

ACCOMMODATION

Hotels in Madagascar are classified by a national star system – five star being the highest, but in my experience this designates price, not quality. In this book I have used three categories: A, B and C. Often B, being less pretentious, are the better hotels. Beach bungalows, which come into all three categories, are usually excellent value.

Category A   Up to international standard in Antananarivo, Tamatave,

Tulear, Fort Dauphin and Nosy Be, but usually large and impersonal. Often overpriced and very run down in other less-visited towns. Prices range from £15 to £53 double.

Category B   More rustic accommodation, as available in the nature reserves, can be just as clean and comfortable with the added attraction (if you have the right attitude) of a certain amount of wildlife in the rooms. Gekkos, in particular, seem to enjoy hotel bathrooms, perhaps because of the prolific insect life found there. Most town hotels in this category have a basin and bidet in the room, and comfortable beds although hard, French-style bolsters take the place of pillows. They are often family-run and very friendly and pleasant. The average price is £8.

Category C   Exhilaratingly ghastly at times but quite charming at others, these are not for the squeamish. There may be rats, cockroaches, and other such creatures sharing your room. The pillows are filled with sisal, and the double beds can be quite amazingly uncomfortable with lumpy mattresses sagging like hammocks so that couples are thrown companionably together in the centre, or thin coverings over slats. During a freezing night on such a bed in Tulear I had a slat-induced dream that I was having a blood transfusion and was being backed into the apparatus like a horse into the shafts so that tubes could be plugged into my shoulder blades.

Some hotels have basins in the room, and occasionally they are clean and excellent value, only earning the C because of their price. In an out of the way place you will pay as little as £1 for the most basic room, although £3 or £4 would be more usual.

Sally Crook points out: '*Toilette* means shower or bathroom, at least in northern Madagascar, so to prevent accidents ask for the W.C. ('dooble vay say'). I only found it by the smell in one small overnight hotel after asking repeatedly for the wrong thing.'

Note: The Malagasy word *Hotely* usually means a restaurant/snack-bar rather than accommodation.

There are no organised campsites in Madagascar, but you can put your tent just about anywhere without danger.

FOOD AND DRINK

Food

Eating well will continue to be one of the delights of Madagascar, since restaurants will be exempt from the tourist tariff. International hotels serve international food, usually with a French bias and often do special Malagasy dishes (such as the Hilton on Thursdays). Lodges and smaller hotels serve local food, sometimes hot and spicy, which can also be excellent, particularly on the coast where lobster and other sea food predominate. Meat lovers will enjoy the succulent zebu steaks. Outside the capital, most hotels offer a set menu (*table d'hôte*) to their guests. Where the menu is *à la carte* it is a great help to have a French dictionary, preferably one with a food section.

Chinese and Indian food is common in many towns, and almost always good and reasonably priced. *Soupe Chinoise* is found almost everywhere, and is filling and tasty. The Malagasy eat a lot of rice (see p. 152) so most dishes are accompanied by a sticky mound of the stuff. It's bland and flavourless, but sops up the tasty sauces.

Butter and cheese used to be almost unobtainable, but are now served in the larger cities. There's usually a good selection of fruit in the markets and fruit is served in most restaurants, along with raw vegetables or *crudités*. From June to August the fruit is largely limited to citrus and bananas, but from September there are strawberries, mangoes, lychees, pineapples, citrus fruit, bananas and loquats. Slices of coconut are sold everywhere, but especially on the coast, where coconut milk is a popular and safe drink, and toffee-coconut nibbles are sold on the street, often wrapped in paper from school exercise books.

Drink
The Malagasy 'Three Horses' beer is very good (the large bottles are known as *grand modèle*), as is the new 'Beeks Brau'. The price goes up according to the surroundings: twice as much in the Hilton as in a *hotely* and there is always a hefty deposit payable on the bottles. Some of the wines from around Fianarantsoa are not bad. Rum, *toaka gasy*, is very cheap and plentiful, especially in sugar-growing areas such as Nosy Be, and fermented sugar cane juice, *betsabetsa* (east coast) or fermented coconut milk, *trembo* (north), make a change. The best drink of all is *punch au coco*, with a coconut milk base, which is a speciality of Île Ste Marie.

Soft drinks are limited to a good but rather expensive springwater, 'Eau vive' and, of course, Coca-cola. The locally produced *limonady* sadly bears no resemblance to lemons.

Malagasy food
After a year of living in Madagascar and travelling in remote areas, David Curl described the standard Malagasy dishes as: 'skin and rice, gristle and rice, fat and rice, and bones and rice', these being chicken, beef, pork and fish respectively. A sometimes true summary for the smaller villages, where basic menus are chalked up on a blackboard outside *hotelys*:

Henan omby (or *Hen'omby*) – beef.
Henam borona (or *Hen'akoho* – chicken.
Henan-kisoa – pork.
Henan drano (or *Hazan-drano*) – fish.

The menu may add Mazotoa homana. This is not a dish, it means *Bon appétit!*.

Along with the meat or fish and inevitable mound of rice (*vary*) comes a bowl of stock. This is spooned over the rice, or drunk as a soup.

Thirst is quenched with *ranovola*, or rice water, obtained by boiling water in the pan in which the rice was cooked. It has a slight flavour of burnt rice, and since it has been boiled for several minutes it is safe to drink.

In smarter restaurants Malagasy food can be very good indeed, and all visitors should at least sample the most popular dish, *Romazava*, a meat and vegetable stew, spiced with ginger. This is usually served with *bredes* (pronounced 'bread'), a variety of greens which often have a pleasant peppery taste. Another good local dish is *ravitoto*, shredded manioc leaves with fried pork.

One of the best restaurants in Madagascar! (Chez Vavate, Île Ste Marie)

HANDICRAFTS AND WHAT TO BUY

You can buy just about everything in the handicrafts line in Madagascar. Most typical of the country are wood carvings, raffia work (in amazing variety), crocheted and embroidered table-cloths and clothes, semi-precious stones, carved zebu horn, Antaimoro paper (with imbedded dried flowers), mounted butterflies, shells, and so on. The choice is almost limitless.

The luggage weight limit when leaving Madagascar is 20 kg (30kg if you are going to Paris which manages to count as a 'national' flight!). Bear this in mind when doing your shopping.

Other local products which make good presents are vanilla pods (although strictly speaking you are limited to 100 grammes), pepper corns, saffron and other spices, and honey.

Do not buy products from endangered species. That includes tortoiseshell, crocodile skins, and, of course, live or stuffed lemurs and other animals. Also prohibited are endemic plants and any genuine article of funerary art.

Some purchases will need an export permit. For animal products such as mounted butterflies apply to room 42 or the 4th floor of the Department dcs Eaux et Forets in Nanasana. Many artifacts and especially wood-carvings need a permit from the Ministere des Arts et de la Culture Revolutionnaire (69 Rue Victoire Rasoamanarivo – near the College de France) but this is rarely asked for at the airport. It is as well to get a receipt for your purchase whenever possible. Semi precious and precious stones may also need a permit from the Ministere des Mines et L'Energie, in Ambohidahy. The rules on permits always seems to be changing, so try to get local advice.

MISCELLANEOUS

Electrical equipment
The voltage in Madagascar is 110. Outlets (where they exist) take 2-pin round plugs.

Communication with home
In 1988 a one minute telephone call to Britain cost 7,000 FMG (from a private phone; hotels add a surcharge).

If you want to receive mail, have your correspondent address the envelope with your initial only, your surname in block capitals, and send it to you c/o Poste Restante in whichever town you will be. It will be held at the main post office.

B.P. in an address is *Boîte Postale* – the same as P.O. Box...

VILLAGE ETIQUETTE

Travellers venturing well off the beaten path will want to do their utmost to avoid offending or frightening the local people, who are usually extremely warm and hospitable. Unfortunately, with the many *fady* prohibitions varying from area to area and village to village, it is impossible to know exactly how to behave; all you can do is watch the villagers and do as they do, and if possible take a local guide. *Vazahas* (white foreigners) and other outsiders are exempt from the consequences of infringing a local *fady*, but of course may inadvertently cause the community to make expensive sacrifices to propitiate the offended *razana*.

On arrival at a village, ask for the 'Ray aman'dreny' (mother and father) of the village. This will be the village elder(s). Another person to introduce yourself to is the *Président du Fokontany* or head of the People's Executive Committee. He will show you where you can sleep (sometimes a hut is kept free for guests, often someone will be moved out for you). You will usually be provided with food, and as an honoured guest may even receive meat (in rural villages the day to day diet is rice and *bredes*). To suggest paying for your board and lodging would be considered an insult, but a small present would be appropriate.

The above applies to very remote areas, inaccessible by vehicle and unaccustomed to foreigners. In other communities you should still make contact with the *President du Fokontany* but may be expected to pay for your lodging. You should certainly offer to do so.

The traveller in Madagascar has a great responsibility. The customs of isolated rural people are very different from the west, but with their warm friendliness it is easy to forget these differences.

Cultural sensitivity is not easy to acquire, but in a country as 'unspoilt' as Madagascar it is essential if tourism is not to change a unique culture. The following example demonstrates the effect a generous-seeming action can have.

I was escorting an American couple from Fort Dauphin to Berenty. Passing one of the sparse collection of huts that make up a Antanosy village we saw that something important was happening: there were drums and dancing. At our request the driver got out to ask what was going on, and we learned that a village woman had become possessed of an evil spirit and the dance was the first stage in a three day exorcism process which would culminate with the sacrifice of a goat. We arranged with our driver to leave Berenty in time to see the closing stages.

Two days later they were still at it. The dance had become a shuffle, but still a remarkably energetic shuffle. Permission was asked, and graciously given, for us to stay and even to take photos. We were objects of mild curiosity but the onlookers were much too involved in the goings on in front of the houses to give us much attention.

After an hour the Americans began to get impatient. It was very hot and nothing new had happened for some time. No sacrifice, no escaping evil spirit. Suddenly I heard a commotion: one of them had produced a packet of balloons and was busy blowing them up and distributing them to the children. 'Kids always love these things' he chuckled. They did indeed love them. We were soon surrounded by first a pleading, then irate group of mothers and wailing children who either had not received a balloon, or whose new and ephemeral toy had burst. The exorcism process was still going on, but most onlookers had now turned their attention to us. The mood was broken.

As we drove away the American was half angry, half amused at what had happened. I was only upset. We had blundered in on a private and solemn event and been unable to resist making an exhibition of ourselves. These villagers would not show the same friendly, disinterested reaction to the next set of tourists.

Yet the giving of presents is part and parcel of modern Third World travel, condoned and encouraged in most guide books. We who venture off the beaten path, who intrude on other cultures, need to ask ourselves who we are aiming to benefit: the recipient of our gifts or ourselves. And if we are honest, would we not say it is ourselves, because to see the brief pleasure we give makes us feel less guilty about our affluent presence in their humble village?

'I thought then how horribly different our encounter would have been in a tourist spot – how those boys would have begged instead of chatting, and whined instead of laughing, and sniggered at our scantily clad bodies instead of stroking my bare white shoulder wonderingly with small black fingers. The distortion of human relationships, rather than the building of Holiday Inns or the sprouting of souvenir stalls, is the single most damaging consequence of Third World tourism.'

Dervla Murphy, *Muddling through in Madagascar.*

as the Zoma (Friday in Malagasy), there are colourful *lamba* cloths for the living and shrouds for the dead. Whole stalls are devoted to school exercise books, for education is at a premium in Madagascar, and its equipment is hard to come by. Everywhere in town and country children come up to you asking quietly for "*monnaie pour cahiers*" or "*monnaie pour stylos*". On my last day in Tana I handed half a dozen ballpoints to a group of soft-spoken nine-year-olds, who immediately turned into small savages fighting over the spoils.

The Times

In the film 'Crocodile Dundee,' the Aborigine stops the New Yorker from pressing the shutter: 'Do you think it will steal your soul?' she asks. 'No,' he says. 'You've got the lens cap on.' Maybe the tribes that believe the camera steals your soul are nearly right, at that—only it is the photographer's soul that suffers, not the subject's.

The Independent

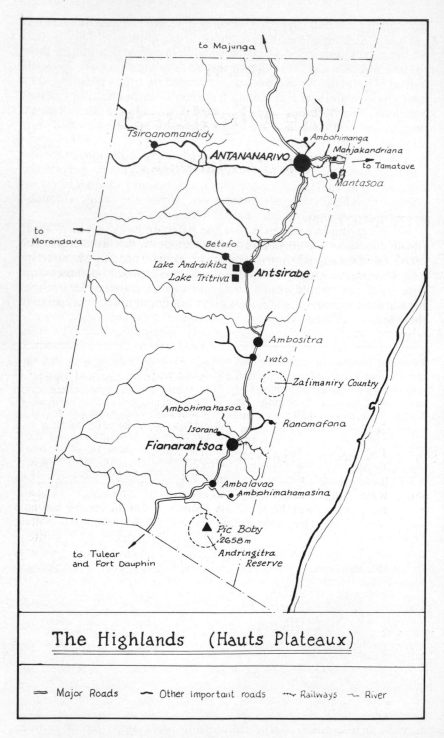

to Majunga

Tsiroanomandidy

ANTANANARIVO

Ambohimanga

Manjakandriana

to Tamatave

Mantasoa

to
Morondava

Betafo

Lake Andraikiba
Lake Tritriva   **Antsirabe**

Ambositra

Ivato

Zafimaniry Country

Ambohimahasoa

Ranomafona

Isorana

Fianarantsoa

Ambalavao
Ambohimahamasina

▲ Pic Boby
2658 m

to Tulear
and Fort Dauphin

Andringitra
Reserve

The Highlands   (Hauts Plateaux)

〜 Major Roads   〜 Other important roads   〜 Railways   〜 River

Chapter 7

The Highlands
(Hauts Plateaux)

INTRODUCTION

The kingdom of Imerina was born in the highlands. Recorded history of the Merina people (also known as the Hova), who are characterised by their Indonesian appearance and exhumation practices (*famadihana*) begins in the 1400s with a chief called Andriandraviravina. He is widely thought to have started the dynasty that became the most powerful in Madagascar, eventually conquering much of the country.

Key monarchs in the rise of the Merina include Andrianjàka, who conquered a Vazimba town called Analamanga built on a great rock thrusting above the surrounding plains. He renamed it Antananarivo and ordered his palace to be built on its highest point. With its surrounding marshland, ideal for rice production, and the security afforded by its high position, this was the perfect site for a Merina capital city.

In the 18th century there were two centres for the Merina kingdom, Antananarivo and Ambohimanga. The latter became the more important and around 1787 Ramboasalama was proclaimed king of Ambohimanga and took the name of Andrianampoinimerina.The name means 'the prince in the heart of Imerina' which was more than an idle boast: this king was the Malagasy counterpart of the great Peruvian Inca Tupac Yupanqui, expanding his empire as much by skilful organisation as by force, doing it without the benefit of a written language (history seems to demonstrate that orders in triplicate are not essential to efficiency). By his death in 1810 Madagascar was firmly in control of the Merina and ably administered through a mixture of old customs and new. Each conquered territory was governed by local princes, answerable to the King, and the system of *fokonolona* (village communities) was established. The new king, Radama I, had a firm foundation on which to build his own successes.

The Merina are still the most influential of the Malagasy peoples (although President Ratsiraka is Betsimisaraka) and dominate the capital. Further south, the highlands are occupied by the Betsileo, who have been heavily influenced by the Merina and also practise *famadihana*. Since the mid 19th century Merina houses have been built of brick or red mud (laterite), often with roofs supported on slender pillars. These typical houses are a feature of the city and its surroundings. Invariably they are of less sturdy construction than the cement tombs that can be seen on the outskirts of town, the dead being considered more important than the living.

There is some splendid scenery on the *Hauts Plateaux*. Route National 7, which runs to Tulear, passes dramatic granite domes and grassy hills, and always the mosaic of paddy fields add colour and pattern to a land journey. These patterns are best appreciated from the air, from where the old defence ditches, *tamboho*, forming circles around villages or estates can be seen. I never tire of staring down as the plane circles before landing at Ivato airport. The aerial view is as exotically different as Madagascar itself.

ANTANANARIVO
History
The city founded by Andrianjaka was called Antananarivo which means 'City of the thousand', supposedly because a thousand warriors protected it. By the end of the 18th century, Andrianampoinimerina had taken Antananarivo from his rebellious kinsman and moved his base there from Ambohimanga. From that time until the French conquest in 1895 Madagascar's history centred around the royal palace or *rova*, the modest houses built for Andrianjaka and Andrianampoinemerina giving way to the splendid palace designed for Queen Ranavalona by Jean Laborde and James Cameron. The rock cliffs near the palace became known as Ampamarinana, 'the place of the hurling' as Christian martyrs met their fate at the command of the Queen.

There was no reason for the French to move the capital elsewhere: its pleasant climate made it an agreeable place to live, and plenty of French money and planning went into the city we see today.

Arriving and leaving
Airport formalities
In its red tape heyday, getting from the aircraft to taxi or bus could take a couple of hours, although the actual process was conducted with a courtesy and patience that some leading airports (Kennedy, are you listening?) could copy. However, recent reports (October, 1988) are that delays at Ivato airport have now been reduced to a minimum. Knowing what to expect and which order to do it in will speed your progress:

1. Police. Have your passport checked and stamped.
2. Douane. Fill in your currency declaration form. Make quite sure it tallies with the amount of money and travellers cheques you have (make a note of the total *before* you get to the airport); the officials may count your money, so have it handy.

3. Santé (Health). You will need your vaccination card here showing that you are up to date with necessary inoculations. You will also be asked to list where you stayed for the last five nights. If one of them includes a malarial area your card may be confiscated and you will be told to report to the health department in 10 days. Malaria is taken seriously; you will be handed an information sheet on the correct prophylactics, and the following message: 'Keep this during one month. If you are ill or you does not feel weel during this time, you should show this ticket to the doctor to help him for taking car of you'.

4. You are ushered into a curtained cubicle (men one side, women another). Residents may get a body search here, tourists only get a smile and a quick check of documents.

You are now out in the main airport! While waiting for luggage to arrive, change money. The bank is on the right at the bottom of the stairs. Remember to have your currency declaration handy (and at all times when you change money).

Uniformed baggage handlers help you to retrieve your luggage (you do not need to tip them). You then take it into the customs area for checking (these days tourists are rarely asked to open luggage) and – congratulations, you are outside!

When leaving the country the situation is, if anything, worse. 'Coming in the airport formalities were very quick (half an hour)... Going out, well, 13 checkpoints and two hours later we were in the departure area. The paperwork needed to leave is *formidable*, especially if you are taking carvings.' (H.S-H). Make sure your paperwork is in order; take the carvings (or whatever) loose in a bag, but bring packing materials so you can pack it all up after customs has chalked you through. See page 91 for products needing export authorisation.

You need to get to the airport *at least* two hours before the flight. In addition to sorting out your purchases before leaving for the airport, make sure your currency declaration tallies with the amount of money you have left (they may check), and reserve 1,500 FMG for the airport tax (but check the current rate when you arrive). There is quite a good souvenir shop (hard currency) after you pass through all the controls, but remember you may not change FMG back to hard currency.

Transport into the city centre (12 km)

There is a very good airport bus service, Air Routes Services, which costs 1,500 FMG to Tana. Or you have the choice of posh taxi, cheap taxi, or local bus.

Posh taxis meet you *in* the airport, and hustle you and your luggage to their vehicle outside. The fare is about 10,000 FMG (bargain hard).

Walk across the road to the car-park where lurk the cheap taxis (understandably they are none too popular with the posh guys). These will cost around 6,000 FMG, but can often be bargained down.

Bare-bones budget backpackers can walk to the nearby town of Ivato – or the road junction (½ km) and get the local bus for 100 FMG.

Antananarivo today

One of the most attractive capitals anywhere, Antananarivo (popularly known as Tana) has the quality of a child's picture book. Brightly coloured houses are stacked up the hillsides, and there are very few of the modern skyscrapers that deface most capitals. Rice paddies are tended right up to the edge of the city, clothes are laid out on the river bank to dry, and ox-carts rumble along the roads on the outskirts of town. It's all deliciously foreign, and can hardly fail to impress the first time visitor as he or she comes in from the airport. The good impression is helped by the climate – during the dry season the sun is hot but the air pleasantly cool (the altitude is between 1,245 m and 1,469 m).

The city is built on two ridges which combine in a V. Down the central valley runs a broad boulevard, Avenue de l'Indépendance (sometimes called by its Malagasy name Fahaleovantena), which terminates at the station. It narrows at the other end to become Avenue du 26 Juin, then dives through a tunnel to reach lake Anosy and the Hilton Hotel (pedestrians make their way breathlessly up and down flights of stairs). The Avenues Indépendance and 26 Juin are the focal point of the Lower Town, lined with shops, offices, hotels, and crammed with market stalls and lower class bustle, but the 'centre of town' could just as easily refer to the Upper Town where the president's palace (no cameras!), the Hotel Colbert, the main post office and other assorted offices are located. This is where you will find the most expensive boutiques.

It is all very confusing, and made worse by streets being unnamed, changing name several times within a few hundred metres, or going by two different names (when reading street names it's worth knowing that *Lalana* and *Arabe* mean Road or Street). Fortunately you can never really be lost since this is a town for wanderers – you are just seeing a new area. As a rough wandering guide, however, I would recommend that lots of time be spent in the Upper Town – and on the opposite side, above the market – but don't venture beyond the station where distances are long and streets dreary.

Sightseeing

As if to emphasise how different it is to other capitals, Tana has very little in the way of conventional sight seeing. It doesn't even have a Tourist Office, although I would bet that this omission will be rectified before too long. There is an archaeological museum at the University of Madagascar that few seem to go to, but which is reportedly well worth the visit for the old photographs of the city. No-one can agree on when it is open: Musèe d'Art et d'Archeologie, 17 Rue Docteur Villette, Isoraka. Tel: 210-47. Hours 15.00 to 17.30 (or 14.00 to 17.30), Thursdays and weekends (or every afternoon except Monday).

Tsimbazaza

Rather a good museum (natural history and ethnology), botanical garden and zoo, well worth visiting as much for the pleasure of seeing the Malagasy enjoying a day out, as for the selection of plants and trees and some species of native Malagasy fauna. The park is open on Thursdays, Saturdays, Sundays and holidays, from 8.00 to 11.00, and 14.00 to 17.00. On other days, however, although not open to the general public, tourists will always be admitted on request (go further down the road to the small entrance).

Some international conservation efforts have gone into improving the zoo, and establishing educational programmes and as more money is made available this trend will no doubt continue. In addition to cages containing a variety of animals including lemurs (and an island of ring-tails), and a lake with hundreds of egrets nesting in the trees. There is a very good vivarium (open only in the afternoon) with a large collection of reptiles and small mammals. The botanical garden is spacious and well laid out, and also displays some reproduction Sakalava graves. It is the museum, however, that attracts the most interest for its excellent selection of skeletons of now extinct animals, including several species of giant lemur and the famous 'elephant bird' or *Aepyornis* which became extinct 800 years ago. It is displayed next to the skeleton of an ostrich, so its massive size can be appreciated. Another room displays stuffed animals, but the efforts of the taxidermist have left little to likeness and a lot to the imagination.

Tsimbazaza is about 4 km from the city centre. There are buses from Avenue de l'Indépendance (no 15), but it is easier to take a taxi there and bus or taxi-be back.

Zoma

No-one should visit Tana without going to the market. *Zoma* means Friday and this is the day when the whole of Avenue de l'Indépendance erupts into a rash of white umbrellas. The market runs the length of the street and up the hillsides, filling every available space with an amazing variety of goods. There are stands selling nothing but bottles, or spare parts, or years-old French magazines; there are men who repair watches, or umbrellas or bicycles; there are flowers and fruit and animals (including cats) and herbal medicines and charms; and there are dozens of varieties of handicrafts, from embroidery to wood carvings, semi-precious stones, raffia goods, and so on.

Bring lots of small change, and nothing else – the *zoma* is notorious for thieves. Carry larger sums of money in a money belt.

Although the *Zoma* proper is on Fridays, there is always a market in Tana, always some white umbrellas shading fruit and vegetables opposite the stairs leading to the upper town, and some handicraft stalls off a side road nearer the station. It is always interesting to wander around on Thursday nights, watching stalls being set up and goods unpacked under the flickering light of paraffin lamps. This is the one bustling evening: Tana is usually very quiet after dark.

The white parasols of the Zoma line Avenue de l'Indepéndance

The Queen's Palace (Rova)

Standing high above the city, this miscellany of mausoleums and palace dominates the skyline (especially when viewed from lake Anosy or the Hilton Hotel).

The energetic can walk there – it's a breathtaking (in both senses of the word) climb which takes about an hour from the town centre, but is well worth it for the views and scenes en route. Start at Lalana Ratsimilaho, near the Colbert, and when in doubt always take the uphill road. The entrance to the *Rova* is topped by a very European-looking eagle; King Radama 1 had his stronghold here guarded by elite troops known as The Eagles. The Queen's Palace, originally built in wood by Jean Laborde at the request of Queen Ranavalona I, is enclosed in a stone structure, designed by James Cameron in 1873 during the reign of Queen Ranavalona II. Laborde's building is perfectly in harmony with Madagascar, Cameron's would be more in keeping with Edinburgh. The main palace, *manjakamiadana* ('where it is pleasant to reign') has long been closed for renovations, but by the time you read this it should have reopened allowing a view of the 39 metre high rosewood pillar, said to have been brought from the eastern forests by ten thousand slaves, several huge rooms full of museum treasures, and the throne itself.

On entering the compound you will see on the left what appears to be two attractive wooden chalets. These are *tranomanara*, sacred houses, over the tomb of the Queens, where the remains of four Queens are interred, and the tomb of the Kings which houses three Kings. Their bodies lie seven metres below the ground.

Another building contains paintings of the monarchs and their advisors, including James Hastie and Sir Robert Farqhuar, military advisors to Radama I, and a fascinating early photo of Jean Laborde.

The reconstruction of Andrianampoinimerina's little palm-thatched house is interesting. The King's bed is high on a platform in the north-east corner, opposite a much wider shelf on which slept eleven of his twelve wives. The lucky twelfth spent one week in the royal bed, no doubt in acts of procreation. A tall column rises to the roof by the King's bed. We are told that on hearing the approach of a stranger, his highness would scramble up this pillar (there are tiny handholds) and if the visitor was welcome he would inform whichever wife was tending the cooking pots beneath the pillar by dropping a pebble on her head. Or so we are told.

Andrianampoinimerina's sedan chair, borne by eight men, is here, and an accompanying litter for his luggage. He travelled widely in his kingdom, exhorting the peasants to greater labours by replacing their worn out agricultural tools.

The *Besekana* contains the litter that carried the bodies of Ranavalona I and II. The royal initials RM (M being Manjaka, the Malagasy version of Regina) said that the monarch was not dead but 'had turned her back'; the reversed letters symbolise this.

Other curiosities in the royal compound are a vaguely Roman-looking Christian church (built in stone for Ranavalona II), and a rather odd pool, made for Queen Ranavalona III, with a statue apparently showing her braiding her hair. Queen Ranavalona III was exiled by the French and it is said that her pool was a misrepresentation by an anxious-to-please Frenchman of a bath used for ritual purification. (Merina royalty bathed ritually at the end of the rainy season, and the water was then distributed to any subjects that were present. The baths were made of silver.)

The *rova* is open Tuesday to Saturday, 14.00 − 17.00, Sunday 9.00 − 12.00, 14.00 − 1700. Closed Monday. You are not permitted to take photos within the compound (cameras are checked in at the gate). However, you can apply for a photo permit (it takes 24 hours) and come back with your camera the next day.

Where to stay

Category A
Hilton Hotel. One of Tana's skyscrapers (as you'd expect), very comfortable with good meals (typical Malagasy food is served one night a week and Chinese another). Its advantages are that Madagascar Airtours has its office in the building (and there are many other convenient offices and shops), and it has a swimming pool. In the pleasantly hot sun of the dry season this is a real bonus. The disadvantage is that it is some way from the centre of town. £53-£64 ($93-$112) double, £42-£51 ($74-$90) single.

Hotel Colbert. Very French, usually full, my choice of the posh Tana hotels for its excellent location in the Upper Town, superb food, and lively atmosphere. £34 ($60).

Hotel de France. The only first class hotel on Avenue de l'Indépendance. (£20, $35). Ask for an inside room – 59, 60, 61, among others. Convenient for those staying only briefly in Tana. Very good meals (but single men be warned − you'll be hassled by the bar-girls!), and a super patisserie with pain au chocolat (great for a breakfast splurge if you're sleeping cheap); very useful for Zoma zombies!

Category B
Solimotel, near Lac Anosy. Said to be very good, with swimming pool.

Le Relais de Pistards. Bungalows on L. Fernand Kasanga (same road as Tsimbazaza), about 1 km beyond the zoo. Owned by Florent and Jocelyne Colney who can organise tours for their guests. Mid price range. Recommended.

Hotel Mellis (2 star), Rue Indira Gandhi (off Ave de l'Indépendance). The most popular in this category, clean and comfortable, 8,000 FMG.

Muraille de Chine (3 star), Avenue de l'Indépendance, near the railway station. More expensive (£10) and not recommended.

Select Hotel (3 star), Avenue de l'Indépendance. Seedy. Poor value.

Hotel Terminus (2 star), Avenue de l'Indépendance (near the railway station). About 9,000 FMG. A popular hotel with *vazahas* but be on your guard for thieves.

Category C
   Hotel Glacier, Avenue de l'Indépendance. Rooms between 4,000 FMG and 8,000 FMG. A popular and central hangout, though some rooms are very sleazy. Avoid nos 12, 14, 22, 23, 24. Ask for 21, 34, 35, 36 which have hot water, or 9 and 10 which overlook the street.

La Rivo Hotel, Lalana Rainampandrandry; (with your back to the station, walk to the big junction, then left, uphill. 2,500 FMG.

Hotel Lapasoa du Bolidor, Ave Andrianampoinimerina. Near the station. Family-run and very friendly. 3,500 FMG to 4000 FMG.

Centre d'Acceuil Malley, 25, Avenue de l'Indépendance (just before Air Madagascar). 2,500 FMG.

Auberge de Jeunesse (youth hostel), 76, Rue Ratsimilaho, Ambatonakanga. (Past the Aeroflot office in the Upper Town near the Hotel Colbert). Very clean and reasonably priced. Meals provided. No YHA membership needed. 4,000 FMG full board. 20 beds.

Where to eat

Apart from the big hotels, Colbert, Hilton, France, all of which serve good food, there are several excellent restaurants.

The two best are under the same management: l'Aquarium (sea food) at Mahavoky, Besarety (take a taxi), tel: 222-66 and La Rotonde (French, everything but seafood), 19, rue Besarety, tel: 207-88.

Relais Normand, (French) 2, Arabe Rainibetsimisaraka, Soarano. Recommended. A few rooms are also available here.

Restaurant de la Grande Ile, beyond the market (away from the station) a little way up Rue Paul-Dussac to the right. Very good Chinese meals. Excellent value.

Restaurant Fiadanana. Near Hotel Lapasoa du Bolidor, and probably the best for Malagasy food.

Restaurant Rivière Parfums. Same street, also good Malagasy food.

La Muraille de Chine, Avenue de l'Indépendance, (on the right near the station) Chinese. Recommended.

Restaurant Minar, Rue Indira Gandhi. Good Indian food.

Two good snack bars on Indépendance: Blanche Neige (fancy, milkshakes) and Bouffe Rapide.

For a cheap meal try the smaller restaurants *hotely gasy* down Ave Andrianampoinimerina. Meals usually include Chinese soup.

Cheapest of all, and very enjoyable, is to have breakfast on Avenue de l'Indépendance. From early morning there are stalls selling bread and yoghurt. The latter seems to be safe providing you bring your own spoon and don't let them put ice in it. Fruit can be bought from numerous stalls.

Transport

Trains run east to Tamatave and south to Antsirabe from the station at the end of Avenue de l'Indépendance.

Buses (local) are always crowded and need some skill to use because of the confusing number of district names. Supposedly, however, you can buy a bus-circuit map from FTM (see below) which would help a lot.

Taxis are plentiful and reasonable. They do not have meters so agree on the price beforehand. Taxis parked outside the large hotels are more expensive and operate on a 'fixed' rate. Bargain hard.

Antananarivo Centre   - Key

① Station   ② Restaurant Grand Orient

③ Hotel La Muraille de Chine   ④ Hotel Terminus

⑤ Institut de Hygiène Social   ⑥ Bank   ⑦ Hotel La Rivo

⑧ Supermarket   ⑨ Hotel Mellis   ⑩ Hotel de France

⑪ French Embassy   ⑫ Air Madagascar   ⑬ Zoma (Market)

⑭ Auximad   ⑮ Patisserie Suisse   ⑯ Place de l'Indépendance

⑰ Restaurant Grand Île   ⑱ Main Post Office

⑲ Hotel Colbert, La Taverne   ⑳ Aeroflot

㉑ President's Palace   ㉒ Hotel Hilton, Madagascar Airtours

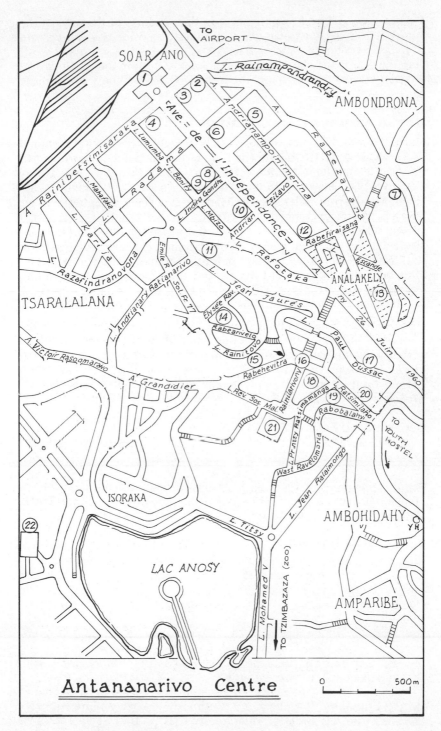

Antananarivo Centre

0   500m

Taxi-brousse and taxi-be parks are on the outskirts of the city, at the appropriate road junctions: Gare du Ouest, Anosibe (Lalana Pastora Rahajason on the far side of Lac Anosy) serving the south and west; Gare du Nord, at Lalana Doktor Raphael Raboto in the north-east of the city, serving the north and the east. Taxi drivers know where these places are.

Useful addresses/information

Maps   A large selection of maps can be bought at the Institut National de Geodesie et Cartographie (its long Malagasy name is shortened to FTM), Lalana Dama-Ntsoha RJB, Ambanidia (Tel: 229-35). Hours 8.30 to 12.00, 14.00 to 18.00. They do a series of 12 maps, scale 1:500,000 covering each region of Madagascar. These are most inviting, but sadly no longer completely accurate, especially in their concept of a village, which may turn out to be one hut which fell down last decade. There are also excellent maps of Nosy Be and Ste Marie. As usual, the staff are extremely pleasant and helpful. The more popular maps can often be bought from a FTM van parked at the top of the steps leading from the Lower to the Upper Town (Place de l'Indépendance), and may also be found in bookshops, but are often out of print.

Bookshops   The best bookshop is Libraire de Madagascar, near the Hotel de France on Ave de l'Indépendance. Another, on the left side of L.Indira Gandhi (just off Ave Indépendance) has a good selection of maps and town plans. In the Upper Town the Lutheran Bookshop (Trano Printy Loterana) opposite the Solimal building sells *English-Malagasy Vocabulary* if you can't get it in the other shops.

Department d'Eaux et Forêts   Nanisana. Open 8.00 − 12.00, 14.00 − 18.00. Apply here for your *Autorisation d'Acces* to visit national parks and reserves (see page 61).

Bank.   For the best rate and least hassle, try the bank near the Ny Havana (Roxy) cinema, half way up the steps to the Upper Town. Banking hours: 8 − 11, 14.00 − 16.30.

Supermarket   Though very poorly stocked by European standards (and zero by American) the supermarket on Ave 26 Juin nevertheless has useful picnic/travel goodies: dried fruit, honey, etc. For a better range of supplies try Prisunic, by Place de l'Indépendance near the Colbert Hotel.

Hairdresser   On Indépendance on the left near the station. Excellent.

Medical Centre   Opposite the French Embassy (1½ blocks away from Ave Indépendance). Very helpful.

British Embassy   (Ambassador Anthony V. Hayday.) Immeuble Ny Havana, Cité des 67 Ha, Antananarivo (B.P. 167). Tel: 277-49 or 273-70.

Excursions from Antananarivo*
Ambohimanga

Lying 21 km from Antananarivo, Ambohimanga, meaning the 'blue city', was for a long time forbidden to Europeans. From here began the line of kings and queens who were to form Madagascar into one country, and it was here that they returned for rest and relaxation among the tree-covered slopes of this hill-top village.

Ambohimanga has seven gates, though several are all but lost among the thick vegetation. One of the most spectacular gates, through which you enter the village, has an enormous stone disc which was formerly rolled in front of the gateway each night. Above the gateway is a thatched-roof sentry post. Inside the village the centre-piece is the wooden house of the great king Andrianampoinimerina (1787-1810).

The simple one-roomed house is interesting for the insight it gives into everyday (royal) life of that era. There is a display of cooking utensils (and the stones that surrounded the cooking fire), and weapons, and the two beds (as in the Tana *rova* with the top one for the king and the lower for one of his wives). The roof is supported by a 10 metre rosewood pole.

Andrianampoinimerina's son, Radama, with British help, went a long way to achieving his father's ambition to expand his kingdom to the sea. After Radama came a number of queens and they built themselves elegant summer houses next to Andrianampoinimerina's simple royal house. Outside influence is strongly evident here, especially British, and you can see several gifts sent to the monarchs by Queen Victoria.

This is a beautiful, peaceful place. Before leaving Ambohimanga you can have a drink at a cafe/bar inside the royal palace area with quite superb views towards Antananarivo. On Sundays there are sometimes displays of traditional dancing.

Ambohimanga is reached on a good road by private taxi (have him wait for you) or taxi-brousse from the Ambodivona/Tana road junction. There are reportedly also buses.

Lake Mantasoa

Sixty kilometres east of Antananarivo is Mantasoa where in the 19th Century Madagascar had its first beginnings of industrialisation. Indeed, historians now claim that industrial output was greater then than it ever was during the colonial period. It was thanks to Jean Laborde that a whole range of industries was started including an iron foundry which enabled Madagascar to become more or less self-sufficient in swords, guns and gunpowder, thereby increasing the power of the central government. Jean Laborde was soon highly influential at court and he built a country residence for the Queen at Mantasoa. Sadly most of the remains of the buildings have disappeared, drowned to make a reservoir. The scenery is spectacular, and camping is permitted

Parts of the following sections were contributed by Damien Tunnacliffe.

THE TWO-MAN INDUSTRIAL REVOLUTION

Technology was introduced to Madagascar by two remarkable Europeans, James Cameron, a Scot, and Jean Laborde, a Frenchman.

James Cameron arrived in Madagascar in 1826 during the country's 'British' phase when the LMS had attempted, with only partial success, to set up local craftsmen to produce goods in wood, metal, leather and cotton. Cameron was only 26 when he came to Madagascar, but was already skilled as a carpenter and weaver, with wide knowledge of other subjects which he was later to put to use in his adopted land: physics, chemistry, mathematics, architecture and astronomy. Cameron seemed able to turn his hand to almost anything mechanical. Among his achievements were the successful installation and running of Madagascar's first printing press (by studying the manual – the printer sent out with the press had died with unseemly haste), a reservoir (now Lac Anosy) and aqueduct, and the production of bricks.

Cameron's success in making soap from local materials ensured his royal favour after King Radama died and the anti-British Queen Ranavalona came to power. Even soap could not extend his stay once the missionaries had been ordered to leave, however, and in 1835 Cameron sailed to South Africa.

He returned in 1863 when the missionaries were once more welcome in Madagascar, to oversee the building of stone churches, a hospital, and the stone exterior to the *Rova* or Queen's palace in Antananarivo.

Jean Laborde was even more of a 'renaissance man'. The son of a blacksmith, Laborde was shipwrecked off the east coast of Madagascar in 1831. Queen Ranavalona, no doubt pleased to find a less Godly European, asked him to manufacture muskets and gun-powder, and he soon filled the gap left by the departure of Cameron and the other artisan-missionaries. Laborde's initiative and inventiveness were amazing: in a huge industrial complex built by forced labour, he produced munitions and arms, bricks, and tiles, pottery, glass and porcelain, silk, soap, candles, cement, dyes, sugar, rum ... in fact just about everything a thriving country in the 19th Century needed. He ran a farm which experimented with suitable crops and animals, and a country estate for the Merina royalty and aristocracy to enjoy such novelties as firework displays. And he built the original Queen's palace in wood (in 1839), which was later enclosed in stone by Cameron.

So successful was Laborde in making Madagascar self-sufficient, that foreign trade was discontinued and foreigners – with the exception of Laborde – expelled. He remained in the Queen's favour until 1857 when, amid the brutal massacre of Christians, he was expelled to Mauritius. The 1,200 workmen who had laboured without pay in the foundries of Mantasoa, rose up and destroyed everything – tools, machinery, and buildings. The factories were never rebuilt, and Madagascar's Industrial Revolution came to an abrupt end.

in the pine forests. One of the fanciest hotels in Madagascar is located here: Hotel de Hermitage (B.P.16, Manjakandriana; tel: 05). The Chalet, run by a Swiss family (tel: 20), is warmly recommended (meal 4,000 FMG in 1986).

Mantasoa can be reached by taking a train to Manjakandriana and then a taxi-brousse for the last 15 km, or a taxi-brousse all the way from Tana.

Tsiroanomandidy

Lying about 200 km to the west of Tana, on a good (surfaced) road (4 hours by taxi-be), this town is worth visiting for its huge cattle market, held on Wednesdays and Thursdays. There is one fairly good hotel ('clean, food OK, and sometimes even hot water in the – only – bathroom.'). Tsiroanomandidy is linked to Maintirano and Majunga by Twin Otter (Tuesdays), and Morondava (Saturdays). See Chapter 11.

ANTSIRABE

Antsirabe lies 169 km south of Antananarivo at 1,500 m. It was founded in 1872 by Norwegian missionaries attracted by the cool climate and the healing properties of the thermal springs. The name means 'the place of much salt', and the hot springs are still one of the town's main attractions. You can take baths at a variety of hot temperatures all for the equivalent of about 20 pence. An experience not to be missed!

This is also one of Madagascar's few elegant cities. A splendidly broad avenue leads from the station to the famous Hotel des Thermes, with a monolith depicting Madagascar's eighteen tribes as added interest. The town is divided into two distinct parts: to the right of the station is the former European quarter with its grid-iron streets, gardens and aura of gentle decay. Norwegians still maintain a presence in the town, both through missionaries and an aid programme. To the left of the station is the Malagasy town, though first you pass a line of banks and shops and the Catholic church. You come to a small market place and in the street beyond that you will find a popular Vietnamese-run restaurant.

On a promontory overlooking the Baths or *Thermes*, as the French call them, stands the Hotel des Thermes: an amazing building both in size and architectural style. It would not be out of place along the French Riviera and must be the most atmospheric colonial-style hotel after the Raffles Hotel in Singapore. It is quite expensive by the standards of Madagascar (15,000 FMG in 1987 but now in hard currency) but probably worth the extravagance.

Saturday is the best time to be in Antsirabe because that is the main market day. Ask for the 'Asabotsy' market on the far side of the lake which is close to the middle of the town. The market is like Antananarivo's *zoma* in miniature but with an even greater cross-section of activities (no handicrafts, though).

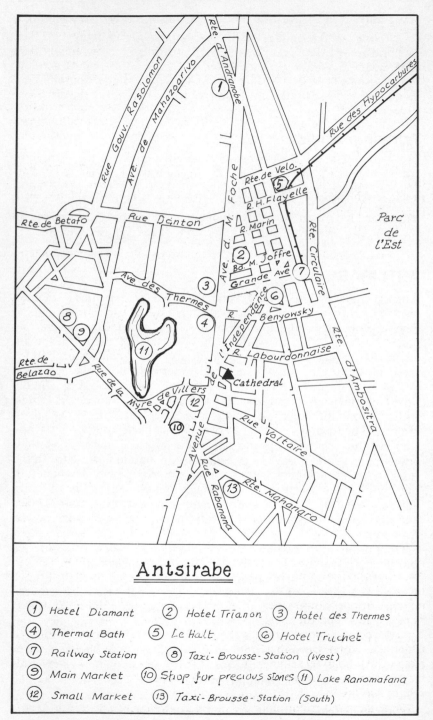

Antsirabe

① Hotel Diamant ② Hotel Trianon ③ Hotel des Thermes
④ Thermal Bath ⑤ Le Halt ⑥ Hotel Truchet
⑦ Railway Station ⑧ Taxi-Brousse-Station (West)
⑨ Main Market ⑩ Shop for precious stones ⑪ Lake Ranomafana
⑫ Small Market ⑬ Taxi-Brousse-Station (South)

Antsirabe is in the heart of one of the more productive regions of Madagascar. You will find a great variety of European and tropical produce on sale. It is a town which is relaxed and relaxing; there is not the 'edge' that is sometimes felt in the capital. People are genuinely friendly. There are a few beggars but not the same distressing poverty as in Antananarivo.

In addition to agriculture, Antsirabe is one of the centres of industry (food processing, aviation), and produces much of the woven cotton goods that are sold throughout the island. Above all it is the home of the excellent Three Horses Beer.

If you are travelling from May to September you will need a sweater or cardigan at night. It really does get quite cold. A stroll at night will be repaid by the sight of the *pousse-pousses* silently moving like fireflies, each with a lighted candle at their back. Unlike the *pousse-pousses* in Antananarivo and on the coast, those of Antsirabe are wellcared-for and there is a feeling of pride about them and the men who pull them. Antsirabe is one of the best places to buy semi-precious stones such as garnets, emeralds, etc. There are a number of little shops where stones are cut and sold, the best being a red-painted restored Colonial house on the road south of Rue de la Myre de Villers (see map).

Getting there.

The more interesting way is by train from Antananarivo. It is (usually) a three and a half hour journey and there are two trains a day, leaving at 06.30 and 13.30. On arrival at Antsirabe you are met by a bevy of *pousse-pousse* drivers who will enthusiastically try to persuade you to use their services. Indeed, this is the *pousse-pousse* capital of Madagascar, and some travellers have resorted to sneaking out of the back door of the hotel to avoid their attentions. Everywhere in Antsirabe is within easy walking distance.

Where to stay

If you want to pamper yourself then simply walk half a mile down the very grand avenue which leads from the station and ends at the Hotel des Thermes (about £20 double). If you want something more modest (6,000 FMG in 1988) then go down the grand avenue and take the last turn on the right before the Hotel des Thermes and walk up the road to the Hotel Trianon which is opposite the Cercle Mixte, an old officers' mess. The Hotel Trianon is run by a Frenchman whose business is mining semi-precious stones. The hotel is a sideline (7,000 FMG 1988) but it is clean and the meals are excellent value.

Also recommended are the Hotel Diamant (mid price range – Chinese), Hotel Baobab (6,000 FMG – 1988 – with shower; good restaurant), Soafytel (near cathedral, 7,000 FMG double, shower) and the Fitsangantsanganana, a family-run hotel with a garden on the far side of the lake.

Recommended restaurants are La Halt, in the European (northern) part of the city, and the Vietnamese Le Fleuve Parfumé.

Excursions from Antsirabe

Lake Andraikiba

About 5 km from Antsirabe you can see one of the several volcanic lakes. In colonial French times, Andraikiba was a popular place for water-skiing and other water sports but it is now rather run down. Like many such lakes it has its legends, the most famous one being the story of the local prince who could not make up his mind which of two women to marry and decided that the first to swim across the lake would be his wife. One of the young women, however, was pregnant with his child and drowned as she tried to swim across. Local people say that every day near dawn a beautiful young woman emerges from the water and rests on a rock, disappearing as soon as anyone approaches.

Lake Tritriva

Continuing past Lake Andraikiba on a dirt road for 12 km or so, you come to another volcanic lake, this one quite dramatic. Deep (80 m), green water is trapped in a perfect volcanic cone, fringed with trees. From the edge of the cone you have views for miles across to Antsirabe in the far distance. It is possible to get down to the water to swim (but very cold!).

Tritriva also has its legends, especially of a young couple whose parents refused to let them marry and who threw themselves to their death in the water. They were changed into two trees whose interlaced branches grow from the rock at the edge of the lake.

This is an excellent place for ornithologists and botanists, and bats live in caves in the cliffs. A highly recommended excursion.

Betafo

About 20 km west of Antsirabe by an excellent tarmac road that goes as far as Morondava, lies Betafo. It is a good example of a town in the highlands with red-brick churches and houses. Dotted among the houses are 'vatolahy', standing stones erected to commemorate warrior chieftains. These standing stones are inscribed and decorated.

At one end of the town is another volcanic lake, Lake Tatamarina, edged with weeping willows and with almost equally bent and silent anglers. From there it is a walk of 2½ km to the Antafofo waterfalls among beautiful views of ricefields and volcanic hills.

Ambositra

If you go south from Antsirabe along Route National 7 for 100 km you come to Betsileo country, and the small town of Ambositra in a beautiful setting surrounded by hills. Ambositra is the centre of Madagascar's wood carving industry, and even some of the houses have ornately carved wooden balconies and shutters.

The reason the wood carving industry is here is the proximity of the small remaining area of primary forest with its rare and beautiful wood and also because to the east of Ambositra live the Zafimaniry people who maintain the real traditions of Malagasy wood carving.

The best place to buy top quality carvings is at the 'Arts Zafimaniry', a co-operative run by a French Catholic mission, and housed in their monastery. This splendid complex of buildings is well worth a visit for its location and views, and is reached from the south side of town, up the hill. The address is ECAR, Boulevard Circulaire. Within the monastery the shop is not easy to find – you will have to ask one of the monks.

There is reputed to be a museum in Ambositra 'on the hill of Ambositra Tompon'anarana' but I haven't checked it out.

With all this carving around, you would expect the town's name to have some connection, but no, it means 'town of gelded cattle' because a former landowner raised admirably plump steers!

Where to stay/eat

Grande Hotel. 'Gently-decaying, colonial style. Good food and the best place for information on the Zafimaniry.' (D.T.)

A cheaper alternative is La Bonne Lave Mahavantana.

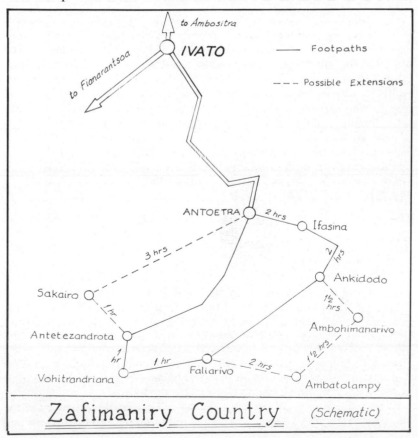

Zafimaniry Country   (Schematic)

Zafimaniry villages

Most of the Zafimaniry villages can only be reached on foot. The starting point is 10 km south of Ambositra at the village of Ivato. From there a good road goes to the village of Antoetra, perched on the mountainside at about 1,874 m. Their elaborately decorated wooden houses have geometrical and figurative carvings. Ifasina is two hours away on foot, and there are other villages in the area (see sketch map) and each has its carving speciality. This is rugged country, between 1,500 m and 1,800 m, and you must be fully equipped and prepared to camp. FTM map no 8 would be very helpful for this trip. Madagascar Airtours do a four day trek in Zafimaniry country: an excellent and safe way of seeing the more remote villages.

Interestingly, the Zafimaniry are unique in Madagascar in using the backstrap loom for weaving. This method of tensioning the warp is unknown in Africa, but common in Asia. Their speciality is woven bark, where the fibres are separated after soaking in water. The resulting cloth is used for burial purposes.

Continuing south down R.N.7, the scenery becomes increasingly spectacular. Just before Ambositra the grassy hills have given way to the western limit of the rainforest, and the road climbs up steep hills where the roadside shrubs are spray-painted red from dust and mud. The steepest climb comes after about two hours, when the car labours up an endlessly curving road, through thick forests of introduced pine, and reaches the top where orange and tangerine sellers provide welcome refreshment. Then it's down through more forest, on a very poor stretch of road, to Ambohimahasoa and more open country of rice-paddies and houses as you begin the approach to Fianarantsoa.

FIANARANTSOA

The name means 'Place of good learning' and Fianarantsoa (Fianar for short) is considered to be the intellectual capital of Madagascar. Queen Ranavalona made it her second capital in 1830, finding it conveniently situated between Antananarivo and the south.

In addition to access by road there are flights five days a week from Tana (£44). Airport to town by taxi: 800 FMG (1986).

Present-day Fianar is as notable for the number of churches, both Protestant and Catholic, as for its confusing lay-out, with the town being situated on three levels. For travellers making only a brief stop this arrangement is daunting, since the lower town, dominated by a huge concrete stadium, is decidedly dreary apart from the station itself which is a splendidly elegant piece of French colonial architecture, and quite out of keeping with the buildings in its neighbourhood.

The upper town, with its narrow winding streets and plethora of churches is said to be worth a visit. It's quite a way – take a taxi up.

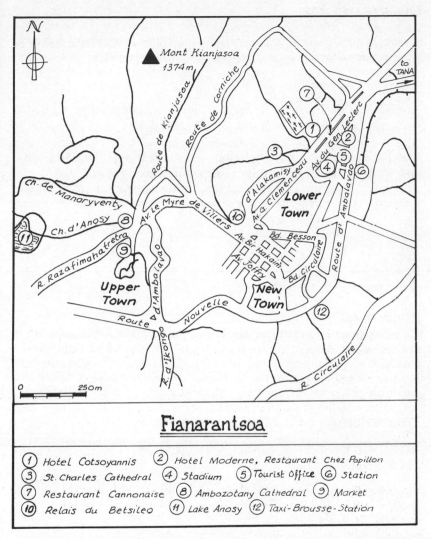

Fianarantsoa

① Hotel Cotsoyannis   ② Hotel Moderne, Restaurant Chez Papillon
③ St. Charles Cathedral   ④ Stadium   ⑤ Tourist Office   ⑥ Station
⑦ Restaurant Cannonaise   ⑧ Ambozotany Cathedral   ⑨ Market
⑩ Relais du Betsileo   ⑪ Lake Anosy   ⑫ Taxi-Brousse-Station

Warning: this map may be inaccurate! Use it as a general guide only, and send any corrections to me for the next edition.

Many Malagasy names begin with RA. This is a respectful prefix, similar to esq. in Britain.

Where to stay
Category A
Sofia Hotel. 'A large building hiding behind high wall on right side of or road from Tana. Very good. Super Restaurant.' (S.H.)

Category B
Hotel Relais du Betsileo. 'Is the one most foreigners go to but it was neither welcoming nor well-run in 1986'. (D.T.)

Hotel Cotsoyannis. Friendly, good value (6,600 — 9,950 FMG 1988) and with hot water in a rather surprising small shower that opens straight out into the corridor, without any place to put your clothes, towel etc. Lots of fun for other guests!

Lotus Rouge. Mid-range in price and comfort.

Category C
Hotel Escale. Cheap and grotty.

Where to eat
Chez Papillon. Treat yourself to 'The best restaurant in Madagascar, if not the Indian Ocean'. Not cheap, but definitely good, and slightly smug with it. I enjoyed my meal, but other travellers have written 'we thought food awful and very overpriced'. *Chacun a son gout*, and certainly I've eaten far better in Majunga and Ste Marie at a fraction of the cost.

Restaurant Maharajah. At the bottom of Rue Pasteur.

Bar Panda. Opposite Cotsoyannis. Good, inexpensive meals.

'Fianarantsoa is at the centre of Madagascar's wine growing industry. Both red and white wine are produced and if one enters into the spirit of the thing both are just about drinkable and one or two of the reds are even palatable.' (D.T.)

Further information
There is a tourist office (Syndicat d'Initiative) near the station run by Stella Ravelomanantsoa. He (sic) speaks English and is very helpful.

Excursions
Wine tasting
The Isandra estate (Domaine Côtes d'Isandra) and the Famoriana estate (Domaine Côtes de Famoriana) are two of the largest and best known wine producers in Madagascar. Both vineyards are open to visitors. Isandra is 20 miles north-west of Fianarantsoa and Famoriana is a little further on beyond the small town of Isorana.

Ranomafana

A pleasant small town, north-east of Fianar, known for its hot springs. Accessible by taxi-brousse (good road). 'I had a whale of a time – or should I say a lemur of a time – in Ranomafana. The road descending to the town follows the course of a spectacular river (with waterfalls) and through some really nice (though all too little) rainforest. There is, of course, the hot-water swimming pool which costs a nominal fee, or you can have a private bath. Officially open from about 7.00 and closed at midday and in the evening.

'There is one western-style hotel in town: Hotel Thermal de Ranomafana (B.P. 13, Tel: 1 (!)). Rooms from 6,500 FMG (1988). A bit damp but quite adequate. Good communal washing facilities, but ironically no hot water despite the name of the town (*Rano* – water, *mafana* – hot). The food is *very* good.' (David Curl).

'The Bobo Hotel, with a sign post of Mickey Mouse outside, is said to be a good place to hang around in the evening if you're looking for a lift in a lorry next day.' (Sally Crook).

Ranomafana is particularly interesting to naturalists since a new species of lemur was recently found there (see Box), although you'd be lucky to see them. Much more common is the red-bellied lemurs (*Lemur rubriventer*). See Addenda for important 1988 information on the rainforest of Ranomafana.

The Golden Bamboo Lemur, and other Hapalemurs

The story of the golden bamboo lemur (*Hapalemur aureus*) goes back to 1972 when another similar Hapalemur, *Hapalemur simus*, thought to be extinct, was re-discovered by André Peyrieras in the south east.

In 1986, two scientists arrived to study this new lemur in the forest near Ranomafana where it had been seen by Corinne Dague, a local French school teacher and lemur devotee. Patricia Wright, from Duke University, North Carolina, did some studies on what she thought were *Hapalemur simus* followed by Bernard Meier from Germany. Both initially assumed that they were observing a different form of the lemur Peyrieras had described. It was only after Ms Wright saw two dissimilar groups sharing the same habitat but feeding on different plants, that she realised these were probably two distinct species; *Hapalemur aureus* are smaller and browner than *Hapalemur simus*, and were later found to have other differences which put them firmly in the category of a new species. The brachial scent gland is in a different location and, to clinch the matter, the golden bamboo lemur has more chromosomes.

The different English names given to the Hapalemur genus are confusing. They are called bamboo lemurs and also gentle lemurs, as well as the more straightforward hapalemur. The three species and their various names are: *H. griseus*, grey gentle lemur, grey bamboo lemur, lesser hapalemur; *H. simus* broad-nosed gentle lemur, greater bamboo lemur, greater hapalemur; *H. aureus*, golden bamboo lemur (no doubt a 'gentle' name will follow).

This is also an excellent area for bird watching. Dick Byrne recommends that you take a guide from the little village a few kilometres up the road towards Fianar. 'These guys really know their stuff but they don't speak much French. Some of them know the Latin names of the birds, however.' (Dick paid 2,500 FMG a day for a guide in 1987.)

Ambalavao

Some 50 km south-west of Fianarantsoa is a town of outstanding interest for its scenery, cultural history and modern handicrafts.

This is where the famous Malagasy 'Antaimoro' paper is made. This 'papyrus' paper impregnated with dried flowers is sold as wall-hangings and lampshades, and the zoma in Tana is full of good examples.

The people in this area are Betsileo, but paper-making in the area copies the coastal Antaimoro tradition which goes back to late Moslem immigrants, who wrote prophesies or verses from the Koran on this paper. This Arabic script was the only form of writing known in Madagascar before the LMS developed a written Malagasy language nearly five hundred years later using the Roman alphabet.

Antaimoro paper is traditionally made from the bark of the havova tree from the eastern forests, but sisal paste is now often used. After the bark is pounded and softened in water, dried flowers are pressed into it before it finally dries. The factory where it is made is behind the church in Ambalavao, but travellers heading south will prefer to defer their shopping until Tana.

Although Ambalavao is on R.N.7, southward bound travellers are advised to make it an excursion from Fianarantsoa, since vehicles heading to Ihosy and beyond will have filled up with passengers in Fianar and you will be in for a long wait.

The town has one hotel, the Verger (tel: 5), and apart from its splendid location and paper, the market is highly recommended. 'Here you can buy very nice handmade silk scarves [these are lamba gasy, which are also used as ancestral shrouds. In the village of Ambinanindovoka, about 20 km to the east, they weave a different style known as lamba Arindrano]. There are many sorcerers [ombiasy] selling medicaments.' (J.L.). The main market is held on Wednesdays, and there is a cattle market on Thursdays.

The area around Ambalavao has arguably the finest mountain scenery in Madagascar. Coming from Fianar the landscape is a fine blend of vineyards and terraced rice-paddies (the Betsileos are acknowledged masters of rice cultivation) then after 20 km a giant rock formation seems almost to hold the road in its grasp. Its name is, appropriately, Tanan'Andriamanitra, or Hand of God.

Beyond Ambalavao, as you continue on the road south-west, granite domes of rock dominate the grassy plain. The most striking one, with twin rock towers, is called Varavarana Ny Atsimo, the 'Door to the South', which dominates the pass of the same name. Beyond is the 'Bonnet de l'Évêque' (Bishop's Hat), and a huge lump of granite shaped like an upturned boat, with its side gouged out into an amphitheatre; streams run into the lush vegetation at its foot. Then comes the flat Horombe plateau and the south.

This area of granite domes and cliffs is of great interest to geologists because the pattern of erosion is almost unique – only Brazil has something similar. Deep vertical channels known as *cunettes* cut into the rock. No-one knows what forces of nature caused them.

Granite mountains in the Ambalavao area

Excursions from Ambalavao
Pic Boby
South of Ambalavao lies the Andringitra massif, crowned by Madagascar's second highest mountain, Pic Boby (2,658 m). The area, which shelters some precious virgin forest, constitutes Réserve Naturelle Intégrale de l'Andringitra, which has recently been given special attention by the government conservation agencies. A permit to visit must be obtained in Tana. Guides may be hired at the village of Antanifotsy, which is 50 km from Ambalavao down a very bad road. There are footpaths in the reserve, including one running 25 km from the village to Pic Boby.

The reserve is rich in endemic fauna and flora, including several species of lemur.

Another more accessible town for mountain excursions is Ambohimahamasina. No permit is needed here.

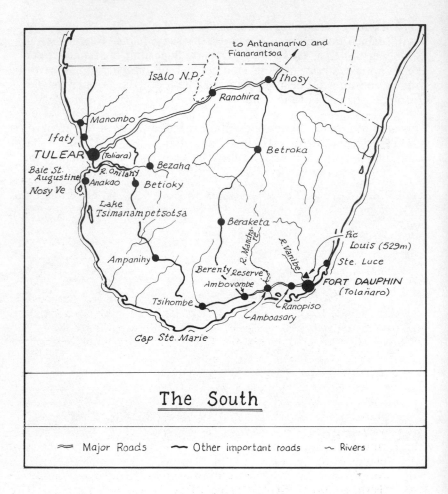

The South

~~ Major Roads   — Other important roads   ～ Rivers

John Mack, the British Museum's expert on ethnology in Madagascar tells the following story to illustrate the sensitivity to local conditions required of those westerners who wish to help the rural Malagasy. Some time ago the government gave the people of rice growing areas extra funds to encourage them to boost rice production. The people did the obvious (to them) thing: they spent the money on cement to improve the tombs of their ancestors. After all, it was the *razana* who were responsible for the quantity and quality of rice produced.

Chapter 8

The South

INTRODUCTION

This is the most exotic and most famous part of Madagascar, the region of 'spiny desert' where weird cactus-like trees wave their thorny fingers in the sky, where pieces of 'elephant bird' shell may still be found, and where the Mahafaly tribe erect their intriguing and often entertaining *aloalo* stelae above the graves.

This is also where Madagascar's most popular nature reserve (Berenty) is found, and arguably the country's most beautiful beach (Fort Dauphin), so no visitor is likely deliberately to omit the south from his or her itinerary.

Europeans have been coming to this area for a long time. Perhaps the earliest were a group of shipwrecked Portuguese sailors. Six hundred men were cast ashore in the south-west in 1527 and some are thought to have taken refuge in the Isalo massif in a cave now known as the *grotte des Portugais* (although a research project in the 1960s concluded that it was probably of Arab origin dating from the 11th Century). Later, when sailors were deliberately landing in Madagascar during the interest in the spice trade in the 16th and 17th Centuries, St Augustine's Bay, south of the modern town of Tulear, became a favoured place. They came for reprovisioning – Dutch and British – trading silver and beads for meat and fruit. One Englishman, Richard Boothby, was so overcome with the delights of Madagascar and the Malagasy, 'the happiest people in the world', that fired by his enthusiasm the British attempted to establish a colony at St Augustine's Bay. It was not a success. The original 100 settlers were soon whittled down to 60 through disease and murder by the local tribesmen who became less happy when they found their favourite beads were not available for trade and that these *vazahas* showed no sign of going away. The colonists left in 1646. Fifty years later St Augustine was a haven for pirates, and by 1754, when a British Admiral called at the Bay, many of the Sakalava aristocracy had English names.

The most important tribes in the south are the Mahafaly, Antanosy and Antandroy, occupying areas along the coast and into the hinterland, and the Bara in the centre. These southern Malagasy are tough, dark-skinned people, with African features, accustomed to the hardship of living in a region where rain seldom falls and finding water and grazing for their large herds of zebu is a constant challenge.

In contrast to the highland people, who go in for second burial and whose tombs are the collective homes of ancestors, those in the south

commemorate the recently dead. There is more opportunity to be remembered as an individual here, and a Mahafaly man who has lived eventfully, and died rich, will have the highlights of his life perpetuated in the form of wooden carvings (*aloalo*) or colourful paintings adorning his tomb. Formerly the *aloalo* were of more spiritual significance, but just as we, in our culture, have tended to bring an element of humour and realism into religion, so have the Malagasy. As John Mack says (in *Island of Ancestors*) '*Aloalo* have become obituary announcements when formerly they were notices of rebirth'.
formerly they were notices of rebirth'.

Antandroy tombs may be equally colourful, if less entertaining. Large and rectangular (the more important the person the bigger his tomb) and like the Mahafaly, topped with zebu skulls left over from the funeral feast. A very rich man may have over 100 skulls on his grave. They usually have 'male and female' standing stones (or in modern tombs, cement towers) at each side. Modern tombs may be brightly painted with geometric patterns on the sides. The Antanosy have upright stones, cement obelisks, or beautifully carved wooden memorials. These, however, are not over the graves themselves. This sacred and secret place will be elsewhere.

Tomb painting showing cause of death and boozy funeral procession.

Getting around

Road travel in the south is a challenging affair (just how challenging is described by Dervla Murphy in *Muddling through in Madagascar*) but roads *are* being improved, and R.N.7 to Tulear is now paved almost its entire length! (Anyone who travelled on it before paving will appreciate the exclamation mark). Apart from this new road, and the road between Fort Dauphin and Ambovombe ('the best in Madagascar') the tracks that link other important towns are abysmal; most people will prefer to fly.

Ihosy

Pronounced 'Ee-oosh', this small town is the capital of the war-like Bara people, who resisted Merina rule and were never really subdued until French colonial times. Cattle rustling is a time-honoured custom in this region. Ihosy is the junction for Tulear and Fort Dauphin; the road to the former is now good, to the latter is terrible. Ihosy is about five hours from Fianarantsoa by taxi-brousse, and in the midst of wonderful scenery.

The expensive (12,000 FMG) but comfortable Zaha Motel is here, plus the Hotel de Ihosy, described as 'a flop house for 1,500 FMG'. There is also a nice little square of open-sided *Hotelys* serving quite good Malagasy food.

Isalo National Park

The combination of sandstone rocks (cut by deep canyons and eroded into weird shapes), rare endemic plants, and dry weather (between June and August rain is almost unknown), makes this park well worth a visit. For botanists there is *Pachypodium rosulatum* or elephant's foot – a bulbous rock-clinging plant, and a native species of aloe, *Aloe isaloensis*, and for lemur-lovers there are sifakas and ring-tails. You might even see a fossa. The landscape is vividly described by Dervla Murphy: 'I've seen the work of erosion in many places but never anything like this. It is, literally, incredible. You don't believe it. You think you're hallucinating … We stared at a row of sculpted 'busts' in the near distance: an Egyptian Pharaoh, a tangle-haired caveman, a neat-headed woman. The hallucinatory feeling strengthened. How can wind and water have done all this? And the lichen colours! Sweeping splodges of yellow and red and green – some monster's palette.'

A permit is best obtained in advance in Tana, but is also available from the Department d'Eaux et Forêts in the adjacent town of Ranohira, 97 km south of Ihosy. Guides can be hired here to show you the park, including a three day trek to the Grotte de Portugais. For any extensive excursion into the park, boots are a must: here even the grass cuts like a knife and the rocks play havoc with ordinary shoes. If exploring without a guide, a compass is essential.

As in all Malagasy parks and reserves, poaching has been a problem here and visitors will help decrease this threat to the flora and fauna. Also the park fee of 1,500 FMG goes directly to the local community.

There is a basic hotel in Ranohira.

Tsy midera vady tsy herintaona.
Don't praise your wife before a year. (Don't count your chickens before they're hatched.)

(Malagasy proverb)

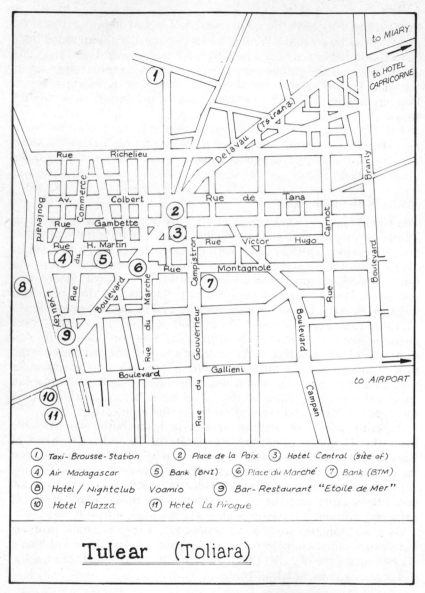

Legend:

① Taxi-Brousse-Station   ② Place de la Paix   ③ Hotel Central (site of)
④ Air Madagascar   ⑤ Bank (BNI)   ⑥ Place du Marché   ⑦ Bank (BTM)
⑧ Hotel / Nightclub Voamio   ⑨ Bar-Restaurant "Etoile de Mer"
⑩ Hotel Plazza   ⑪ Hotel La Pirogue

Tulear (Toliara)

Warning I'm having problems co-ordinating the old street names on my source map with my notes. If Ave Philbert Tsirana is *not* ex Blvd Delavau, my apologies to confused readers!

My omby singorana amin' ny tandrony, ary ny olona kosa amin' ny vavany.
Oxen are trapped by their horns and men by their words.

(Malagasy proverb)

TULEAR (TOLIARA)

Getting there

Road   Now that Route National 7 has been improved, access by taxi-brousse is not bad. After Ranohira the rugged mountains give way to grasslands with flat-topped mountains (what would be called mesas in American) topped with forest. On the last stretch you pass the forest of Zombity where there are lemurs. Keen naturalists might like to stop off here.

Air   There are flights five days a week (£80, $148), but be careful: these are often fully booked, and in the high season the Air Mad office in Tulear is full of desperate *vazahas* trying to get back to Tana. Air Mad sometimes do six day excursion rates from Tana to Tulear (30% off).

Tulear today

Tulear's history is centred on St Augustine's Bay, described at the beginning of this chapter, although the name of the town is thought to derive from an encounter with one of those early sailors who asked a local inhabitant where he might moor his boat. the Malagasy replied: *Toly eroa*, 'Mooring down there'. The town itself is modern – 1895 – and designed by an uninspired French architect. His tree-planting was more successfully aesthetic, and Tulear's shady tamarind trees, *kily*, give welcome respite from the blazing sun.

There are two good reasons to visit Tulear: the rich marine life with superb snorkelling and diving, and the Mahafaly tombs. Places of interest in the town itself include the small museum of the Sakalava and Mahafaly culture on Blvd. Philibert Tsiranana. The museum occupies the upper storey of the building and the exhibits are labelled in English and French. There are some Sakalava erotic tomb sculptures here. Near the sea boulevard on the way to the post office is a (tourist) shell market, and further up the same street there is – at weekends – a charming 'amusement arcade' constructed mainly from bamboo.

The beaches north and south of Tulear have fine white sand and are protected by an extensive coral reef. However, this is too far from shore to swim out to – a *pirogue* (for hire at the beach hotels) is necessary. Tulear itself, regrettably, has no beach, just mangroves and mudflats.

Where to stay

(Hotels and beach bungalows are expensive in and around Tulear.)

In town:

Category A
Hotel Plazza. B.P. 362. Tel:427-66. Was 18,000 FMG (air conditioned) to 15,000 FMG,(fan-cooled so better for keeping mosquitoes at bay) but now hard currency prices. Central (fronting the ocean). Hot water. Good food. Recommended.

Category B
Hotel Capricorne, B.P. 158, tel: 414-95. 9,000 FMG. About 2 km from the town centre (Betania), but fewer mosquitoes and friendly (English spoken). Very good food.

(Since the Hotel Central was burnt down in the 1987 anti-Indian race riots there are at present no hotels in this price range in the centre of town.)

Category C
La Pirogue. 6,500 FMG. Pleasant 'beach' bungalows near the Hotel Plazza. Good food and atmosphere.

Hotel Voamio. 5,000 FMG. Very primitive bungalows and noisy (this is one of Tulear's main night clubs), but friendly.

Hotel Soava Dia, on the main road into town near the bus station. 2,500 FMG (1985). Corrugated iron roof, so hot. 'Cats jump onto the tables to finish off the scraps from the plate as soon as a customer leaves. Nobody else shooed them away, and they weren't very impressed with my efforts.' (S.C.)

Warning   In the cool season (May to October) the nights in Tulear are very cold. The cheaper hotels rarely supply enough blankets.

Beach accommodation out of town:
Mora Mora, Ifaty (26 km north of Tulear). B.P. 41. Tel: 410-71. Half-board 11,000 FMG. Full board 15,500 FMG. Very comfortable beach bungalows, good food, and equipment for snorkelling, scuba diving or deep sea fishing (but the beach itself is unpleasant – covered with dried sea-weed). Highly recommended. Reached by taxi-brousse (frequent) heading for Manombo or with Mad Airtours.

Note: The formerly popular Zaha Hotel, also in Ifaty, has reportedly closed down. Check this with Madagascar Airtours.

Safari Vezo. Run by Jean-Louis Prevot, this unpretentious set of beach bungalows by an unspoilt Vezo fishing village (Anakoa) costs 12,500 FMG full board. The two hour *pirogue* journey is organised by M.Prevot and costs 14,000 FMG. Details from Madagascar Airtours (Hotel Plazza) or write to B.P. 427. (Tel: 41381).

Where to eat
The best meal (seafood) in town is in an unpretentious wooden building on the sea front, the Etoile de Mer, between the Plazza Hotel and the Voamio. In 1987 this was reportedly 'deserted', but hopefully this was only a temporary condition.

Golden City. Chinese restaurant near the Capricorne. Recommended.

There are several Indian restaurants in the centre of town, but they may not have survived the riots.

A little thatched kiosk at the junction of the seafront and the main boulevard serves good *pommes frites* and sandwiches.

Excursions from Tulear

Madagascar Airtours has an office in the grounds of the Plazza Hotel and run some very good tours. Given the problems of public transport, these are well worth considering. They include St Augustine and Ankilobe (fishing village), and Betioky (about 15,000 FMG per person; minimum of four. See below).

St Augustine and Anakao

Accessible by *vedette* or *pirogue* this historically important spot is also a very pleasant beach resort. St Augustine was the haunt of pirates and was mentioned by Daniel Defoe in *The King of Pirates*. Anakao has beach bungalows (see *Accommodation*) and a Vezo fishing village.

Off shore is the island of Nosy Ve. The first landing there was by a Dutchman in 1595, and it was officially taken over by the French in 1888 before their conquest of the mainland.

Nosy Ve is said to be a lovely little island, of particular interest to ornithologists because there is rumoured to be a breeding colony of red-tailed tropic birds.

Note: the area immediately adjacent to Tulear is not a good example of spiny desert. For Didicrcaccac and Euphorbia you need to get away from the coast.

Lake Tsimanampetsotsa (nature reserve)

100 km south of Tulear, and difficult to reach other than by private vehicle or tour, is the brackish lake set in spectacular spine desert. Didiereaceae and Euphorbia are much in evidence, and there are flamingoes in the lake and many other water birds. Both ring-tailed lemurs and sifakas are found here.

Betioky

A very dusty 138 km (four hours each way) trip that can be made by taxi-brousse or through Madagascar Airtours which gives you a chance to see the Mahafaly tombs for which the area is famous.

The surrounding landscape is dry scrub and gentle hills. The first tombs that you come to, after about an hour, are painted with scenes from the life of the deceased, and his often sticky end, shot or run over by a truck. On one of these the cost of building the tomb is boldly painted on the side (200,000 FMG). I was told that these are Bara, not

ROBERT DRURY

The most intriguing insight into 18th century Madagascar was provided by Robert Drury, who was shipwrecked off the island in 1701 and spent over 16 years there, much of the time as a slave to the Antandroy or Sakalava chiefs.

Drury was only 15 when his boat foundered off the southern tip of Madagascar (he had been permitted by his father to go to India with trade goods). The shipwreck survivors were treated well by the local king but kept prisoners for reasons of status. After a few days they made a bid for freedom by seizing the king as a hostage and marching east. They were followed by hundreds of warriors who watched for any relaxation in their guard, they were without water for three days as they crossed the burning hot desert, and just as they came in sight of the river Mandrare (having released the hostages) they were attacked and many were speared to death.

For ten years Drury was a slave of the Antandroy royal family. He worked with cattle and eventually was appointed royal butcher, the task of slaughtering a cow for ritual purposes being supposedly that of someone of royal blood – and lighter skin. Drury was a useful substitute. He also acquired a wife.

Wars with the neighbouring Mahafaly gave him the opportunity to escape north across the desert to St Augustine Bay, some 250 miles away. Here he hoped to find a ship to England, but his luck turned and he again became a slave, this time to the Sakalava. When a ship did come in, his master refused to consider selling him to the captain, and Drury's desperate effort to get word to the ship through a message written on a leaf came to nothing when the messenger lost the leaf and substituted another less meaningful one. Two more years of relative freedom followed, and he finally got away in 1717, nearly 17 years after his shipwreck.

Ever quick to put his experience to good use, he later returned to Madagascar as a slave trader!

'The boat tomb' near Fort Dauphin by the Anosy sculptor Fasira.

Mahafaly. Most of the huts beside the road have tall sacks of charcoal for sale: a source of income for the impoverished people, but more damage to the environment. In this arid area water must sometimes be trucked in from Tulear.

After the simple rectangular tombs come classical (but unpainted) *aloalos* or stelae, topped with zebus, wrestlers, and a taxi-brousse. The most magnificent tomb is on the edge of a village off the road to the left. Well worth scrambling down to. The deceased was evidently an extremely wealthy man, there are numerous brightly painted *aloalos* on his tomb, showing all sorts of things: soldiers, cattle, houses, cars, horse and rider, aeroplane... That man had really *lived*! And died: the list of animals slaughtered for his funeral, and proudly noted on the side of the tomb, comes to 116.

There is nothing much at Betioky except cheerful people and a little *Hotely* serving passable food. Tours take you there mainly because

The Hotely *at Betioky.*

there is a craft centre which the guides like to call a museum. It isn't, it's a souvenir shop, and the quality is not particularly good. If you decide to spend the night at Bezaha (see below) on the great river Onilahy, then there is no reason to make the journey all the way to Betioky. Harry Sutherland-Hawes writes: 'We got an overnight stop in Bezaha, a town selected by the government for electrification (hydroelectricity), to try to convince the southern Malagasy that they are doing something for them. The hotel was very basic – though it did have a four poster bed!! Well, an iron frame. It was so hot in the room we didn't fall asleep, we passed out. The loo is a hole in the ground. If you open a window a swarm of mosquitoes dance in looking for yummy foreigners. A hotel for the tough. Very good food though, and a great bar adjoining. Everyone very friendly, and it's very very cheap – 2,000 FMG for the night'. (See Addenda for more on Betioky and Ampanihy.)

If you continue by road beyond Betioky you will begin to enter large areas of spiny desert. The next town of importance is Ampanihy.

Ampanihy

'I had been looking forward to getting to Ampanihy ('the place of bats') on the rough road between Fort Dauphin and Tulear because a male friend had stayed there a few weeks earlier and found the hotel room came complete with female companion. I was curious as to what I would be offered in this line but, being female, was told that there were 'no hotels' and sent to sleep in the office of Air Madagascar (one flight every fortnight) in a room full of cockroaches next to the almost bare room of a young lady with chronic catarrh.

'The one tourist hotel had not been in use for a while and was being slightly improved and solar panels were being set up when I was there in 1985. Nobody knows how to maintain the panels, though. They are trying to restart the tourist industry with the enticement of beautiful mohair carpets made in the town.' (Sally Crook)

Mohair goats were introduced to the Ampanihy area in French colonial times. Carpet weaving is therefore not a traditional craft, but the Malagasy have taken to it happily. The goats are no doubt also happily increasing the desertification of the area.

After Ampanihy you enter Antandroy country and will understand why they are called 'People of the thorns'. Continuing on R.N. 10, you reach **Tsihombe**, which was a French military post until 1946 and is more Frenchified than most small towns of this area. Dervla Murphy reports having an *Haute Cuisine* (relatively) meal here in 1982, and maybe that restaurant is still going strong. For an account of what the journey between Tulear and Fort Dauphin is (was) like, read *Muddling through in Madagascar*!

The road improves and at Ambovombe reaches glorious perfection (for Madagascar) in its home run to Fort Dauphin.

Ambovombe

The junction for R.N.10 and R.N.13, which runs to Ihosy and, if anything, is in even worse condition than R.N.10. Taxi-brousses to Ihosy cost 13,000 FMG in 1985. There is a cheap hotel by the taxi station and a decent meal is available nearby at Hotel du Musulman which seems to serve non-stop turkey. 'You can watch the birds pecking away in the yard while you're eating their brother.' (Sally Crook).

FORT DAUPHIN (TAOLAÑARO)

History

The remains of two forts can still be seen in or near this town on the extreme south-east tip of Madagascar: Fort Flacourt, built in 1643, and the oldest building in the country erected by shipwrecked Portuguese sailors in 1504. This ill-fated group of 80 reluctant colonists stayed about fifteen years before falling foul of the local tribes. The survivors of the massacre fled to the surrounding countryside where disease and hostile natives finished them off.

1642 saw a French expedition, organised by the Sociéte Française de l'Orient and led by Sieur Pronis with instructions to 'found colonies and commerce in Madagascar and to take possession of it in the name of His Most Christian Majesty'. An early settlement at the Bay of Sainte Luce was soon abandoned in favour of a healthier peninsula to the south, and a fort was built and named after the Dauphin, (later Louis XIV) in 1643. At first the Antanosy were quite keen on the commerce part of the deal but were less enthusiastic about losing their land. The heavily defended fort only survived by use of force and with many casualties from both sides. The French finally abandoned the place in 1674, but their 30 year occupation formed one of the foundations of the later claim to the island as a French colony. During this period the first published work on Madagascar was written by Promis's successor, Etienne de Flacourt. His *Histoire de la Grande Isle de Madagascar* brought the island's amazing flora and fauna to the attention of European naturalists, and is still used as a valuable historical source.

Getting there

The overland route is reportedly best done with a company called Sonatra, which operate from the taxi-brousse station on the far side of Lake Anosy in Tana. They go via Ihosy, Betroka and Ambovombe. You should book your seat as far in advance as possible.

For the wimps, there are flights to Fort Dauphin, via Tulear, Tues., Thurs., Sat., £80. Sit on the right for the best views of Fort Dauphin's mountains and bays. Flights are usually heavily booked. The airport is chaotic. It's tiny and looks as though it has recently been bombed (it hasn't) and there's always an exceptionally long wait for luggage. Take a taxi into town; the 'courtesy' bus to the big hotels was reported in 1987 to cost 2,500 FMG!

Fort Dauphin today

With the possible exception of Diego Suarez, this is the most beautifully located of all towns in Madagascar. Built on a small peninsula, the town is bordered on three sides by beaches and breakers and backed by high green mountains which dwindle into spiny desert to the west. More geared to tourism than any other Malagasy mainland town, Fort Dauphin offers a variety of exceptionally interesting excursions (Berenty, the spiny forest, the Portuguese fort, the bay of Sainte Luce) and arguably the country's most beautiful beach, Libanona.

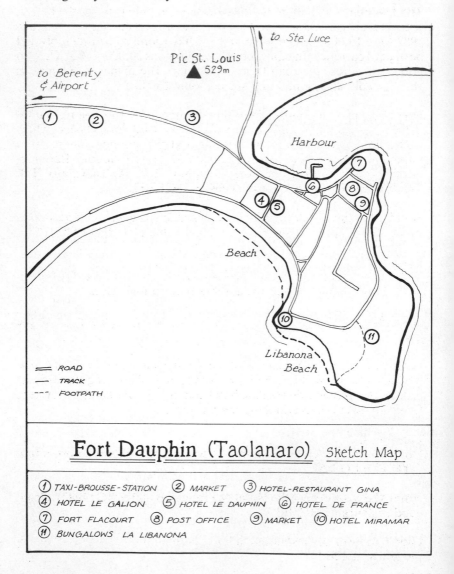

Fort Dauphin (Taolanaro) Sketch Map

① TAXI-BROUSSE-STATION   ② MARKET   ③ HOTEL-RESTAURANT GINA
④ HOTEL LE GALION   ⑤ HOTEL LE DAUPHIN   ⑥ HOTEL DE FRANCE
⑦ FORT FLACOURT   ⑧ POST OFFICE   ⑨ MARKET   ⑩ HOTEL MIRAMAR
⑪ BUNGALOWS LA LIBANONA

Where to stay

Most of Fort Dauphin belongs to M. Jean de Heaulme, the owner of Berenty reserve, who has done so much for conservation and scientific study of wildlife in Madagascar. His hotels are the Dauphin, the Galion, the Miramar, and – most recently – the Hotel de France. You are expected to stay in one of these if you want to visit Berenty, but it is not compulsory. See Addenda for updated details of hotels.

Category A

The Dauphin and Galion. Of the two, the Dauphin is by far the better, with a lovely garden, a crocodile pool, and a good restaurant. Prices in 1987 were 15,000 FMG double, but will have gone up considerably and be in hard currency. Inexplicably, the Galion was 20,000 FMG. The two hotels are across the road from each other. The manager, Saymoi, is very friendly and helpful and speaks some English.

Hotel Miramar. The most beautifully situated hotel and best restaurant in Fort Dauphin. On a promontory overlooking Libanona beach, which is excellent for swimming, sunbathing and tide-pooling. There are a limited number of rooms costing 20,000 FMG (1987) double. Bookings must be made through the hotel Dauphin (B.P. 54, Taolañaro. Tel: 210-48). Meals (oysters, lobster) cost 3,750 FMG.

Hotel Libanona. Near the Libanona beach and the only independently owned hotel in this category. Very good value at 17,000 FMG.

Category B

Motel Gina. Six pleasant thatched bungalows on the outskirts of town. 6,000 FMG double. Good restaurant. Will arrange tours.

Hotel Casino. A little further out of town and a similar price to the Gino.

Hotel de France. Formerly one of the worst value hotels in Madagascar (though interesting through their recycling of the Hotel register as toilet paper), this is now a de Healme hotel and in 1987 was being renovated. Centrally located, overlooking the harbour.

Category C

Hotel Henriette. Good value but only has a few rooms so often full. 4,000 FMG (1985).

Hotel Mahavoky (near the Hotel de France). 6,000 FMG (1987), clean, good restaurant. Helpful.

I don't know of any restaurant in Fort Dauphin that is not part of one of the above hotels.

Excursions

Berenty reserve

'*Kill* to get to Berenty!' (H.S-H). I've never known a visitor – traveller or tourist – who hasn't felt this way. The danger is that Berenty is already becoming overcrowded, with reports of up to 50 visitors descending on the place at a time. Fortunately there is (at present) only a limited amount of accommodation, so if you can arrange to spend a night or two you can still have the reserve to yourself in the magic hours of dawn and dusk.

Visits to the reserve must be organised through the Hotel Dauphin. 1987 prices were: 30,000 FMG per person using group transport; 80,000 FMG (1 – 3 people) with private transport; 13,000 FMG per night in simple but clean accommodation (no hot water). The food is excellent and there is a very good small museum.

The reserve lies some 80 km to the west of Fort Dauphin, amid a vast sisal plantation, and one of the most exciting aspects of a visit to Berenty is the drive there. For the first half of the journey the skyline is composed of rugged green mountains often backed by menacing grey clouds or obscured by rain. Groves of travellers palms (*ravenala*) dot the landscape and near Ranopiso (which has a road-side fruit stand) is an example of the very rare three-cornered palm *Neodypsis decary* (your driver should be able to show you, and if you miss it there is another example near the Berenty restaurant). He will certainly show you the grove of pitcher plants – *Nepenthes Madagascariensis* – whose nearest relatives are in Asia. The yellow 'flowers' (actually modified leaves) lure insects into their sticky depths where they are digested, probably for their nitrogen content.

Shortly after Ranopiso there is a dramatic change in the scenery: within a few kilometres the hills flatten and disappear, the clouds clear, and the bizarre fingers of Didierea appear on the skyline, interspersed with the bulky trunks of baobabs. You are entering the spiny desert, and have made the transition from eastern climatic zone to southern. The most common spiny tree is the *Alluaudia* or 'octopus tree' with sharp spines alternating with tough little leaves up its many fingers. In this area there are five species of *Alluaudia*, all members of the Didiereacea family. Though often mistakenly called cacti, and bearing many similarities, a close inspection will show that these plants are like nothing else you've ever seen. They are taller, too, than any cactus – fifteen metres high or more. Shorter, but equally spiny plants provide ground cover. The strange thing about the spiny forest is that the lack of large native browsing animals makes one wonder what the Didierea are protecting themselves from? (Alison Jolly speculates that this protection evolved when giant lemurs could have posed a danger by fracturing the precious water-storing stems.)

Soon after the beginning of the spiny desert you will be taken to see an Antanosy 'tomb' (actually the dead are buried elsewhere), with some beautiful carved wooden figures. There are zebu, 'the tomb of Ramaria (she has a bible and cross), someone losing a leg – or worse – to a crocodile, and the most famous piece – an exquisitely carved boatload of people. This has been described as portraying the soul voyage of the dead, but in fact – more prosaically – is a memorial to a group who died in a canoe accident. These were done by the famous Antanosy carver Fesira who worked on a series of commemorative sculptures shortly after the war.

In the area are other memorials, but without carvings. These cenotaphs commemorate those buried in a communal tomb or where the body could not be recovered, and look like clusters of missiles lurking in the spiny forest.

Amboasary is the last town before the bridge across the river Mandrare and the turnoff to Berenty. The rutted red road takes you past acres of sisal, beautiful in the evening light, to the entrance of the reserve.

Ring-tailed lemurs at Berenty.

Berenty is famous for its population of ringtailed lemurs and sifakas. Henri de Heaulme and his son Jean have made this the best protected and studied 100 hectares of forest in Madagascar. Although in the arid south, its location along the river Mandrare and the introduced shady tamarind trees ensure a well watered habitat (gallery forest) for the large variety of animals that live there. The forest itself is threatened by the rampant spread of the cactus-like 'rubber vine', *Cissus quadrangularis*. Scientist are studying ways to check their growth.

The following species of lemur are sure to be seen: brown lemur (*Lemur fulvus*), ring-tailed lemur (*Lemur catta*) and sifaka (*Propithecus verreauxi*). Most lemurs here are well-used to people and the cocky ringtails will eat bananas from your hand. They have an air of swaggering arrogance, are as at home on the ground as in trees, and are highly photogenic with their black and white markings and waving striped tails. These fluffy tails play an important part in communication and act as a benign weapon against neighbouring troops which might have designs on their territory. Ring-tailed lemurs indulge in 'stink fights' when they scent their tails with the musk secreted from wrist and anal glands and wave them in the neighbours' faces; that is usually enough to make a potential intruder retreat. There are approximately 160 ring-tailed lemurs in Berenty, and the population has stayed remarkably stable considering that only about a quarter of the babies survive to adulthood. The females, which are dominant over the males, are receptive to mating for only a week or so each year, in April/May, so there is plenty of competition amongst the males for this once a year treat. The young are born in September and at first cling to their mother's belly, later climbing onto her back and riding jockey-style.

Attractive though the ring-tails are, no lemur can compete with the sifaka for soft-toy cuddliness with their creamy white fur, brown cap, and black faces. Sifaka belong to the same sub-family of lemur as the indri (seen in Perinet). Unlike the ring-tails, they rarely come down to the ground, but when they do the length of their legs in comparison to their short arms necessitates a comical form of locomotion: they stand upright and jump with their feet together like competitors in a sack race. The best place to see them do this is across the road near the aeroplane hangar near the restaurant/museum. Sifaka troop boundaries do not change, so your guide will know where to find the animals. The young are born in July. Sifaka make a speciality of sunbathing – spreading their arms to the morning rays from the top of their trees. They feed primarily on leaves so are not interested in the tourist-proffered bananas that so excite the ring-tails and brown lemurs.

The brown lemurs of Berenty were introduced from Analabe, near Morondava, and are now well established and as tame as the ring-tails.

There are a few other lemurs which, being noctural, are harder to see: the mouse lemur (*Microcebus murinus*), and lepilemur (*Lepilemur leucopus*) which may be seen peering out of its hollow tree nest during the day.

Apart from the lemurs, another striking mammal is easily seen in the reserve – fruit bats or flying foxes. Thousands of them live in noisy groups on 'bat trees' in one part of the forest; with their wingspan of over a metre they are an impressive sight.

Bird watching is rewarding in Berenty, with 56 species recorded. You are likely to see several families unique to Madagascar, including the hook-billed vanga (*Vanga curvirostris*) and couas – the crested coua (*Coua cristata*), and the giant coua (*Coua gigas*) with its handsome blue face-markings. The cuckoo-like coucal (*Centropus toulou*) is common, as are grey-headed love-birds (*Agopornis cana*) and the beautiful paradise flycatcher with its long tail feathers (not endemic – these birds occur in East Africa). The most common bird of prey in Berenty is the Madagascar buzzard, *Buteo brachypterus*.

Excursions from Berenty include an area (within the reserve) of spiny desert, and a visit to the sisal factory, which sounds boring but is, in fact, very interesting and enjoyable.

Fort Portuguese (Île aux Portuguaise)
A tour to the old fort, built in 1504, is well worthwhile. It involves a *pirogue* ride up the river Vinanibe, about 6 km from Fort Dauphin, and then a short walk to the sturdy-looking stone fortress (the walls are one metre thick) set in zebu-grazed parkland. Arrange through Madagascar Airtours. 35,000 FMG per person (1986 prices).

Baie Sainte Luce
About 65 km north-east of Fort Dauphin is the beautiful and historically interesting St Luce Bay where the French colonists of 1638 first landed. I haven't been there, but met a couple who raved about the beach, the lobster, and the swimming in a natural pool. You can go there on a tour (one to four people, 60,000 FMG. Madagascar Airtours) or, if you have a tent, make your own way as best you can.

The area around Fort Dauphin is excellent for walking, with isolated villages in the green hills, and the mountain of Pic Louis. This is an easy climb, and you are rewarded with superb views, and perhaps some lemurs (and leeches in the rainy season).

LAMBAS

The colourful cotton wraps known as *lamba* (or, to be more precise, *lamba wan*, since *lamba* is the white shawl worn in the highlands) are worn by both men and women in Madagascar. In some rural parts of the country men wear their *lamba* as a kind of wraparound skirt, and women use it in a variety of ways, often as a baby-carrier.

Even small shops in eastern Madagascar have a good selection of *lambas* which make attractive and versatile souvenirs. The designs are bright and cheerful and most *lambas* have a Malagasy slogan at the edge of the fabric. If you buy one, ask the shop manager to translate it for you.

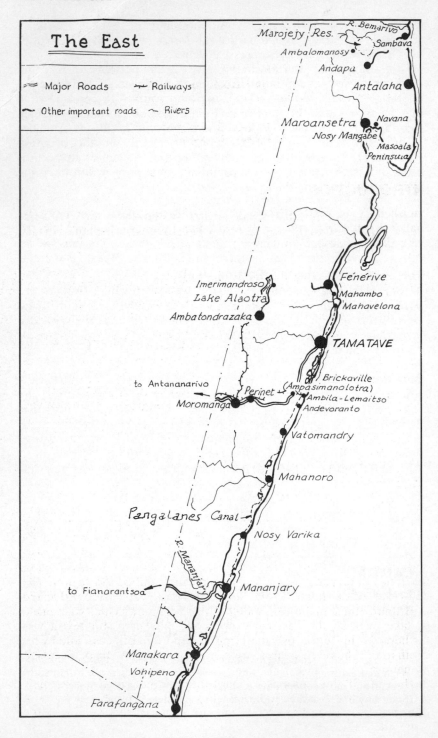

The East

≈ Major Roads   ⊢ Railways
~ Other important roads   ~ Rivers

R. Bemarivo
Marojejy Res.
Sambava
Ambalomanosy
Andapa
Antalaha
Maroansetra   Navana
Nosy Mangabe   Masoala
    Peninsula

Fénérive
Imerimandroso
Lake Alaotra   Mahambo
    Mahavelona
Ambatondrazaka
    TAMATAVE

to Antananarivo   Brickaville
    (Ampasimanolotra)
Perinet   Ambila-Lemaitso
Moromanga   Andevoranto

    Vatomandry

    Mahanoro

Pangalanes Canal

    Nosy Varika

R. Mananjary

to Fianarantsoa   Mananjary

Manakara
Vohipeno

Farafangana

Chapter 9

The East

INTRODUCTION

Punished by its weather (rain, cyclones), the east coast is notoriously challenging to travellers. In July 1816 James Hastie wrote in his diary 'If this is the good season for travelling this country, I assert it is impossible to proceed in the bad'. This statement still holds true. There is no point in visiting this region during the months of heaviest rainfall (December, January, February). The driest months are September, October and November, with March, April and May being fairly safe, apart from the possibility of cyclones. From June to August you take your chance – and you may well be rewarded by a fine spell.

The east coast has another problem: sharks (see page 147). So despite beautiful beaches swimming is only possible in areas protected by reefs.

Weather and sharks apart, there are plenty of good reasons to visit this region. Much of Madagascar's unique flora and fauna is concentrated in the eastern rain forests and any serious naturalist will pay this area a visit. So should others for the rugged mountainous scenery with rivers tumbling down to the Indian Ocean, the balmy (and sometimes barmy) tropical atmosphere, friendly people, abundant fruit and seafood, and the supremely unspoilt island of Sainte Marie (Nosy Boraha).

The chief products of the east are coffee, vanilla, bananas, coconuts and cloves.

This region has an interesting history dominated by European pirates and slave traders. Unlike other parts of the country which were ruled by powerful clans or tribes, the east was settled by adventurers and entrepreneurs who cared little for power, only for riches. It was not until the 18th Century that one ruler, Ratsimilaho, unified the region. The half-caste son of Thomas White, an English pirate, and briefly educated in Britain, Ratsimilaho responded to the attempt by chief Ramanano to take over all the east coast ports and his successful revolt was furthered by his judiciously marrying an important princess, and by his death in 1754 he ruled an area stretching from the Masoala peninsula to Mananjary.

The result of this liaison of various tribes was the Betsimisaraka, now the second largest ethnic group in Madagascar. Some (in the area of Maroansetra) practise second burial, although with less ritual than the

Merina and Betsileo. The Betsimisaraka use *ombiasy* (native healers) for foretelling the future as well for diagnosing illnesses and prescribing cures which may involve rituals as well as the use of appropriate herbs.

Getting around
Although the map shows roads of some sort running almost the full length of the east coast, this is deceptive. Rain coupled with cyclones regularly destroy roads and bridges so it is impossible to know in advance whether a selected route will be usable, even in the 'dry' season. The rain-saturated forests drain into the Indian Ocean in numerous rivers, many of which can only be crossed by ferry. And there is not enough traffic to ensure a regular service.

BY TRAIN TO THE EAST COAST

The train from Antananarivo to Tamatave is considered to be one of the great railway journeys of the world. Between 1901 and 1913 thousands of Chinese coolies laboured to complete the line, and, as with its counterpart in East Africa, many lives were lost in the process. For 375 km the railway runs through tunnels, over viaducts, and on the edge of cliffs overlooking tumbling rivers.

After a dawn start from Tana, the train goes south, circling the city before heading east through typical scenery of the *Hauts Plateaux* – paddy fields, villages, and rocky outcrops. Then comes an area of forest before it climbs up to the Angavo massif, gateway to the eastern rainforest. Here it reaches its highest point, just before Anjiro, where the railway makes a huge hairpin bend. From there it is downhill all the way. The scenery gradually changes, from the transition zone of bamboo, to evergreen rainforest (moist montane forest). Look out for the large river Mangoro which you cross soon after Ambohibary. Moramanga is reached in four hours, and Perinet (Andasibe) in another half hour. Here the train takes a leisurely lunch break, to allow the first class passengers to dine at the Hotel de Gare (see p.158). After Perinet the railway leaves the road (R.N.2) which it has hugged since Tana, and strikes out on its own following the river Sahatandra (Vohitra). Wise passengers sit on the left for this leg of the journey; the views are spectacular. This is the stretch with tunnels and bridges every kilometre or so – an impressive feat of engineering. Passing through the remnants of virgin rainforest, you don't need an experienced eye to see the ravages of slash-and-burn agriculture.

Shortly before dusk the train stops at Vohibinany (Brickaville – but it seems to be called Ampasimanolotra on maps), then passes through groves of traveller's palms before heading north to its destination. The map shows the tracks running right along the edge of the sea, up the narrow ribbon of land isolated by the Pangalanes lakes and canal. Sadly the view is obscured first by dense brush and then by darkness, and the arrival in Tamatave, after a journey of twelve hours, comes as a relief.

There are two other eastern railways, one a branch from Moramanga to Lac Alaotra, and the other from Fianarantsoa to Manakara. Opinions vary as to whether the latter is even better than, or not as good as, the Tana to Tamatave route. It is certainly shorter.

TAMATAVE (TOAMASINA)

History

As in all the east coast ports, Tamatave began as a pirate community. In the late 18th Century its harbour attracted the French, who were already a presence on Île Sainte Marie, and Napoleon I sent his agent Sylvain Roux to establish a trading post there. In 1811, Sir Robert Farquhar, governor of the newly British island of Mauritius, sent a small naval squadron to take the port of Tamatave. This was not simply an extension of the usual British/French antagonism, but an effort to stamp out slavery at its source, Madagascar being the main supplier to the Indian Ocean. Slavery had been abolished by British Act of Parliament in 1807. The attack was successful, Syvain Roux was exiled, and a small British garrison remained. During subsequent years trade between Mauritius and Madagascar built Tamatave into a major port. Farquhar, through creative interpretation of the 1814 Treaty of Paris which ceded Mauritius to the British, tried to persuade his government that Madagascar was a dependency of the new colony and continued energetically to cultivate royal Merina favour. Westminster was not enthusiastic, however, and eventually the French re-established themselves in the area, but only after the flowering of Anglo-Malagasy relationships during King Radama's reign.

In 1927 a catastrophic cyclone hit Tamatave flooding the town to a depth of three metres. With the sea came large ships that had been lying in the harbour and ended up in the centre of town.

Theories on the origin of the name Toamasina vary, but one is that King Radama I tasted the sea-water here and remarked 'Toa masina' – It's salty.

Getting there

In 1985 the long-awaited new road from Tana to Tamatave was completed, thus halving the time to go by car to the coast. Chinese work crews spent nearly ten years on the project, with further felling of the depleted eastern rainforest, but few will begrudge the benefits to the local population.

Taxi-brousses leave Tana throughout the day, and the journey takes from six to eight hours. It's best just to go along (by taxi) to the taxi-brousse departure point in the east of the city.

There are daily flights between Tana and Tamatave (£32), and the port is linked by air to Diego Suarez (although there may not be a direct flight) via Maroansetra, Antalaha, and Sambava –£80, and also to Île Sainte Marie. Taxis from the airport cost 1,500 FMG.

If you need to wait at Tamatave airport, go to the very pleasant bar upstairs.

Most visitors, however, take the train. The railway from Tana to Tamatave via Perinet (Andasibe) is justly famous. The train leaves

Tana at 6.00 and is due to arrive at Tamatave at 18.30. There is one first class carriage with 54 seats which can (should) be booked in advance. The fare used to be 7,000 FMG plus 200 FMG booking fee, but must now be paid in hard currency. Third class is always tremendously crowded, involves queueing from about 4.00am and is only for the wilfully self-destructive. I did it once – and once was enough, but undoubtedly some of the discomforts are counterbalanced by the delightful Malagasy and their offspring who will be your cheek-by-jowl co-passengers. Price 4,000 FMG.

The train back from Tamatave to Tana leaves even earlier: 5.30 am.

The train to Tamatave: third class compartment.

Tamatave today
Tamatave has an agreeable look of shabby elegance, with some fine palm-lined boulevards and once-fine colonial houses. As befits the country's main port, it is always full of foreigners. Sailors speaking a variety of languages hang around the bars and tea shops, and the hotels are often full to bursting since tourists from Tana also spend their holidays here. Consequently there is a good variety of bars, snackbars and restaurants, but hotels may be full.

Unlike most Malagasy towns, Tamatave is a pleasant place to stay for a day or two (although as usual there are no specific 'tourist sights'). The market *Bazar be* is colourful and interesting, and a good place to buy vanilla, cloves, black pepper, etc. Distances are large, and the footsore should take a *pousse-pousse*; an enjoyable way of getting an overview of the town is to have a *pousse-pousse* tour.

Where to stay
Category A
Neptune, 35 Boulevard Ratsimilaho (on the seafront). The poshest hotel in town. 26,000 FMG (but now payable in hard currency). Very pleasant but impersonal. Full meal, 5,500 FMG.

Hotel Joffre (Boulevard Joffre) and Hotel Flamboyants (Av. de la Libération). Around 18,000 FMG (converted into hard currency). Both pleasant but often booked up.

Hotel Miramara. 9 Bungalows and 7 chalets a couple of kilometres north of Tamatave, on the beach road. 4 people sharing bungalow – 15,000 FMG. One room chalet with 3 beds – 12,000 FMG. Very good value. Large swimming pool, tennis and basketball.

Category B
Hotel Etoile-Rouge, 13 Rue de Lattre de Tassigny. 8,000 FMG to 12,000 FMG. Highly recommended – very friendly and comfortable (but no mosquito nets). Only 6 rooms so often full. Excellent restaurant.

Category C
Hotel Plage, Boulevard de la Libération (round the corner from the Neptune. Very noisy (night club downstairs) but clean and comfortable, and they serve breakfast at 4am to rail travellers. 8,000 FMG – 15,000 FMG, 1988.

Hotel Bebelle, Rue de Commerce. 12 rooms. Quiet. 4,000 FMG.

Hotel L'Escale. Near the station so convenient for 5.30 train to Tana. 3,500 FMG. Dirty. Also in the station area and the same price: Hotel Niavo.

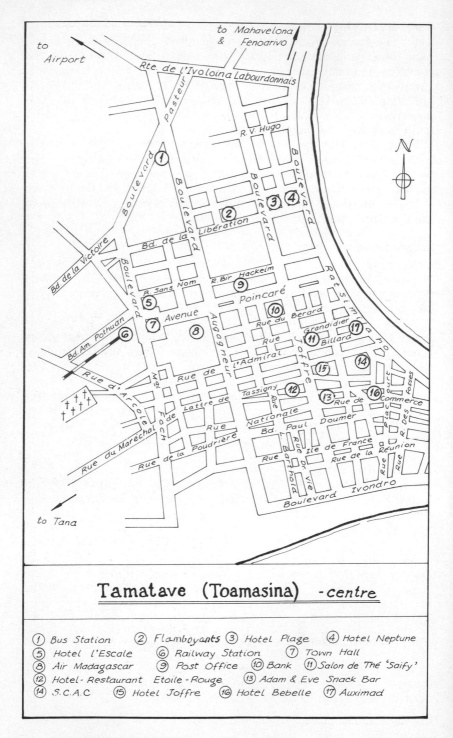

Tamatave (Toamasina) -centre

① Bus Station   ② Flamboyants   ③ Hotel Plage   ④ Hotel Neptune
⑤ Hotel l'Escale   ⑥ Railway Station   ⑦ Town Hall
⑧ Air Madagascar   ⑨ Post Office   ⑩ Bank   ⑪ Salon de Thé 'Saify'
⑫ Hotel-Restaurant Etoile-Rouge   ⑬ Adam & Eve Snack Bar
⑭ S.C.A.C   ⑮ Hotel Joffre   ⑯ Hotel Bebelle   ⑰ Auximad

to Mahavelona and Fenoarivo

Rte de l'Ivol. Laboud

R V Hugo

Boulevard

③ ④

Avenue Poincaré

⑩ R du Bérard ⑰ Grandidier

⑪ Billard

R. de l'A

Rue Joffre

⑬ ⑭

⑫ ⑮ ⑯ Rue

R Nationale

Daumer

Bd. Paul

R. Berthold Rue du Vie

Ile de France

Rue de la

Boulevard

Ivondro

Rue du Fosses

Rue des Fosses

Place du Court

Rue du Commerce

Région

R. Roux

R. B Bleve

Bd. Albert 1er

Rue de la Marine

Harbour

Pier

N

Tamatave (Toamasina) - waterfront

(See map of Centre for key)

Where to eat

Apart from the hotels, most of which serve good food, the best restaurants are on Boulevard Joffre near the Joffre Hotel.

Best hotel food: Hotel Etoile-Rouge and Hotel Neptune. The Neptune does a good all-you-can-eat-buffet for Sunday lunch.

Restaurant Fortuna. Highly recommended Chinese restaurant near the Joffre Hotel. Exact address unknown – ask a *pousse-pousse* driver to take you there.

Restaurant Chinois, Madame Chen Kuotsiao, 20 Boulevard Joffre.

Tahiti Kely. On the road to the airport. Said to have the best seafood in town.

Salon de Thé Saify (near Hotel Joffre). Excellent selection of cakes and snacks.

Adam & Eve snack bar. Near Hotel Joffre. 'Best cuppa in Madagascar'.

Warning   Beware of thieves in Tamatave: never leave your hotel room unlocked.

Excursions from Tamatave

Jardin de Ivoloina   Once grand and enormous Botanical Gardens, created in 1898, now very run down but being rehabilitated by conservation groups. 11 kilometres north of town: taxi drivers are reluctant to go all the way because of the atrocious road. Good botany and bird watching, and some captive and semi-tame brown lemurs.

North towards Fenoarivo Atsinanana (Fénérive)   The road north is mostly in good condition – although a recent cyclone washed away part of it – and a taxi or bus ride at least as far as Mahavalona is recommended. This can be done in a day, but for those with more time there are some excellent beach bungalows for eating and relaxation.

It is an interesting drive (and for a day trip worth going by taxi so the driver can point out things of interest). You will pass cinnamon trees, palms, bananas, tropical fruit trees such as lychee, breadfruit, mangoes, and perhaps the vine that produces pepper, and clove bushes. About 30 km from Tamatave, on the left, you will see some open-sided sheds with corrugated iron roofs. These are Betsimisaraka grave sites: not, as sometimes stated, 'canoe burials' but the exposed part of wooden coffins containing several bodies (which are buried underground). In this area the Betsimisaraka do not practise second burial.

Note: A recent traveller reported that the bridges along this stretch were is very poor condition (September, 1988).

JAWS

Sharks are a real danger to swimmers in unprotected bays on the east coast. Shark associated deaths seem particularly high in Tamatave – everyone has a gruesome story. Jytte Larson met several such people on her east coast travels: 'A Tamatave man told me that one week ago four professional divers (hunting for lobster for the restaurants) had been taken by sharks. The owner of Chez Vavate, on Ste Marie, told me that her husband, who goes out beyond the protective reef for seafood, was recently held up for an hour by a shark. He had to remain completely motionless and at last the shark lost interest and disappeared.'

So, however inviting the water, only swim in areas protected by a coral reef or artificial shark barrier. Menstruating women should be particularly careful. Ask local advice – the French for shark is *requin* and in Malagasy *Antsantsa*.

Mahavelona (Foulpointe) The town itself is unremarkable, but nearby is an interesting old circular fortress with mighty walls made from an iron-hard mixture of sand, shells and eggs. There are some old British cannons marked GR. This fortress was built in the early nineteenth century by the Merina governor of the town, Rafaralahy, shortly after the Merina conquest of the east coast. There is a splendid contemporary picture of Rafaralahy in all his finery in John Mack's book *Madagascar, Islands of the Ancestors*.

Before reaching the town you will pass once-named Motel Hotel, now rebuilt after cyclone damage and called Hotel Manda. I have no reports on price or quality; see Addenda for other accommodation in this protected area with safe swimming.

Mahambo A beach resort with safe swimming and two groups of chalets, Le Recif and Le Gîte 'Fantastic; an old Indian couple run it. A chalet with shower, toilet, and two and a half double beds is 9,000 FMG. The food is brilliant. Fish in white wine, langouste in coconut sauce. Don't take a taxi, you'll have to wait to be ferried at the broken bridge. By bus you can cross the bridge by foot and take another bus/taxi brousse.' (Bob Gillam).

Sadly, the otherwise excellent – and safe – beaches in the area are plagued by sand-fleas.

Beyond Mahambo is Fénérive, formerly capital of the Betsimisaraka empire (basic hotels) and continuing north on a very poor road you finally reach Soanierana-Ivongo and Manompana – possible departure points for Sainte Marie.

OTHER PLACES OF INTEREST

North of Tamatave (towns accessible by air)

Maroansetra

The rainiest place in Madagascar (you'd know that without reading the record books) but the Mecca of naturalists and wildlife enthusiasts because of the nearby island reserve of Nosy Mangabé which has been set aside to protect the very rare aye-aye.

As so often happens in Madagascar, I spent rather longer than planned in Maroansetra, so got to know the town quite well. I liked it. There is a modest air of prosperity (relatively speaking), a small but bustling market selling a wonderful variety of fish, including little hammerhead sharks, vanilla laid out to dry in the sun, and a shop selling beautiful hardwood furniture which sets up an anguish of conscience in

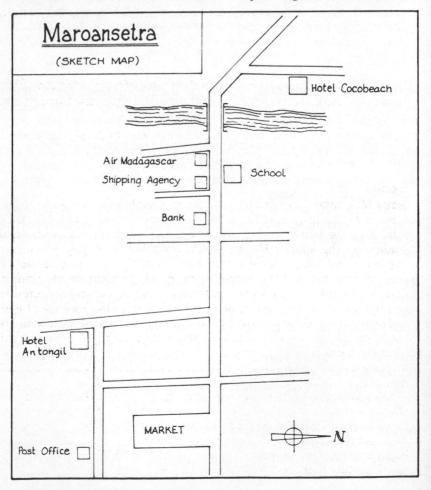

Maroansetra (SKETCH MAP)

Hotel Cocobeach
Air Madagascar
Shipping Agency
School
Bank
Hotel Antongil
MARKET
Post Office
N

conservation-minded visitors.

The airport is 8 km from town. There may or may not be a taxi, but it is a pleasant walk.

There used to be a regular ferry service (crowded, unpleasant) from Maroansetra to Île Sainte Marie and Tamatave, but this has been discontinued. However, there is always plenty of activity in the port and you may find a boat to somewhere. Enquire at the shipping office on the main street.

Where to stay/eat

The best place is the Motel Coco Beach, on the outskirts of town. This is a typical series of beach bungalows (4,500 FMG with cold-water shower, 3,500 FMG without), well set up but with inadequate facilities (one loo for everyone) and a rather dingy dining room. Its shortcomings are more than compensated for by the very helpful manager, Monsieur Fidel. He will arrange excursions (including Nosy Mangabe) and do everything in his power to ensure that you have a relatively trouble-free stay. His address is B.P. 1, Maroansetra (512). Tel: 18. Fidel speaks some English.

Under the same management but in the centre of town is the Antongil. Now renovated, and classed by recent travellers above the Coco Beach. Lively and full of character. 7,000 FMG, 1988.

There is reportedly an excellent restaurant in town called the Cousteau. Also a 'new juice-bar-cum-cafe on the main street'.

Excursions

Nosy Mangabe To visit the island you must have a permit from the Eaux et Forêts people in Tana, but there should be no problem getting this, even for non-scientists. There is usually a naturalist doing field studies on the island. He/she would probably be happy to answer questions, but remember that they have work to do. A simple shelter may be available, but those wishing to spend the night should bring a tent (the Dept Eaux et Forêts could advise you). Aye-ayes are secretive and nocturnal, so you will be lucky if you see one (the zoologist I met had been on the island two weeks and had yet to see one of these lemurs) but Nosy Mangabe has a wealth of other creatures: ruffed lemurs (two species), brown lemurs, bright red frogs, and reptiles such as the marvellous leaf-tailed lizard *Uroplatus fimbriatus*, chameleons, and snakes.

Nosy Mangabe is also an extraordinarily beautiful island, with sandy coves (no swimming, alas, because of sharks) and a hill (a very hard, slippery climb) topped by a lighthouse with lovely views.

To get there you are at the mercy of local boat owners, and this may be expensive. One traveller had to pay 45,000 FMG. Obviously it is worth getting a group together to save costs. (See also Addenda.)

Another very worthwhile tour (which can be arranged by M.Fidel) is a pirogue trip up the Andrianofotsy river to the village of the same name. The vegetation and river life viewed on the way is fascinating, and the unspoilt (so far) village, with its inquisitive inhabitants, is peaceful and endearing. There is also a very interesting Betsimisaraka cemetery nearby where 'second burial' takes place.

Bob Gillam recommends the following trip: 'Follow the coast towards Navana, a beach backed by thickets, waterways clogged with flowering water-hyacinth and lots of forest. You need to cross a lot of water on a pirogue, a regular local service. It takes an hour through little canals and costs 500 FMG.'

Finally there's an excursion of another sort – the tough sort. It's possible to walk across the **Masoala Peninsula**, from Maroansetra to Antalaha. It's a distance of 152 km, takes five days with one tramp of 48 km, and involves much walking along river beds or ankle deep mud in the pouring rain or baking heat – around 35°. Added to this, the path is mostly by rice fields so doesn't cross large areas of virgin forest. However, I haven't done it, so don't let me put you off! The trek can be arranged through Madagascar Airtours, who describe it evocatively in their brochure as going through 'dense underwoods bearing orchids, villages, rivers and streams ... the contact with the forest inhabitants takes smoothly back to the well-spring of life'. If I were to do it I'd insist on taking longer than five days, even though it meant backpacking with a tent rather than using local villages. At least it's a way of getting to Antalaha!

Olivier Langrand tells me about another, more interesting trans-Masoala path to Andapa. It takes about 6 days and is seldom used, even by locals, so finding a guide for the whole distance may be difficult (Olivier hasn't done it himself). Real adventure stuff.

Antalaha

'Quite a pretty town dominated by the vanilla industry. The European-run Hotel de Centre is 3,500 FMG but comfortable. Meals 2,000 FMG (1985). Bus to airport 1,500 FMG – same as taxi price'. (Sally Crook)

Sambava

A straggling town in the centre of the vanilla and coconut growing region. It is also an important area for cloves and coffee production, and a base for exploring the eastern rain forest.

The airport is 1.5km to the south of the town. The market is at the north end.

Where to stay/eat
Category A
Hotel Carrefour. (1988 prices) 16,000 FMG, 24,000 FMG and

28,000 FMG (air conditioned). Restaurant. Poor value.

Category B
Orchidea Beach (B.P.86. Tel: 128) Very pleasant new bungalows overlooking the ocean. 10,000 FMG (1988). Excellent meals. Friendly. Very good value and highly recommended. Run by an Italian, M. Filosi, and his family.

Calypso Hotel. 11 rooms: 4 at 6,500 FMG, 3 at 7,500 FMG, and 3 at 10,000 FMG (1988). Clean. Recommended.

Category C
Hotel Pacifique. 3 rooms at 3,500 FMG. Bungalows at 6,500 FMG and 5,000 FMG.

Dragon d'Or. 6 rooms at 3,000 FMG. Central. Basic. Good restaurant. Nearby is Chez Sam, a good Chinese restaurant.

Excursions
A travel agency, Sambava-Voyages (B.P. 28a. Tel: 110) not far from the Air Madagascar office at the south end of the town, will organise excursions by *pirogue* on the nearby river Bemarivo to an island rich in birdlife, Nosiharina, or to the Réserve Naturelle Intégrale of Marojejy. For the latter, give them plenty of advance warning and preferably get your own permit in Antananarivo. The trip to Marojejy takes at least three days. A tent is needed plus provisions. The reserve is tough going and for serious naturalists. For one thing the rainfall on the eastern slopes is thought to reach 3,000mm a year! But the reserve is extremely rich in endemic species of flora and fauna, some unique to the massif.

Sambava Voyages have now increased their operations to include a variety of river and hiking trips which sound ideal for those wishing to get off the beaten track but not quite ready to go it alone.

The Manageress of Sambava-Voyages is Mme Seramila. She speaks a little English, and a good catalogue — in English — is available.

Boats also go up the Bemarivo to the village of Amboahangibe to transport coffee. You may be fortunate enough to get a lift, or arrange your own pirogue.

An interesting visit in town is to the vanilla factory. To find it follow your nose!

The relative prosperity of the area is shown by the rather good road to **Andapa**. When I went there twelve years ago I was enchanted by the villages en route: Manantenina and Andranomifototra. I remember tracks leading to the villages, and masses of butterflies. And friendly people. I also remember my attempt to walk west from Antanimbaribe (see page 153). However, I still believe this area has a lot to offer explorers; or at least I still find the 1:500,000 scale Antalaha map (no 4) as tantalising as ever, so it's a good thing I'm writing this in England!

RICE

The Malagasy have an almost mystical attachment to rice. King Andrianampoinimerina declared 'Rice and I are one' and the loyalty to the Merina king was symbolised by industry in the rice paddies. Today the Betsileo are the masters of rice cultivation, but it is grown throughout the island (except in the dry south west), either in irrigated paddies or as 'hill rice' watered by the rain. Rice accounts for half the country's agricultural produce.

The Malagasy eat rice three times a day, the annual consumption being 135 kg per person (about a pound of rice a day!). Rice marketing was nationalised in 1976, but this produced such a dramatic decline in the amount of rice reaching the open market that restrictions were lifted in 1984. However, many small farmers grow rice only for their own consumption. The government is making great efforts to increase rice production (yields are very low compared with other countries) and to make Madagascar once more sufficient in this staple food. Once an exporter of rice, their needs must now be met by imports.

VANILLA

Not a native Madagascar species, vanilla is an orchid from Mexico. Because the insect necessary for pollination stayed behind in its native country, all vanilla in Madagascar must be pollinated by hand.

Vanilla is grown in the north and east of Madagascar; almost the entire crop goes to the United States for ice cream. The government sets the price for vanilla; in 1986 this was about £8 (7,500 FMG) per kilo.

Indri

A CAUTIONARY TALE

I first came to Madagascar in 1976 with an insatiable appetite for seeing wildlife. In those days you could fly direct from East Africa to Majunga, so George and I started our clockwise exploration of the island without going to Tana. No Tana meant no official permits for visiting nature reserves. No problem in Montagne d'Ambre – we got our permits in Diego – but *beaucoup de problèmes* in our next choice, Maronjejy, which attracted us because our map showed a footpath running right across the reserve: just right for a two day backpacking trip.

As we made our way to the trail head we tried hard to get a permit. We spent three days walking to sundry villages on the edge of the reserve, meeting some delightful Malagasy and equally appealing chameleons and butterflies, but failing to find a representative from *Eaux et Forêts* willing to give us the necessary permission. When an *Eaux et Forêts* man appeared on the scene – while we were being told of the comparative merits of cat and lemur meat by our otherwise charming hosts in Antanimbaribe – we were amazed. And when he asked for our passports and started to write out a permit, (laboriously copying all our passport details such as 'Name and address of bear') we were thrilled. When we gathered that he also intended to accompany us into the reserve we were less happy, normally prefering to follow our own route at our own pace. However, local information was that the path was not easy to follow, so it seemed sensible to have expert guidance.

Our Man (we never learned to pronounce his name) was not really equipped for backpacking; he had plastic sandals, a brief case containing three hats, two clean shirts, and about 5 lbs of official papers. He carried no food or bedding so I had to add a blanket to my already laden pack, and George crammed in some extra biscuits. We were also carrying a fair bit of unnecessary weight – our packs (the old-fashioned external-frame variety) weighed around 35lb, and I was further hindered by a movie camera with which to make a David Attenborough style record of the wildlife.

Unencumbered, Our Man took a bold route up the side of the mountain, through vanilla groves, while we sweated in the rear. I'd forgotten how exhausting it is climbing steeply in very hot, very humid weather. When we caught up with him he was gazing possessively at a distinctive stone. 'This marks the edge of the reserve', he told us. And added that it was the furthest he'd been. He'd never actually tried to walk 'our path'. We felt a twinge of doubt. Another twinge came when we met our first fallen tree; we'd known about the recent cyclone – indeed we'd caught the edge of it in what had seemed the very appropriately named Hell-ville – but we'd forgotten the effect cyclones can have on trees. This shows the effect Madagascar can have on one's grey cells since we'd looked down in amazement at the spilt-matches effect as the plane flew over the forest on its approach to Sambava.

By the time we'd crawled under, or teetered over, our fifth or sixth fallen giant, I was in a thoroughly bad mood. With sweat running down my face, ants dropping down my neck, and my hateful pack and even more hateful movie camera throwing me off balance, it didn't seem that I was having much fun.

We camped by the river, pitching our tent across the path, this being the only flat space available, and cooked a rather sumptuous meal. We deserved a treat, and our map showed that tomorrow would be downhill all the way. We should reach our destination in the early evening. No need to save any food, apart from our emergency nuts and raisins. Our Man, miserable for lack of rice, nevertheless had a hearty appetite for freeze-dried food.

After breakfast and self-reminders that we should spend more time looking for wildlife we set off. The path evidently crossed the river so we obediently did likewise, and equally obediently followed our man as he decided to follow the river when the path disappeared. This was fine for him in his plastic sandals, but dodgy when we wished to keep our hiking boots dry. We boulder-hopped athletically until we came to a high, vine-draped cliff. There was no way round the base, we had to climb up the slippery, steep sides and let ourselves down, Tarzan-style, on the lianas.

'*Ou est le sentier?*' we asked Our Chap. We asked him the same question in increasing desperation for the next two days. I expect he was asking himself where the path was; after all, he probably wasn't very happy either at being lost in the eastern rain forest without cigarettes or rice and with two stroppy *vazahas* who never should have been there in the first place. However, I bet he wasn't as unhappy as I was. Certainly he wasn't stumbling along sobbing quietly. I'd given up being brave when the first fire-ants landed down my neck. Up until then I'd been quite stoical, taking a detached scientific interest in the leeches that decorated our legs and hands (what do they eat when there aren't juicy tourists stumbling past their bushes?) and even allowing something approaching joy at the sight of a rare *Brookesia* chameleon.

The terrain we were struggling through deserves some description. In fact there *is* a description in the *Flora* section. I note with interest that we were floundering through moist montane forest where there is 'more undergrowth [than lowland forest] ... and abundant epiphytes, ferns and mosses, and large lianas and bamboo. As the altitude increases, so the height of the canopy decreases,... permitting the growth of epiphytes and shrubby, herbaceous undergrowth with an abundance of moss.' Yes, I remember it well. The large lianas had a habit of snagging our pack frames, bringing us to an abrupt halt, and the bamboo had tiny cactus-like hairs that became imbedded in our hands if we grabbed bamboo for support. The shrubby, herbaceous undergrowth with an abundance of moss formed a safe-looking carpet over treacherous drops into hidden streams, and rotting logs that broke when we stepped on them. And they are certainly right about the density of this rain forest being greater than in other parts of the world. Without a panga to cut our way through the obstructing vegetation, we had to sidle, push and thrust our way through.

People ask if being lost in the jungle of Madagascar wasn't frightening. No, it wasn't frightening. When you're as miserable as I was, there isn't the leisure to be frightened as well. Apart from the hostile plants, almost all of which seemed to sting, slice, prick or trip, and the sweat running into our cuts and scratches, there was the effort of climbing near-vertical hillsides to cut off loops of the river, then easing ourselves down again, clinging onto whatever booby-trapped plant happened to be handy. At least we became blasé about crossing white water on moss-slicked tree trunks (a mild death-wish does wonders for your balance) and stopped caring about whether we got our boots wet. Since we were sometimes wading through waist-deep water it hardly seemed to matter. We had to follow the river, since the only certainty was that eventually we would come to a village.

After twelve hours of unmitigated effort we stopped for the night. Supper was broth, nuts and raisins. We passed the map wordlessly between us, and gave up guessing our location. With the knowledge of what was to come, breakfast (a cup of tea) was even less cheerful, and with nothing to eat we felt exhausted by ten. Then Our Man gave us a surge of hope and energy when he pointed to something in the soft sand at the edge of the river. A human footprint! If you've ever thought how splendid it must be to set foot where no white man has trod – forget it. It's greatly over-rated. But a footprint in the sand? We were unequivocally excited. No matter that we saw no other, and that our progress was as slow and painful as before, we had seen the light at the end of the tunnel. At noon (no lunch) we saw another, even more cheering sign of human life: an abandoned hut on the hillside. It took four hours to reach it, and much to our disappointment there was no clear trail nearby, but at least there was a flat area for our tent, and sugar cane and tobacco, much to Our Man's delight. He hastily picked some and dried it by the fire before smoking it. He also found leaves for *bredes* and gave a great shriek of excitement at his tastiest find: inch-long weevils with long snouts. We helped him collect the revolting creatures in a plastic bag.

Our fourth day in the jungle started in extreme gloom. We expected a village to lie just below the rim of the hill beyond the hut, but on reaching the top we saw ... miles and miles of forest. There was also the twinkling silver of a corrugated iron roof, but the sight of the distance between us and it and the hilly nature of the intervening jungle sapped our energy before we started. We were both getting very, very tired. The jungle was the densest, steepest, nastiest yet, with more fallen trees and more thorny branches than any before. Every step had to be carefully judged, every forward progression forced through the dense vegetation. Six hours later when we found a path we had no energy left for elation or even relief. We just walked numbly on, and it was only when a voice greeted us from behind that we could take in that we really had made it. We sat down and let Our Man and the woman jabber away. 'She knows my family', he told us excitedly 'My wife's wondering where I am!'.

The woman led us to her neat thatched hut made from woven bamboo, and we sank thankfully onto the clean floor mats. Our Man had regained all his old aplomb and described our adventures at length, with illustrative gestures. The family regarded us with gratifying respect and sympathy, tut-tutting in horror at our festering cuts and leech bites. We let the condolences wash over us until roused by a marvellous sound – the clinking of cutlery. Mats were spread on the floor and an enormous bowl of rice was carried in, followed by two different kinds of greens. We ate huge quantities, but Our Man filled his plate again and again. We were feeling almost human when he said jovially: 'You remember that little house we slept near last night? They say it's only half an hour over that hill.' We didn't laugh.

As we followed the path to Ambatobe we felt physically and mentally renewed and for the first time realised how we must appear to others. Our shirts had been wringing wet with sweat for four days; we were smelly, grubby and scabby, and we badly needed a bath. When we came to a stream we told Our Man to go on ahead.

The river formed a deep pool with a natural rock seat. It was hard to tear ourselves away but eventually, with clean bodies and fresh clothes, we approached the village. All the inhabitants were lined up on both sides of the path to greet us. 'Salama, salama!' we called, shaking the outstretched hands, sometimes twice as people raced round to have another turn.

Reverently we were guided to the biggest hut and two chairs were drawn up. In the dim light we could see our man already comfortably enthroned and surrounded by an admiring audience. The villagers crowded in and gazed at us in awe. Our story was told again and again, and when every detail had been lovingly described and all questions answered, supper arrived. A veritable banquet, with chicken stew, many varieties of greens, and the inevitable mound of rice. A plateful of small brown objects was added. Good heavens, we'd completely forgotten the weevils! Here they were, nicely roasted, and it seemed ungrateful not to try them. They had an agreeable nutty flavour. Forgetting my former disgust, I ate my share.

After supper Our Man changed his shirt, produced an official hat from his briefcase, and started reading to the villagers from one of his many papers. They listened respectfully, nodding at intervals. Eventually the audience trickled away and we could climb into our sleeping bags and sink into blissful sleep.

Next day two stalwart youths were enlisted to carry our packs and we practically floated down the wide trail to the road. The view was magnificent, birds sang, butterflies danced and a rustle in the trees made us look up: a troop of lemurs gazed mockingly down at us. We arrived at the road in just under two hours. The distance covered in that time was rather more than we'd gone in the three previous days.

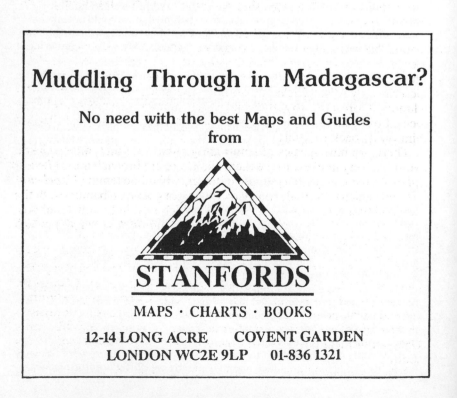

West of Tamatave

Perinet (Andasibe)

A visit to Madagascar's most accessible Special Reserve, Perinet-Analamazoatra, is a must for anyone interested in the flora and fauna of the eastern rainforest (moist montane forest at this altitude: 930 – 1,049 m). Perinet protects the largest of the lemur family, the indri.

About three feet tall, with barely visible tails, black and white markings and surprised teddy-bear faces, the indri looks more like a gone-wrong panda than a lemur. The long back legs are immensely powerful, and an indri can propel itself backwards thirty feet, execute a turn in mid-air, and land face-forward to gaze down benevolently at its observers. And you will be an observer: most people see indris in Perinet, and if they don't see them they hear them. For it is their voice that makes this lemur extra special: whilst other lemurs grunt or swear, the indri sings. It is an eerie, wailing sound somewhere between the song of a whale and a police-siren, and it carries for up to two miles as troops call to each other across the forest. The indris are fairly punctual with their song: if you are in the reserve between eight and ten in the morning, and shortly before dusk you should hear them. There's no point in looking for indri at other times of the day; being leaf-eaters and so devoid of excess energy, they spend much of the day dozing in the tops of trees.

In Malagasy the indri is called *Babakoto*. There are various legends connected with the indri, and explaining the esteem with which the local people hold them (it is *fady* to kill an indri). One that links the indri with the origin of man (thus supporting modern evolutionary thought) is described by Alison Richard, another popular legend tells of a man who climbed a forest tree to gather wild honey, and was severely stung by the bees. Losing his hold, he fell, but was caught by a huge indri who carried him on its back to safety.

There are nine species of lemur altogether in Perinet, although you would be very unlikely to see them all. There are brown lemurs (*Lemur fulvus*) or you may get a glimpse of the grey bamboo lemur (*Hapelemur griseus*) which is diurnal, and feeds you might guess, on bamboos. In the same habitat there are mouse lemurs, which nest in hollow bamboos. Then there's the greater dwarf lemur (*Cheirogaleus major*) which hibernates during the cold season.

Lemurs are only a few of the creatures to be found in Perinet. There are tenrecs, beautiful and varied insects and spiders, and lots of reptiles. One of Madagascar's biggest chameleons lives here: *Chameleon parsonii*, which is bright green, about two feet long and has twin horns at the end of its snout. Local boys often collect chameleons for tourists to photograph. They expect a tip. With Malagasy help you may also see a Uroplatus or leaf tailed lizard. Boas are quite common and more easily spotted.

This is a splendid place for bird watching. Near the forester's house there are flowering trees of a species much favoured by the Madagascan green sunbird (*Cinnyris notatus*) which has an iridescent green head and throat, and sucks nectar like the New World hummingbirds. There are also plenty of the cuckoo-like blue couas, blue pigeons, paradise flycatchers, two species of falcon (Newton falcon and Madagascan falcon), two species of black vasa parrots, and many others.

Botanists will not be disappointed either. In French colonial days an orchid garden was started by the lily pond to the right of the road to the reserve, and a variety of species flourish here although most flower in the warm wet season. For a detailed description of the flora found in moist montane forests such as Perinet, see page 50.

To visit the Reserve you need a permit from Eaux et Forêts in Tana, and a guide. The warden's two sons, Maurice and Bedo, have become expert guides. What they lack in language skills they make up with keen eyesight and an infallible instinct on where to find indris. Until recently it was hard to know how much to pay these young guides, but there is now a book by the park entrance with guide-lines for tourists and suggested payment for guides – at the time of writing (November, 1988) this ranges from 1,000 FMG to 2,000 FMG ; no doubt the prices will be kept abreast of inflation.

There is only one place to stay in Perinet: the Hotel Buffet de la Gare, which at first sight is mistaken for the station itself, and where you eat lunch on the Tana to Tamatave train journey. It seems to be one of those places you either love or hate (although it can't be *too* bad – Prince Philip has stayed here). Gerald Durrell described it as having 'a sort of decaying grandeur about it that was irresistible'. I agree, but I escorted one couple to Perinet who had such withdrawal symptoms for the Hilton that they had to leave a day early. The hotel is old (1938), it needs some paint and some new beds and better plumbing, but it is clean and run by Monsieur Joseph with an old world charm and courtesy that more expensive hotels would do well to emulate. Joseph's attention to his guests was demonstrated when someone asked for a hot bath. Fifteen minutes later I watched a team of men running up and down the stairs carrying buckets of steaming water.

The dining room is truly elegant – fresh flowers on the tables and a marvellous rosewood bar. The food is very good, too.

There are eight rooms costing 15,500 FMG (1988), and plans to build a series of bungalows which should be around 20,000 FMG. With the increasing popularity of Perinet, they will be needed.

Perinet is not popular with everyone. Non nature-lovers find the village itself depressing, the rain dreary, and the leeches disgusting. The latter are not a problem on the broad main paths, but if you've pushed through vegetation and it's been raining recently, *prenez-garde*! Tuck your trousers into your socks and carry salt; this usually dislodges the creatures before they get dug in. A lighted cigarette or petrol does the same trick. Malagasy leeches are very small – not African Queen proportions – but the anti-coagulant they inject when they bite means you bleed dramatically.

Lake Alaotra

A spur of the railway runs from Moramanga (which supposedly means 'where the mangoes are cheap') to Lac Alaotra and the village of Imerimandroso. This is the start of the so-called Smugglers Path to the Indian Ocean – a five-day walk. Like the similar path across the Masoala peninsula this sounds both unpleasant and difficult. It is described in the German guide *Madagaskar* (published by DuMont, Cologne) but the Germans I met who had attempted it had all turned back. However, perhaps I just didn't meet the successful ones, so if you're enthusiastic, well equipped, and adventurous by all means give it a try. It goes to Antsikafoka, just south of Fénérive and has a romantic history: before the road and railway this was the normal route for smuggled goods from Reunion and Mauritius to be brought to the highlands. Now there is talk of making a road along this route – it may even be under way. Since reports of Lac Alaotra are not particularly enthusiastic (I haven't been there myself) my recommendation is to give the area a miss unless you have lots of time and have heard on the grapevine that it really *is* worth it and/or the road has made it easier. If you make this decision you will need map no 6, Toamasina.

If you only go as far as Ambatondrazaka, there is a Chinese-run hotel for 6,900 FMG, with just adequate food. The Salon du Lac opposite is a good patisserie. The road goes right round the lake but there is no public transport much of the year.

South of Tamatave

Pangalanes

This series of lakes was linked by artificial canals in French Colonial times for commercial use, a quiet inland water being preferable to an often stormy sea. Over the years the canals became choked with vegetation and no longer passable, but attempts are now being made to rehabilitate the canals and re-establish the unbroken waterway which stretched from Tamatave to Vangaindrano.

It is possible to travel stretches of the canal yourself on barges carrying cargoes of bananas, coffee, etc. This is particularly attractive for fishing enthusiasts since there are many deep-sea fish in the the lakes. There are no sharks, so swimming is safe. Bird watching is also rewarding and crocodiles may be seen, especially at night with the use of a torch.

Some companies run escorted trips to the Pangalanes: Turisma, 15 Ave de l'Indépendance, Antananarivo (B.P. 3997). Tel: 289-11/287-57. Telex 22366 Somatram and Caravanserai, B.P. 627, Antananarivo. Tel: 302-79. Turisma has a three and five day itinerary, the latter allowing a two and a half day stay at the village of Ankanin'ny Nofy, 61 km south of Tamatave.

There is also a hotel near Ambila Lemaitso, Les Everglades, on Lac Rasoabe (Tel: 442-97 in Tana for further information and bookings). It is reportedly a rather sad, gloomy place, but perhaps it just needs more visitors. Excursions can be arranged from the hotel.

Both Ankanin'ny Nofy and Ambila Lemaitso are on the Tana – Tamatave railway.

Andevoranto, south of Ambila Lemaitso, is said to be a cheerful, friendly small town. There may not be accommodation however (but camping would be no problem).

You can continue travelling down the coast as far as Mahanoro (occasional transport) and can sometimes find a *pirogue* to take you to Nosy Varika and Mananjary, which is linked by road to Fianarantsoa. This is adventurous stuff, and not for those with limited time.

Mananjary

A centre for coffee, vanilla, and pepper. Accessible by good road and taxi-brousse, this town is famous for its circumcision ceremony which takes place every seven years: most recently in October, 1986.

Hotels: Jardin de la Mer (Ambinany) and Solimotel (Bd Maritime). 'Solimotel food awful except for the occasional French bread for breakfast' (S.Crook). Camping is an alternative.

'In this area you can see a stone sculpture called "The White Elephant". Since there are no elephants in Madagascar, some historians think that people from India or Africa made this elephant just after their arrival 1,000 years ago. You need a guide and three days to go to this sculpture.' (Jytte Arnfred Larson).

Fianarantsoa to Manakara by train

Not as popular as the Tana-Tamatave train, this is nevertheless a spectacular railway trip, especially the early part. The train leaves every other day at 7.00 and takes six hours to reach Manakara. Tickets (1986) cost 6,725 FMG (1st class – but now payable in hard currency), 3,625 FMG (3rd class); 1st class can be reserved in advance. There are also taxi-brousses at roughly the same price as a third class train ticket.

Manakara

There are three hotels: Hotel Manakara, Super Hotely (basic, clean) and Sidi Hotel (14,000 FMG – 1988 – food poor and expensive. Disco Fri & Sat). From Manakara you can continue south by taxi-brousse to two towns described here by Jytte Arnfred Larson of Denmark.

Vohipeno   'About 30 km south of Manakara. No hotels, only a very small Malagasy *hotely* with one room (only for adventurers). This area is inhabited by the Antaimoro tribe who came from Arabia about 600 years ago, bringing the first script to Madagascar. Originally Moslems,

most of them have now been converted to Christianity. From Vohipeno you can walk about 5 km to Ivato, where you can visit the old Antaimoro kings' tombs. But first you must go to the office of the *president du Fokontany* to get permission. The substitute for the *president* who gave me the permit was a passionate lover of Malagasy history and told me stories about the kings and queens for one hour, although I was anxious to start the excursion. The path to Ivato goes through several small villages – very unspoilt. All over I met very friendly people. In Ivato I met a man who spoke some French and was willing to guide me to the present king. There was a big gathering for a funeral so many local village chiefs were in the king's house. I was invited to enter and after greeting ceremonies, we sat down to negotiate a price for permission to take photos. I was asked to pay 3,000 FMG – but was only allowed to take photos of the tomb from the outside.'

The Antaimoro people also demonstrate their Islamic history through their clothing (turban and fez, as well as Arab-style robes). They are the inheritors of the 'great writings' *sorabe*, written in Malagasy but in Arabic script. *Sorabe* continue to be written, still in Arabic, still on 'Antaimoro paper'. The scribes who practise this art are known as *katibo* and the writing and their knowledge of it gives them a special power. The writing itself ranges from accounts of historical events to astrology, and the books are considered sacred.

Farafangana

Accessible by taxi-brousse from Manakara. Nice fishermen's cottages. Restaurant Le Lac. Good Malagasy *hotely* near some *bungalows administratifs* and a *Vazaha* hotel by the sea (15,000 FMG 1988).

Warning: To vary the route back to the *Hauts Plateaux* there is a temptation to take the very rough – but marvellously scenic – road from Farafangana to Ihosy. The advice is don't: this road is notorious for bandits.

SAMBATRA IN MANANJARY

By Sally Crook

Sambatra means 'blessed' or 'happy' in Malagasy, and it is the word used for the circumcision ceremonies which are performed in much of Madagascar. The Antambahoaka, probably the smallest tribe in Madagascar, live around Mananjary on the east coast, and young boys and their families from the surrounding villages congregate every seven years for a communal circumcision ceremony there. They become 'blessed', though the actual deed of removal of the penis foreskin is now performed at a different time, usually in the hygienic conditions of a hospital.

In October 1986, the week-long celebrations commenced at a leisurely pace and culminated (after a Thursday of inactivity, due to the *fady* nature of this day) on a Friday. Women collected reeds and wove mats in preparation for the big day, and later men carved and painted wooden birds, three of which were fixed on the roof of each *trano be* (literally 'big house'), facing east. This in itself caused much excitement and some unwished for precipitous descents from the sloped, thatched roofs, while the men continued to beat their oval wooden or hide shields with sticks wielded like swords. Similar activity, drumming and chanting continued below, and the women chanted as they stepped from side to side in their dance. A boy standing astride a barrel on a wheeled cart, brandishing shield and stick gave the most fiery display, encouraging the crowds around.

The fathers of boys to be circumcised wore long colourful robes, gathered at the neck. The *trano be* in which the people drink and talk for days, should not be entered by foreign females, and even the Malagasy women must wear their hair in the traditional style – the many plaits on each side of the centre parting being drawn to a cluster at each side of the neck.

In the afternoon of the Wednesday, women shuffled around the *trano be* in an anti-clockwise direction, chanting and holding aloft the white braided and tasselled red ceremonial caps of their young sons. At the front and back of the procession, the rolled mats woven especially for the occasion were held aloft. After several circuits of the house, the crowds proceeded to the beach where, apparently spontaneously, the women's cries were periodically renewed.

The excitement spilt over into a kind of fighting between men with green pointed sticks cut from the mid ribs of palm fronds, and soon the fathers of the circumcision candidates were being routed and chased back into town as the green sticks were hurled at their retreating backs. The apparent terror with which men fled from these harmless weapons indicates a far greater symbolic significance than their physical power.

As Thursday became Friday at midnight, sacred water was collected from the wide River Mananjary where it enters the sea. In the morning gloom nine zebu were sacrificed – one for each clan – by the cutting of the jugular vein after prayers. Some escapees caused excitement before the animals could be bound and lain on their sides with a piece of wood between the teeth. At the first sight of blood, little boys rushed forward to collect it in buckets or in bamboo pipes, just as their 'cousins' in Toraja, Sulawesi, do to this day.

Dancing, music and the women's chant of 'Eeee-ay' changed to processions and a chorus of 'Aaa-ooh' as crowds converged once again on the beach. The young boys, in red and white smocks and wearing their tasselled caps, were carried on their fathers' shoulders. The mind-dulling chant continued as the separate clans were herded along like sheep by men with sticks, following the man with the sacred water held in a small pot on his head, protected by a movable 'hedge' of four poles carried by other robed men.

That night, the boys, bearing white marks on their faces to indicate their clan, were carried on the shoulders of adults around the *trano be*. Each was passed through the west door of the house, and, wearing a string around the waist, was sat upon the severed head of a fine male zebu for a while in the presence of the clan leader, adorned with colourful striped cloth and a fez. The virility of the animal was thus conferred on the boy, and, as he was passed through the east door he had become a man.

These tiny men were almost dropping with exhaustion as they were paraded once again near the house, whose outside northern end had been cordoned off and guarded from trespass throughout the ceremonial days. The joy of their mothers was vocal and infectious as if they were relieved to have their sons now accepted as adults.

ÎLE SAINTE MARIE (NOSY BORAHA)

History

The origin of the Malagasy name is obscure. It either means Island of Abraham or Island of Ibrahim, with probable reference to an early semitic culture.

It was re-named Île Sainte Marie by Christian missionaries, but was more often called *Île aux Forbans*, being the major hideout of pirates in the Indian Ocean. From the 1680s to the mid-18th Century these European pirates dominated the seas around Africa. There was a Welshman – David Williams, Englishmen – Thomas White, John Every, William Kidd, and an American – Thomas Tew, among a Madagascarn pirate population which in its heyday numbered nearly one thousand. Then came a Frenchman, Corporal Jean-Onésime Filet ('La Bigorne') who was shipwrecked on Ste Marie while escaping the wrath of a jealous husband in Réunion. La Bigorne turned his amorous attentions, with remarkable success, to Princess Bety, the daughter of King Ratsimilaho. On their marriage the happy couple received Nosy Boraha as a gift from the king, and the island was in turn presented to the mother country by La Bigorne (or rather, put under the protection of France by Princess Bety). Thus France gained its first piece of Madagascar in 1750.

Île Sainte Marie today

A cliché of a tropical island with endless deserted beaches overhung by coconut palms, bays protected from sharks by coral reefs, hills covered with luxuriant vegetation, and – in 1987 – an absence of unsightly tourist development and of vehicles: there are five on the island. The serpent in this Garden of Eden is the weather: as in all the eastern region, cyclones strike regularly (an exceptionally bad one in 1986 did a great deal of damage) and you can expect several days of rain and wind all year round, but interspersed with calm sunny weather. The best months for a visit seem to be June and Mid-August to November.

The only real town in Ste Marie is Ambodifototra. Other small villages are comprised of bamboo and palm huts.

Ste Marie attracts a more rugged breed of visitor than its island rival, Nosy Be. This is partly because of the weather, partly because there is more choice of low-cost accommodation and an absence of tourist hoo-ha, and partly because it can seem almost impossible to get there, and quite impossible to leave. Travellers have demonstrated the heights of initiative in finding transport off the island when planes are habitually booked solid for months in advance.

Getting there and back

By boat   A very crowded and uncomfortable passenger boat leaves Tamatave once a week, usually on a Tuesday at 6.00. (But note: this boat used to go on to Maroansetra; the cancellation of this leg of the journey may well mean a change of timetable. Boats may even go more

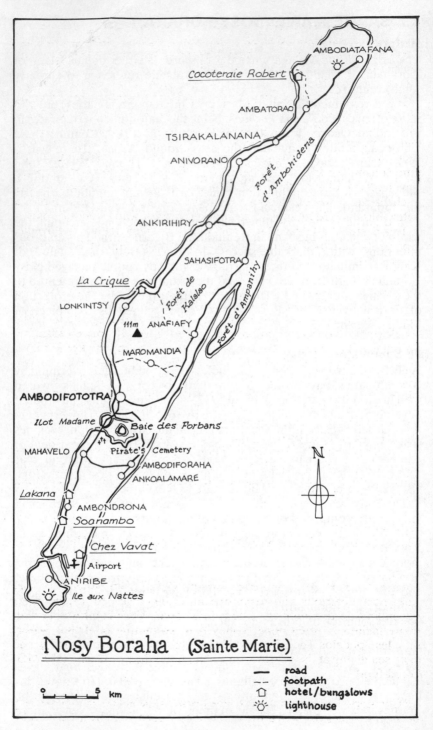

Nosy Boraha   (Sainte Marie)

——	road
– –	footpath
⌂	hotel/bungalows
☼	lighthouse

0 _____ 5 km

frequently). The shipping line is SCAC, a couple of blocks behind AUXIMAD, along the seafront, who used to operate these boats. Price 7,000 FMG for an often rough ten hour crossing, leaving at 6.00 am. It returns on Fridays, leaving at midnight.

It is also possible to take a boat from Manompana, on the mainland opposite, but reports vary. 'I met a Swiss couple who had taken a weekly (approx.) taxi-brousse to Manompana and caught an infrequent boat to the island, and sat on the deck for seven hours in the rain during the night-time crossing.' (S. Crook). I have also met several people who tried and failed to find a boat (disappointing after the tough and time-consuming trip to Manompana). However, reports by a recent traveller (end of 1987) indicate the boat is once again in operation. Try to check the travellers' grape-vine before risking it, though. There is a hotel (basic) in Manompana and the proprietor knows about boats.

Those stuck on Ste Marie can even consider taking a *pirogue*, reportedly run by Hotel Atafana, which drops you at Soanierana-Ivongo.

By plane   Air Madagascar flies to Ste Marie every day except Tuesday and Thursday, £44 ($81) from Tana, £20 ($36) from Tamatave. All flights are heavily booked, especially in July and August, and you should make your reservations well in advance. If you go standby, Monday and Friday are the best bets, when 40 seater Hawker Siddeley planes are used instead of the 17 seater Twin Otter. As soon as you arrive, reconfirm your return flights. However adamant the Air-Mad people are that the flight is full, it is worth going standby. I have got on twice this way, and other travellers report the same success. It's a nerve-racking business, though.

There are no taxis on the island. The few available vehicles are owned by hotels and meet the incoming planes. You therefore need to know where you are staying and if possible have a reservation. (August is the peak month in Ste Marie.) Check with the 'courtesy vehicles' if there is room at their hotel before climbing aboard.

Where to stay
There are no large hotels on Ste Marie, only palm-thatched bungalows.

Category A
Soanambo (B.P. 20). 3 km from airport; 10 km from Ambodifototra. The most luxurious and expensive at 11,000 FMG to 15,000 FMG depending on the number of beds in a room. Very comfortable with many facilities – ping pong, volley ball, swimming pool, hot water, bicycles, 'pedalos' (pedal boats) for hire, plus sailing, wind-surfing and deep sea diving at the nearby Centre Nautique. Main meal 5,000 FMG. Good food.

La Cocoterie Robert. In the extreme north of the island, said to be very beautiful. Access by land difficult, but a boat goes there from Soanambo

(it's run by the same French family). Bungalows 5,500 FMG –
7,000 FMG. Meals 3,500 FMG.

Category B
Lakana. Six simple but very comfortable bamboo and palm bungalows,
5 km from the airport, and including two perched along the jetty. About
6,000 FMG. Meals 3,500 FMG. 10 speed bicycles for hire. Some
English spoken. Near the Centre Nautique.

La Crique. 10,000 FMG per bungalow. The most beautifully located of
all the bungalows, by a beach in the rugged north of the island, a
kilometre north of Lonkinsky. (A vehicle meets the plane and
transports guests to the hotel.) The most popular of all the hotels, so
often full. Try to book ahead (B.P. 1).

Atafana. A new Malagasy-run hotel about 4 km south of La Crique.
7,000 FMG per room. Good food.

Category C
Chez Vavate. 6 rooms/bungalows. 4,500 FMG – 6,000 FMG. On first
appearance an unprepossessing collection of local huts built on a ridge
overlooking the airstrip. Don't be taken in by first impressions, the food
here must be some of the best in Madagascar (and the *punch coco*
ensures that you spend your evenings in a convivial haze) and the
relaxed family atmosphere makes this a very popular place with young
travellers. The only catch is you must walk 1½ km from the airport.
There is no road, and the 'courtesy vehicle' from the airport is a man
with a wheelbarrow! If you miss him take the wide grassy track which
runs parallel to the airstrip then veers to the left up a steep hill, but be
warned – if Chez Vavate is full you will have missed the vehicles going to
the other places. Camping is usually permitted here.

Lafalafa. This restaurant in Ambodifototra also has a few rooms for
2,500 FMG.

Bety Plage. This previously popular hotel 3 km north of Ambodifototra
was demolished in the cyclone of 1986. It may be rebuilt.

Excursions around Ste Marie

From Chez Vavate, Soanambo or Lakana
Île Aux Nattes. A population of some 300 live on this island off the south
of Ste Marie so transport by *pirogue* is easy and frequent. Cost
250 FMG approx. *Pirogues* leave from the southernmost tip of Ste
Marie (the path there is an extension of the airport runway) and will
land you near the little village of Aniribe. From here it is a short walk to
the lighthouse (a villager will show you the path) which can be visited
both for the view and for the fascination of seeing a 1914 model of a

petrol-powered lighthouse still in operation – when there is petrol. Walk back along the very beautiful beach.

Île Aux Nattes was the home of 'Napoleon', a larger than life chief who used to enjoy entertaining *vazahas*. Napoleon held various offices from village chief in pre-independence days to *President Fokotany* in latter years. He died in colourful circumstances in 1986.

In Aniribe you can order *Poulet au coco* (chicken in coconut milk) a day in advance. There is a sort of 'restaurant' where this scrumptious dish has become a tradition. It's a lovely, and still unspoiled, place.

Two walks from the south

1. Two hours. Take the ridge path leading from Chez Vavate for about 2 km to an intersection. The path to the right takes you down to the beach, and that to the left crosses the narrow tail of the island and brings you out on the coastal road a couple of kilometres from the airport.

2. Six to seven hours. At low tide it is possible to walk up the almost deserted east coast (great swimming) of Ste Marie to the village of Ankoalamare and to the motorable track which crosses the island, winding round the rim of steep cultivated valleys and past small settlements. (You can also pick up one of the transverse paths). Return by the coastal road.

Bike rides

Bikes can be hired from many of the hotels, and from the little village near the airport. This way you can see quite a lot of the island (but don't reckon on covering much ground – the roads are very rough and the bikes often very bad). The main town, Ambodifototra, shows signs of past elegance, and two restaurants (Lafalafa recommended for good food and fruit juice) make it a suitable place to stop for lunch.

Pirates' Cemetery   This can only be visited at low tide since there are several tidal creeks to be crossed. Just before the bay bridge to the town is a track leading off to the left. Children will guide you (whether you want them to or not) to the pirates' cemetery, 20 minutes away. This is quite an impressive place, with grave stones dating from the 1830s, one with a classic skull and cross bones carved on it.

Harry Sutherland-Hawes writes 'Check out the local graveyards on the island, especially the one north of Ambotifototra. Keep an eye out on the right hand side of the road and you will suddenly see a stone coffin or two through the leaves. If you wander in, it will surely give you a fright: hundreds of coffins, all laid next to each other, some with carvings next to them. One of the locals who took me there was going to open a couple up to show me, but I declined his kind offer!'

Warnings: There are no facilities for changing money on Île Ste Marie. There is talk of 'developing' Île Ste Marie as a major tourist resort.

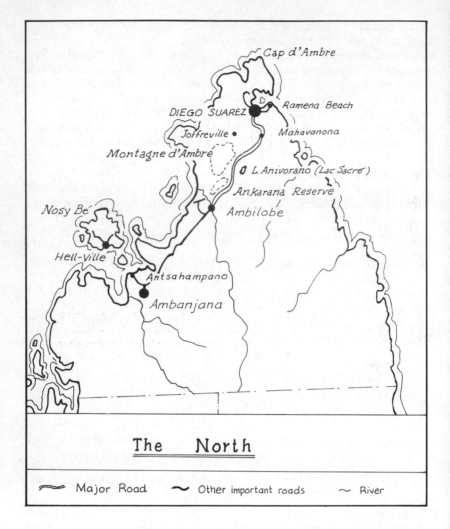

The North

~~~ Major Road   ~ Other important roads   ~ River

Galidia elegans

Chapter 10

The North

INTRODUCTION

The northern part of Madagascar is the domain of the Antakarana people. Cut off by rugged mountains, the Antakarana were left to their own devices until the mid-1700s when they were conquered by the Sakalava; they in turn submitted to the Merina king Radama I, aided by his military advisor James Hastie, in 1821.

The north is characterised by its variety. With the Tsaratanana massif (which includes Madagascar's highest peak, 2880 m) bringing more rain to the Nosy Bé area than is normal on the west coast, and the pocket of dry climate around Diego Suarez – seven months of dry weather; ninety percent of the 900 mm of rain falling between December and April – the weather can change dramatically within short distances. With changes of weather go changes of vegetation and its accompanying fauna, making this region particularly interesting for botanists and other naturalists, as well as straight forward holiday makers.

Getting around

The area retains its isolation and there are few good roads. Although you *can* get just about everywhere by taxi-brousse in the dry season, most people prefer to fly.

DIEGO SUAREZ (ANTSIRANANA)

History

Forgivingly named after a Portuguese captain, Diego Suarez, who arrived in 1543 and proceeded to murder and rape the inhabitants or sell them into slavery, this large town has had an eventful history. (There is no truth, however, to the often claimed story that the Republic of Libertania was founded here by pirates in the seventeenth century.)

The Malagasy name simply means 'port' and its strategic importance as a deep water harbour has long been recognised. The French installed a military base in 1885, and Britain captured and occupied the town in 1942 (Madagascar was then under the control of the Vichy Government) to prevent any Japanese designs on the island as an Indian Ocean base.

Getting there and back

The best way is by air; the only reasonable road is from Nosy Bé via Antsahampano (a popular route with travellers wanting a short taste of the thrills of taxi-broussing). This trip is described under Nosy Bé. There is also a rough overland route to Vohemar, Sambava and Antalaha, travelled by car-brousse twice a week. There are two *gare routières* in Diego, on the Route de l'Ankarana (south) and the Route de la Pyrotechnie (west).

Flights go from Tana (returning the same day) via Nosy Bé every day except Thursdays and Saturdays; £86 ($160). There are also flights from Majunga (£62, $115). The once regular service from the east coast has been cut to one a week (Sundays), from Sambava.

Diego today

Rated second in beauty after Rio de Janeiro (but like Rio this beauty can only be appreciated from the air or a hill-top) the harbour is encircled by green hills, with a conical 'sugar loaf' plonked in one of the bays to the east of the town. Diego's isolation behind its mountain barrier and its long association with non-Malagasy races, has given it an unusually cosmopolitan population. There are Arabs, Creoles (descendants of Europeans), Indians, Chinese, and Comorans.

The name Joffre seems to be everywhere in and around Diego. General Joseph Joffre was the military commander of the town in 1897 and later became Maréchal-de-France. In 1911 he took over the supreme command of the French armies, and was the victor of the battle of the Marne in 1914.

Stratton's description in *The Great Red Island* (1965): 'I have never heard a good word said for the port city. It is safe to say that Diego ... is the worst place in Madagascar. And why limit it? It is one of the worst places in the world.' Well, that's one view, but I find it is lively and interesting. Besides, there are some wonderful seaviews, a good climate, an excellent beach, and the magnificent national park Montagne d'Ambre: something for everyone.

Diego taxis are plentiful and cheap. They cost a set 250 FMG for any destination in the town centre. They usually operate on a shared system, so flag one down even if there's someone in it.

(*Much of the following information was provided by David Curl and Jane Wilson.*)

Where to stay

Category A

Hotel de la Poste (Near Clemenceau square, overlooking the bay. Postal address B.P. 121. Tel: 214-53). The best in town. Air conditioning. 13,500 FMG double (but now hard currency). All rooms have hot water, shower, WC etc. Recommended.

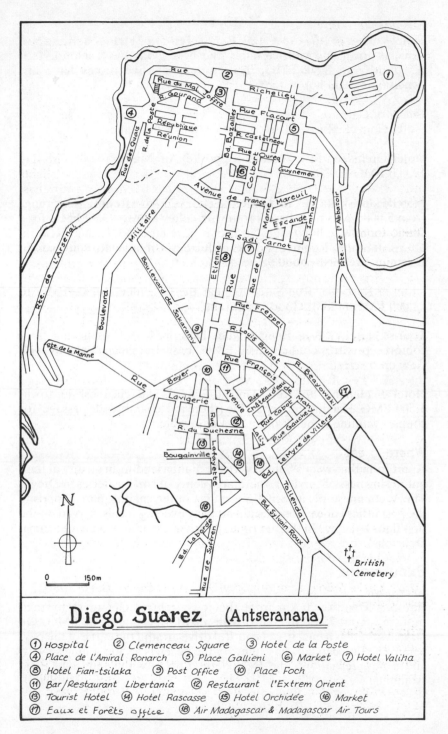

Diego Suarez (Antseranana)

① Hospital ② Clemenceau Square ③ Hotel de la Poste
④ Place de l'Amiral Ronarch ⑤ Place Gallieni ⑥ Market ⑦ Hotel Valiha
⑧ Hotel Fian-tsilaka ⑨ Post Office ⑩ Place Foch
⑪ Bar/Restaurant Libertania ⑫ Restaurant l'Extrem Orient
⑬ Tourist Hotel ⑭ Hotel Rascasse ⑮ Hotel Orchidée ⑯ Market
⑰ Eaux et Forêts office ⑱ Air Madagascar & Madagascar Air Tours

Category B
Hotel Valiha, 41 Rue Colbert (B.P. 270. Tel: 215-31). Probably the best value in town and with certainly the best food. Very helpful staff. 6,500 FMG to 8,500 FMG. The more expensive rooms have air-conditioning and hot water.

Category C
Hotel Nouvel, Rue Colbert. 5,000 FMG. Good value.

Hotel Orchidée, Rue Surcouf (opposite Air Mad). 10,000 FMG to 12,000 FMG (1988).

Hotel Fian-tsilaka, 13 Bvd Etienne (tel: 223-48). Room prices range from 5,000 FMG for a basic room with cold water to 9,800 FMG for a studio room with hot water. No rooms have air conditioning. Reasonable restaurant. 'Rooms are dark; awful views, if any, into courtyard or reception area. Not good value' (D.C.).

Hotel la Rascasse, Rue Surcouf, near the Orchidée. 10,000 FMG to 12,000 FMG (1988). Good restaurant.

Tourist Hotel, 7 Rue Bougainville. Describes itself as having 'tout confort – prix très etudié'. 4,000 FMG, basic but clean. Balcony with view onto street.

Hotel Fiadanana. 9, Rue Amiral Pierre. The cheapest in town. 3,500 FMG. Friendly, disreputable (there are 'chambres de passage' for couples wanting a 'quick one') and enjoyable.

Where to eat
Apart from the various hotels (with the Valiha leading in quality of food but in slowness of service), there are plenty of small eateries in Diego. The Vietnamese restaurant (Libertalia) in the main square (opposite the post office) does economical and tasty evening meals, served on the first floor balcony. In the bar try a 'punch au coco' (coconut and rum). Delicious!

Excursions
Near town
Ramena Beach   20 km from the town centre. Get there by taxi-brousse (about 750 FMG) or private taxi for around 8,000 FMG. On Sundays there is a bus. It's a beautiful drive around the curve of the bay, with some fine baobabs en route. By the beach is a shop selling snacks, and a new restaurant, the Belvedere. Lovely white sand and good swimming.

Montagne de Français (French Mountain) A tough but rewarding climb up to a high point with splendid views, caves, and interesting vegetation – baobabs local to the area and pachypodium. Take a taxi along the road to Ramena beach and get out after 8 km. The driver should be able to show you one of the several footpaths up the hill, or you may prefer to take a guide. It will take one to one and a half hours to climb to the top.

The British Cemetery Less strenuous, and a pleasant oasis of green, is on the road to Ambilobe (near the Ministère de Éducation Base).

Here is a sad insight into Anglo-Malagasy history, as you walk round the graves of the mainly East African and Indian soldiers who served in the British army during the Second World War and were killed in the battle for Diego in 1942.

Further afield

Don't be tempted to explore the northern tip of Madagascar, Cap d'Ambre, unless you have a motorbike or are prepared for a very long walk. Olivier Langrand reports: 'With a motorbike it takes 4 hours of dangerous driving. I reached the place in May, 1987, but it took 96 hours after I fell into a ravine with my car. It was the first car that the lighthouse keeper had seen for several years! Scenic landscape, strong winds.'

Lac Sacré

The sacred lake (Lac Anivorano) is about 75 km south of Diego. It attracts visitors more for its legends than the reality of a not particularly scenic lake and the possibility of seeing a crocodile. The story is that once upon a time Anivorano was situated amid semi-desert and a thisty traveller arrived at the village and asked for a drink. When his request was refused he warned the villagers that they would soon have more water than they could cope with. No sooner had he left than the earth opened, water gushed out, and the mean-minded villagers and their houses were inundated. The crocodiles which now inhabit the lake are considered to be ancestors (and to wear jewellery belonging to their previous selves. So they say).

The two occasions I have been there I have seen no crocs (and there are reported to be only three left now), but other travellers have been luckier. The crocodiles are sometimes fed by the villagers – some people say on Fridays and Saturdays – and you may do best to book a tour with Madagascar Airtours in Diego; they should know when croc feeding day is.

Personally I feel that Anivorano is not worth a special trip (unless you can be sure of seeing crocodiles) but is an interesting stop if you are coming by road from the south.

Parc National Montagne d'Ambre

A splendid example of upland moist forest, this national park ranges in altitude from 850 m to 1474 m and has its own micro-climate with rainfall equal to the eastern region. There are tall trees, orchids, unusual birds, an exciting assortment of reptiles and lemurs – Sanfords lemur, (*Lemur fulvus sanfordi*) and crowned lemurs (*lemur coronatus*). Sanfords lemur is grey, the males having white side-whiskers and ear-tufts. Crowned lemurs get their names from the triangle of black between the ears of the male; the rest of the animal is brown, whilst females are grey, larger, and have no crown. Young are born in September.

Unlike the reserves, Montagne d'Ambre was set up for visitors to enjoy, and has 30 km of well-maintained paths, labelled trees, and a mighty waterfall (Cascade Grande).

You need a permit to visit the park (available from the Direction des Eaux et Forêts in Diego or in Tana). Although the park can be done in one day with Madagascar Airtours, it is really much too nice a place to hurry through. It's best to spend the night in nearby Joffreville (Ambohitra), or better still, camp in the park (assuming it is still permitted – check with the Eaux et Fôrets people). There is also a simple shelter (no beds) where visitors may sometimes sleep if it is not occupied by scientists.

There are plenty of taxi-brousses (600 FMG) going to Joffreville, and even – supposedly – a bus. In the 'town' (no great metropolis) you will find two mouldering hotels: the Joffre (central) and Centre de Repos Marine, formerly a retreat for French officers, and which sometimes tries to be closed but is worth seeking out for its amazing atmosphere of colonial decay.

From Joffreville it is 7 km to the park entrance.

Ankarana

About 75 km south of Diego Suarez is a small limestone massif, Ankarana. An 'island' of *tsingy* (limestone karst pinnacles) and forest, the massif is penetrated by numerous caves and canyons. Some of the largest caves have collapsed, forming isolated pockets of river-fed forest with their own perfectly protected flora and fauna. The caves and their rivers also are home to crocodiles, some reportedly six metres long.

After a preliminary look in 1981, The Crocodile Caves of Ankarana Expedition, led by Dr Jane Wilson, spent several months in 1986 exploring and studying the area. Their findings excited considerable scientific interest and have been followed by a specially made television film.

Ankarana is a Special Reserve but hitherto has received poor protection. Hopefully the recent interest in the area will improve this. There is also talk of opening the massif to controlled tourism – an exciting prospect. Ask Madagascar Airtours in Tana for information.

Intrepid explorers (with a permit) can start from the village of Matsaborimanga. It is opposite the largest piece of forest with high lemur populations and the villagers know the forest well. For caving, you should approach from the village of Adrafiabe. The locals will show you the entrance of the largest cave, Grotte d'Andrafiabe, but will not accompany you inside. With 11 km of passages, caving experience and reliable caving lights are essential.

NOSY BE

History

Nosy Bé's charms were recognised as long ago as 1649 when the British colonel Robert Hunt wrote 'I do believe, by God's blessing, that not any part of the World is more advantageous for a Plantation, being every way as well for pleasure as well as profit, in my estimation.' Hunt was attempting to set up an English colony on the island, at that time known as Assada, but failed because of hostile natives and disease.

Future immigrants, both accidental and intentional, contributed to Nosy Bé's racial variety. Shipwrecked Indians built a magnificent settlement several centuries ago in the south east of the island, where the ruins can still be seen. The crew of a Russian ship that arrived during the Russo-Japanese war of 1904-5 with orders to attack any passing Japanese, and were then forgotten, are buried in the Hell-ville cemetery. Other arrivals were Arabs, Comorans, and – more recently – Europeans flocking to Madagascar's foremost holiday resort.

When King Radama I was completing his wars of conquest, the Boina kings took refuge in Nosy Bé. First they sought protection from the Sultan of Zanzibar, and he obliged by sending a warship in 1838, then two years later they requested help from Commander Passot, who landed his ship at Nosy Bé. The Frenchman was only too happy to oblige, and asked Admiral de Hell, the governor of Bourbon Island (now Réunion), to place Nosy Bé under the protection of France. The island was formerly handed over in 1841.

Getting there

By road and ferry From Diego take a taxi-be (Peugeot 404) or taxi-brousse (always *very* crowded, about 4,000 FMG), to Ambanja on the mainland opposite Nosy Bé (six hours. Hotel Patricia). The road is good as far as Anivorano, then terrible to Ambilobe from where it improves (of course, it all may have changed by the time you read this). From Ambanja take a taxi the following morning about 18 km to Antsahampano, the departure point for the ferry.

There are two ferries a day; the sailing times depend on the tide. The ferry costs 600 FMG and takes two hours. You have the alternative of going by small steam boat *vedette*. Being smaller, they are less tied to the tides. 'They don't look too safe, although there is more shade from the weather than on the ferry. I managed to burn my elbow on the exhaust pipe leading up through the roof and had to keep my toes tucked away from the spinning motor shaft exposed by removal of deck boards to

Nosy - Bé

① Andilana Beach Hotel (Holiday Inn)   ② Airport
③ Hotel Les Cocotiers   ④ Hotel Palm Beach
⑤ Residence d'Ambatoloaka   ⑥ Mont Passot (329m)
⑦ Oceanographic Institute

facilitate repairs. This small boat stopped first at Nosy Komba, which the big boat bypasses.' (Sally Crook). If you've got time and are tough, like Sally, you can also go by road from Tana: 'Peugeot 404 to Ambanja from Tana cost 22,500 FMG in 1985 (the worse the roads, the more expensive the transport). Lots of getting out to dig the car out of the mud once we'd left the tarmac road to Majunga. Took me three days and two nights to Nosy Bé'.

Air   There are regular flights from Tana and Diego to Nosy Bé. These are heavily booked at weekends and during the peak holiday season. season.

Nosy Bé today

This is very much a holiday island, and deserves its popularity if you can face all the tourists after the emptiness of the rest of Madagascar. Blessed with an almost perfect climate (sunshine with brief showers), fertile and prosperous, with sugar, pepper, and vanilla grown for export, and the heady scent of *ylang-ylang* blossoms giving it the tourist-brochure name of 'Perfumed Isle', this is the place to come for a rest.

Most of the easily accessible beaches on Nosy Bé have been taken over by hotels, but adventurous visitors can find completely unspoilt places. The FTM map of Nosy Bé (scale 1:80,000) which is readily available in Tana is very detailed and marks beaches.

Nosy Bé even has good roads (money from sugar and tourists has helped here). Transport around the island is by taxi-be or private taxi (of which there are plenty). Around town a taxi costs 200 FMG, and from Hell-ville to the Holiday Inn, 5,000 FMG. The usual price from the airport is 2,500 FMG. All these prices are negotiable. Surprisingly, no-one so far has thought of opening up a bike-hire shop. It's such an obvious need that I would expect it to happen soon. Meanwhile bicycles and mopeds are occasionally available from the bigger hotels, and make getting around much easier and more fun. And of course you can get around on foot. With the help of the map and a tent, a backpacking trip of a few days would be a wonderful way to escape the crowds.

Where to stay

There are several beach hotels, none of which is cheap:

Andilana Beach Hotel (ex Holiday Inn). Tel: 61-176. 117 characterless rooms with air conditioning. Swimming pool, tennis, etc. About 25,000 FMG. Nicest location, worst architecture. Madagascar Airtours has its office here.

Les Cocotiers. About 17,000 FMG for a beach bungalow. My favourite for its well-designed buildings and excellent food.

Hotel Palm Beach. Bungalows 15,000 FMG, double rooms

Hell-Ville

1. Taxis
2. Market, Theatre
3. Hotel Trans 7 Stop
4. 'Air Madagascar'
5. Hotel de la Mer
6. Bureau de l'Eaux et Forêts
7. Ferry to Antsahaparo

13,000 FMG. Popular. Very good food. Casino. Swimming pool. Beach not as nice as Cocotiers.

Residence Ambatoloaka. 13,000 FMG. The most popular with budget travellers. Camping is sometimes permitted nearby. In the area is the highly acclaimed restaurant Chez Angeline which does a suberb set meal (3,000 FMG) of sea food. You must book a table, and are served in the order of booking, a course at a time, with everyone waiting for the last-comers to finish their first course before the next can be served.

Hell-ville (Andoany)

The name comes from Admiral de Hell rather than an evocation of the state of the town. Hell-ville is quite a smart little place, its main street lined with boutiques and tourist shops. There is a market selling fresh fruit and vegetables (which may also be purchased from roadside stalls), and an interesting cemetery neatly arranged according to nationality.

You can stay in Hell-ville, but of course the hotels are nowhere near as nice as the ones on the beach, and are all overpriced:

Hotel de la Mer, Boulevard du Docteur Manceau. 'Sitting alone between the devil (a fair description of most of the cheaper hotels) and the deep blue sea (which is all the more expensive ones have to offer)' (David Curl). The only middle-range hotel in town. Rooms vary from very nice with a view of the sea, to squalid. Prices (1988) range from 20,000 FMG to 5,000 FMG.

The remaining hotels in town are fairly awful. You have a choice of Hotel 'Trans 7 stop' at the far side of town (away from the harbour, 3,500 FMG, 6 rooms), the Hotel Venus (3,000 FMG, 4 rooms) and the Saloon Hotel (4,000 FMG).

Although the best restaurants are at the beach hotels and Chez Angeline, there are one or two good places on the main street of Hell-ville. The best are L'Arlequin opposite the cinema, and Restaurant Express, a popular meeting place for travellers. To eat really well, order your meal a day in advance. Chez Looky, a couple of doors down from the Arlequin is more modest.

If you are taking the ferry back to Antsahampano, check the board outside the ferry office (A.M.Hassanaly et fils) a few doors up from Air Madagascar.

Excursions

Mont Passot

The highest point of the island (315 m), affording marvellous views of a series of deep-blue crater lakes. These are said to contain crocodiles (though I have never seen one in half a dozen visits) and to be sacred as the home of the spirits of the Sakalava and Antakarana princes. It is *fady* to fish there, or to smoke, wear trousers or any garment put on over the feet, or a hat, while on the lakes' shores. It is, in any case, difficult to get down to the water since the crater sides are very steep.

The best road to Mont Passot runs from near the Holiday Inn, but the more adventurous can try walking (10 km) up the track from Djamandjary, the island's second biggest town. (Note: much has been made in some tourist literature of the 'unusual houses' at Djamandjary. You are led to believe that these are some quaint ethnic curiosity. The ugly cement igloos were, in fact, part of a foreign aid project following devastation from a cyclone. They offer no wind resistance, so do not blow down easily.) Most people come to Mont Passot to see the sunset so you may be fortunate enough to get a lift down, but you risk walking down in the dark. In any case, in the clear air of Nosy Bé the sunset is generally less than spectacular, so if you are on foot make a day excursion of it and take a picnic.

Ampasindava

From Hell-ville a road runs from the north end of the quay, hugging the north-east shoreline to the village of Ampasindava, 7 km. away, where it abruptly ends – at a beautiful sandy beach, ideal for picnics and swimming or for camping (not on the beach which is almost covered at high tide, but nearby, after asking permission.) The very friendly Bachelier family owns the largest property there. There is fresh water, large shady rocks, and nothing else.

The walk there, (or taxi, if you prefer) is varied and interesting. Just outside Hell –ville you pass some mangrove swamps. Stop and look at the mud-skippers – fish that are as at home outside the water as in it! The bulbous cheeks hold water which is washed over the gills allowing it to breathe. The mud-skippers' pectoral fins are formed into a sucker for clinging onto the stems of mangroves.

After 5 km of winding tree-lined road (where I found three chameleons) you arrive at the Centre National de Recherches Oceanographique on the right. This beautifully located Research Institute has a small museum. There is a   good collection of shells and coral, although perhaps really only of interest to marine biologists since most of the fishy specimens are in bottles and the famous Caeleocanth is now at the museum in Tsimbazaza in Tana.

A few kilometres further on you come to the remains of an early Indian settlement and graveyard. The buildings are completely in ruins, the 30 cm thick sand and coral wall in the grip of strangler figs, and flame trees thrust up through the once fine architecture. The story of the builders having been shipwrecked Indian sailors is only hearsay: one wonders if sailors would be such competent architects. It is a mysterious and beautiful place, providing a refreshing symbol (for Madagascar) of the power of nature over the work of man.

Finally, before you get to Ampasindava, you will pass the edge of the reserve of Lokobe. (To visit this you should have a permit – sometimes available from Eaux et Forêts in Hell-ville). A path runs up the steep hillside, and you have a good chance of seeing black lemurs (*Lemur macaco*) and other creatures. Even without going into the forest you may have exciting encounters – I saw two large snakes beside the road.

Traditional village and sacred lemurs
Another way to visit Lokobe is with Jean-Robert who works for Madagascar Airtours, speaks English, and charges 19,200 FMG (1987) to visit his village. Dick Byrne has sent the following description which I endorse, having also done the trip and greatly enjoyed it.

First a bus takes you to the village of Ambatozavavy, amongst mangroves in a shallow bay. Then you start to *earn* your pleasure: paddling elegant outrigger dugouts along the coast! It's great fun, and actually if you get tired you don't have to paddle, it's just quicker. This gets you to Ampasipohy, Jean-Robert's home, a small traditional village. He explains the *fady*, the local crops, the produce villagers get from the forest, and so on. They grow ylang-ylang (which is used for perfume-making) and vanilla. He's also a dab-hand at finding the local species of lepilemur (*Lepilemur dorsalis*), which unlike other lepilemurs spends the day in thick bushes not in holes; they have tiny ears, a rusty coat and very big, round heads and huge eyes. We saw it. We also saw a hefty boa constrictor, thanks to the villagers who all keep a close watch for wildlife to show visitors when Jean-Robert runs a tour (he'll award their diligence from the profits, so it's a great way to channel money to village level without profiteering middlemen, *and* helps boas to stay away from handbags). Back to the canoes, but on the way back you'll stop at an ancient royal burial ground, so sacred that you have to walk barefoot, and search for black lemurs. They're not fed as on Nosy Komba, so are more shy, but good views are nearly guaranteed all the same. A great day out, and lunch is well-cooked traditional Malagasy food, eaten under the palms at the top of the beach.

Jean-Robert will take any number of people from two up, but too many would tend to reduce the enjoyment. He can easily be contacted through your hotel.

Nosy Komba (Nosy Ambariovato)
A 'must' for most visitors to Nosy Bé, but less popular with budget travellers who dislike the air of commercialism that has inevitably spread to this island paradise. Certainly Nosy Komba has changed since we first hitched a lift there with a missionary in 1976, to find nothing but sand, sea, shells, and lemurs. We didn't even see the village! I still find it a magical place, though one should go the whole hog and make an excursion there through one of the hotels. Independent travellers can usually get a *pirogue* to take them, but a solo woman traveller wrote 'As soon as we reached the village (Ampangoriña) the Président du Fokontany met me and took me to one of the huts where I could hire a small bed. The président was constantly following me, and I resented all the constraints put on me. The atmosphere between us became very cool...'. Of course, everyone's experience is different, and I have also met a couple who stayed several days in the président's house and loved

it, but generally speaking I would recommend that you go as a Tourist and pay the villagers for taking their photos, buy vanilla, clay animals and hand-carved model outrigger canoes, eat magnificently, feed the lemurs and be photographed with them all over you, and swim and snorkel, and your 'but I'm a traveller not a tourist' scruples be damned!

Tours to Nosy Komba are arranged through the various hotels. Probably the best bet is through the Hotel Residence Ambatoloaka, since its Italian owner, Paolo, also owns the restaurant A'Paziella in Nosy Komba which is in the most idyllic location on a promontory above the beach (it only serves meals to Ambatoloaka tour guests). Paolo is adding some accommodation to the restaurant, so it will soon be possible to stay on the island in comfort. How would one ever leave?

Female black lemur

Nosy Komba's main attraction is undoubtedly the black lemurs (actually, only the males are black, the females are chestnut brown with white eartufts). To visit them you must pay a small entrance fee. They have always been fearless, being held sacred by the villagers so unmolested, but with the advent of tourists bearing bananas, they have become quite assertive. Lemurs always seem to possess beautiful manners and even assertive lemurs never snatch and bite; they just reach out their black-gloved hands for the treat, and ten or so hands – while the owners are sitting on your head and shoulders and covering your eyes – means you are divested of your bananas pretty quickly. So cameras at the ready!

Black lemurs mate in April and give birth to one baby in September.

When you are done with the lemurs and shopping for souvenirs in the village, the swimming is excellent. The best snorkelling is around the rocky promontory which juts into the sea. The water is not as clear as Nosy Tanikely, but there is plenty to see. Beware of sunburn!

Nosy Tanikely

To me this is as close to paradise as you can get. At the time of writing Nosy Tanikely is a tiny island inhabited only by the lighthouse keeper and his family, unspoiled by any of the trappings of tourism. It is unrealistic to hope that this state of affairs can last, but I do... The island is a marine reserve and it is for the snorkelling that most people visit it. And the snorkelling is stupendous. In crystal clear water you can see an amazing variety of marine life – coral, starfish, anemones, every colour and shape of fish, turtles, lobsters... It is totally mind boggling. The underwater world is always astonishing; perhaps because we see less of it on television than other natural wonders, or perhaps that there is just so *much* there, so much variety, so much colour, so much weirdness. The Madagascar Airtours brochure has got it right when it says 'If you are eager for unreal surprises and pleasant emotions, make up your mind now and discover our new world ...'

With this new world beneath your gaze there is a real danger of forgetting the passing of time and becoming seriously sunburnt. Even the most carefully applied sunblock tends to miss some areas, so wear a tee-shirt and shorts.

Don't think you have finished with Nosy Tanikely when you come out of the water; at low tide it is possible to walk right round the island. During your circumambulation you will see (if you go anticlockwise): a broad beach of white sand covered in shells and bleached pieces of coral, a couple of trees full of flying foxes (*Pteropus rufus*), and graceful white tropic birds (*Phaethon lepturus lepturus*) flying in and out of their nests in the high cliffs. At your feet will be rock pools and some scrambling, but nothing too challenging.

Then there is the climb up to the top of the island for the view and perhaps a tour (tip expected) of the antique and beautifully maintained lighthouse.

Most hotels arrange trips to Nosy Tanikely. The cost used to be 13,000 FMG, but I suspect it has gone up.

Further away are two more islands, seldom visited, and reportedly even more paradisal: Nosy Mitsio (60 km north-west – an uninhabited archipelago) and Nosy Iranja (60 km south-west – a turtle nesting reserve). Both islands are reached in four hours by fast boat.

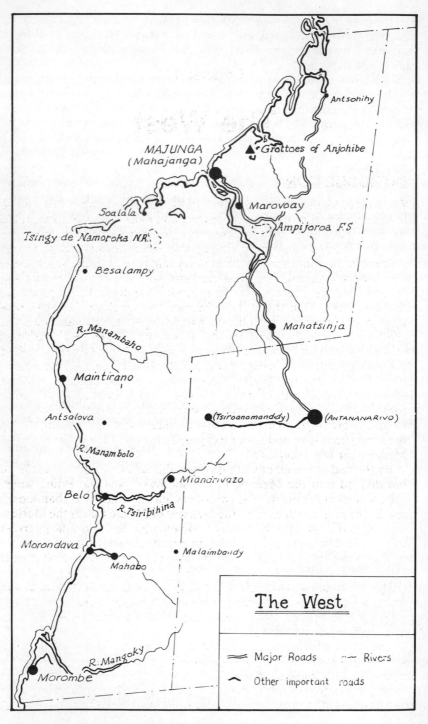

The West

Major Roads   ~~ Rivers
Other important roads

Chapter 11

The West

INTRODUCTION

The west of Madagascar is the home of the Sakalava people. For a while in Malagasy history this was the largest and most powerful tribe, ruled by their own kings and queens. The Sakalava originate from the Menabe, the first kingdom in Madagascar, which began in the sixteenth century in the south east of the country and spread to the south west. The kingdom became progressively stronger and by the end of the century, under the rulership of King Andriamandresy, had reached the Sakalava river. Thus the Menabe became the Sakalava. In 1610 a new king, Andrianahifotsy, became the first Malagasy ruler to use firearms, acquired from traders working the Mozambique Channel. With this new battle weapon conquest became easier, and the Sakalava pushed northward until they occupied the whole western part of the island, from the Onilahy river to the Manambolo river. The unification of the tribe under one king did not last, however, and Andrianahifotsy's three sons divided up the kingdom and started their own expansion. The Boina, a new kingdom in the north (around present day Majunga), was the most successful, and under its king, Tsitavana, the northern part of Madagascar was conquered.

By the end of the eighteenth century, the Sakalava empire was huge but divided into the Menabe in the southwest and the Boina which occupied all of the north. The two rulers fell out, unity was abandoned, and by the nineteenth century the area was under the rule of the Merina. The Sakalava did not take kindly to domination and sporadic guerrilla warfare continued in the Menabe area until French colonial times.

The Sakalava kingdom bore the brunt of the first serious efforts by the French to colonise the island. For some years France had laid claims (based on treaties made with local princes) on parts of the north and north west, and in 1883 two north west fortresses were bombarded, followed by Majunga. This was the beginning of the end of Madagascar as an independent kingdom.

The modern Sakalava have relatively dark skins. Understandably the west of Madagascar received a number of African immigrants from across the Mozambique Channel. Their influence shows not only in the racial characteristics of the people of this region, but in their language and customs. There are a number of Bantu words in their dialect, and their belief in *tromba* (possession by spirits) and *dady* (royal relics cult) are of African origin.

The Sakalava do not practise second burial. The quality of their funerary art (in one small area) rivals that of the Mahafaly: birds and naked figures are a feature of Sakalava tombs, the latter frequently in erotic positions. Concepts of sexuality and rebirth are implied here. The female figures are often disproportionately large, perhaps recognising the importance of women in the Sakalava culture.

Sakalava royalty does not require an elaborate tomb, since kings are considered to continue their spiritual existence through a medium, who have the power to heal, and in royal relics. These relics are ritually washed in September every ten years (and 1988 is the year!).

The west offers a dry climate, deciduous vegetation, endless sandy beaches with little danger from sharks – although the sea can be very rough – and fewer other visitors than most parts of the country. Adventurous travellers will have no trouble finding their own deserted beach and some spectacular landscapes. And sun.

Opposite major rivers, the seawater along the west coast is a brick red colour: 'like swimming in soup', as one traveller puts it. This is the laterite washed into the rivers from the eroded hillsides of the highlands and discharged into the sea; Madagascar's bleedings wounds.

Getting around

Going from town to town in the west is even harder than in the east: in much of the area the roads simply aren't there (apart from the Tana to Majunga road) so flying is essential. There is a thrice weekly service (Twin Otter: unreliable) from Majunga to Tana, via Soalala, Tambohorano, Maintirano, Belo, and Morondava. The Twin Otter also stops at other small western towns from Majunga – Morafenobe and Ambatomainty. Majunga and Antsohihy are served by the larger Hawker Siddeley planes.

MAJUNGA (MAHAJANGA)

History

Majunga has always been a cosmopolitan city. Ideally located for trade with east Africa, Arabia and western Asia, it has been a major commercial port since the eighteenth century, when the Boina capital was moved here from Marovoay. Majunga was founded in 1745. One ruler of the Boina was Queen Ravahiny, a very able monarch who maintained the unity of the Boina which was threatened by rebellions in both the north and south. It was Majunga which provided her with her imported riches and caught the admiration of visiting foreigners. Madagascar was at that time a major supplier of slaves to Arab traders and in return received jewels and rich fabrics. Indian merchants were active then, as today, with a variety of exotic goods. Some of these traders from the east stayed on, the Indians remaining a separate community and running small businesses. More Indians arrived during colonial times.

Madagascar's importance as a port also attracted the French, and in 1883 an expeditionary force landed there at the beginning of the conflict that ended with Madagascar being declared a French Protectorate.

After 1895 the French set about enlarging Majunga and reclaiming swampland from the Bombetoka river delta. Much of today's extensive town is on reclaimed land.

Getting there and back
Majunga is accessible from Tana by good road or by plane.

Road   I took the Air Route Service minibus which was remarkably comfortable. It leaves three times a week in the mid afternoon from Behoririka (the area beyond and to the right of the station) on Ar. Rainizanabololona near Giraud Vinet (the glass factory – most taxi drivers know it). It costs 8,000 FMG for the 14 hour trip and seats should be booked in advance.

There are also regular taxi-brousses from Ambodivona. They also seem to leave mid-afternoon and drive through the night. But check. It would be sensible to break the trip at Maevatana, 7 to 8 hours from Tana.

It's a lovely trip (at least until it gets dark) which takes you through typical *Hauts Plateaux* landscape of craggy, grassy hills, rice paddies, and characteristic Merina houses with steep eaves supported by thin brick or wood pillars.

The taxi-brousse station in Majunga is on the wide boulevard leading towards the sea from the statue of Tsiranana. Most leave around 7.00.

Plane   There is a daily flight from Tana to Majunga, £50 ($92); also flights between Majunga and Nosy Bé (Mondays and Fridays).

A taxi from the airport into town should be 1,500 FMG. A bus also passes the airport every half hour or so.

Majunga today
A hot but breezy town with a large Indian population and enough interesting excursions, high quality beach bungalows and sun to make a visit of a few days well worthwhile. Besides, you can eat one of the best meals in Madagascar here!

The town has two 'centres', the town hall (Hotel de Ville) and statue of Tsiranana (the commercial centre), and the baobab tree on the seafront boulevard (some offices, including Air Madagascar are near here). It is quite a long walk between the two – take a 'pousse-pousse', of which there are many. There are also some smart new buses, and taxis (*taxi-ville*) operating on a fixed tariff of 300 FMG.

A wide boulevard follows the sea along the west part of town, terminating at a lighthouse. Along this boulevard is the famous

Majunga baobab, said to be hundreds of years old with a circumference of fourteen metres.

In March 1984, Cyclone Kamisy struck Majunga, damaging 90% of the buildings, and completely destroying the hitherto popular 'Village Touristique' on the beach to the north of the town. This has now been partially rebuilt.

Where to stay
Category A
La Zaha. At Amborovy beach (not far from the airport, and 8 km from Majunga). Beach bungalows, 12,000 FMG. Excellent swimming and all tourist amenities.

Village Touristique. On a long windy stretch of beach. Not my favourite, but some travellers like it. 10,000 FMG with shower and WC.

Hotel de France, Rue Maréchal Joffre. 10,400 FMG & 10,500 FMG. Shower and WC in all rooms plus air conditioning, but rather rundown. Poor value.

Category B
Hotel Nouvel. 13, Rue Henri Palu (one block up from sea front), 7,500 FMG and 6,400 FMG. Its prices put it in the B category but the Nouvel seems the best hotel in town. Clean, attractive, with air conditioning and mosquito nets. 16 rooms.

Kanto Hotel. The best hotel out of the town and excellent value at 4,600 FMG for cabins (only 4) set on a hill overlooking the sea about 1 km north of the town (300 FMG by *pousse-pousse*). Good open air restaurant and bar. The perfect place to relax in comfort for a few days.

Hotel Restaurant Bombetoka. Along the seafront 1½ km from town. Bungalows 8,000 FMG, poor value but good restaurant.

Category C
Hotel Continental, Rue de la République. Central, very friendly. 3,500 FMG. Shower, fan.

Yaar Hotel. (Near Nouvel) 3,000 FMG − 3,500 FMG. Shower and bidet in each room but no mosquito nets or screen.

Hotel Boina, Rue Flacourt. 4,000 FMG. 12 rooms. Pleasant, screened, good value.

Chez Chabaud (see Katsepy) 2,500 FMG for rooms in Majunga (near Hotel de Ville) or bungalows in Katsepy.

Majunga (Mahajanga)

1. Hotel Kanto
2. Hotel/Restaurant Bombetoka
3. Baobab
4. Air Madagascar
5. Hotel Boina
6. Hotel France
7. Restaurant Pakiza
8. Restaurant Sampon d'Or
9. Yaar Hotel
10. Hotel Continental
11. Lighthouse

Where to eat

Good food in the seafront restaurants of Bombetoka and Kanto (see *Where to stay*).

Hotel-Restaurant de la Plage (Chez Karon) in the Village Touristique serves good food. Closed Mondays.

Le Sampon d'Or. Near the Hotel Continental. Chinese.

Restaurant Vietnamese. Near the Hotel de France.

Restaurant Chez Thi-San, Rue Marechal Joffre.

There are several Indian restaurants serving 'carry' (curry) and Samosas (sometimes called Sambros); usually good value.

The Salon de thé Baba opposite Hotel Continental serves excellent snacks and breakfast (try their pan au chocolat).

'Had our best meal in Madagascar in Bhauna Salon de thé: a curry, mango lassi and an orgasmic cup of tea' (B.G.).

Many small shops sell yoghurt. Good and cheap.

Night Club
La Ravenala. Near the quay. Lively.

Excursions from Majunga
Katsepy
No visit to Majunga is complete without a meal chez Madame Chabaud. She runs a small beach hotel at Katsepy, a tiny unspoiled fishing village across the bay from Majunga, and also a restaurant of the same name near the Hotel de Ville in Majunga. Trained as a cook in France (Nice) she returned to her home town to practise her art to weekend visitors and the occasional tourist. You are unlikely to dine better in Madagascar.

Katsepy is an hour's journey by ferry (leaves at 7.30 and 3.30 – but check at the quay as these times are flexible) and costs 200 FMG. The sign on the quay confusingly calls Katsepy 'Avotra'. There is sometimes a noontime boat on Sundays. Be prepared for a 'wet landing' if you arrive at low tide.

On arrival there are rows of stalls selling basic food and coconut milk if you don't want to splash out at the restaurant. Chez Chabaud is signposted. There are ten rather basic bungalows (bring mosquito coils or your own mosquito net) costing 2,500 FMG, and three vast meals a day (breakfast 600 FMG, lunch and dinner 3,500 FMG, and a special Sunday lunch for 5,000 FMG). There is one large self-catering bungalow for families or small groups and even a fully equipped tree-house!

In between eating you can lounge or walk on the miles of deserted beach (and perhaps accept an invitation to visit a fishing community), watch mud-skippers (tree-climbing fish!) hopping around the mangroves, and swim in the murky-red sea.

Except at weekends, it is best to make a reservation in advance (not because Katsepy will be crowded, but Mme Chabaud may not be there) through Chez Chabaud in Majunga (near the Hotel de Ville).

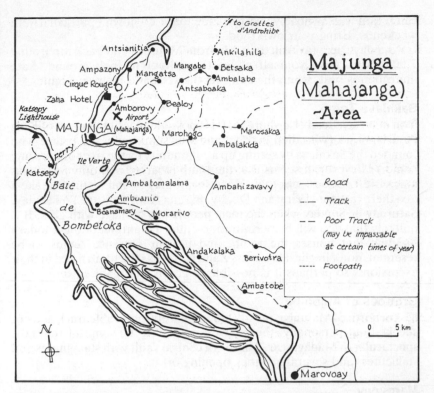

From Katsepy there are several adventurous possibilities for onward travel: vehicles that arrive on the ferry will be bound for Mitsinjo and most take passengers. From Mitsinjo you can visit lake Kinkony (now a protected area) or go on to Soalala, from where there is an air service, (and the possibility or visiting the nature reserve of Tsingy de Namoroka), or you can continue to Besalampy (which is also served by Air Madagascar). Then you can continue to make your way down the coast, taking cars, *pirogues* or whatever transport presents itself. This route is only practical in the dry season and for rugged and self-sufficient travellers. You can fly out of Maintirano, Antsalava, or Belo Tsiribihina. Good luck! If you make it, write and tell me about it.

Cirque Rouge

12 km from Majunga and about 2 km from the airport (as the crow flies) is a canyon ending in an amphitheatre of red, beige and lilac coloured rock eroded into strange shapes – peaks, spires, and castles. The canyon has a broad, sandy bottom decorated with chunks of lilac-coloured clay. It is a beautiful and dramatic spot and, with its stream of fresh water running to the nearby beach, makes an idyllic camping place for a few days (but be careful of swimming in the sea – there's a danger of sharks).

The area, a few kilometres north of the Zaha Hotel, is popular with Majungans who have holiday beach bungalows there, so if you decide to camp you can probably hitch a ride back to town, particularly at weekends. Bring your own food.

As a day trip a taxi will take you from Majunga and back for around 7,000 FMG. Give yourself at least one hour to look around. Late afternoon is best, when the sun sets the reds and mauves alight.

Sakalava Tomb

You may have read elsewhere that it is possible to visit the tomb of King Andriamisara (who died in 1650 and was supposedly the prince who founded the Sakalava by setting up a community by the river of the same name.) However, it seems that the tomb is sacred and only Sakalavas may visit it. Or so I was told. However, it may be interesting to take a taxi there (ask for 'Tsararano Doahy, Fasana Andriamisara') on Friday, Saturday or Sunday when the local people pay homage with gifts. It is unlikely that you will be permitted to enter the unremarkable modern building that houses the tomb, and if your presence seems to be resented, don't linger. However, Zaha Hotel has the tomb listed in their excursions, so perhaps it is possible to go on an organised tour.

Grottoes of Anjohibe

85 km north of Majunga, mostly along a barely motorable track and not checked out personally, these caves are said to be some of the most spectacular in Madagascar. There is a central vault with stalagmites and stalactites, and several grottoes opening off it.

Marovoay

Formerly the residence of the Boina kings, the town's name means 'many crocodiles'. When the French attacked the Malagasy forces assembled in Marovoay in 1895, in their successful drive to conquer Madagascar, it is reported that hundreds of crocodiles emerged from the river to devour the dead and dying. Malagasy hunters have since got their revenge, and you would be lucky to see a croc these days.

Marovoay is accessible by road (72 km) or river from Majunga (*pirogue* or barge). Reportedly a very enjoyable river trip (but don't take my word for it – I haven't done it and have no idea how long it takes!) through the numerous channels of the Bombetoka estuary, and up the Betsiboka river, past a variety of scenery. Probably the most sensible course is to take a taxi-brousse to Marovoay and enquire about river transport there. At least, then, you would be taking advantage of the current and the natural friendliness of a small, and seldom-visited town.

'*The Good Old Days*'. *The* filanzana *was used to transport high officials until the 1940s. This tomb carving shows a pith-helmeted* Vazaha *so bored with the journey that he is reading a book.*

OTHER PLACES OF INTEREST
South of Majunga

The Forestry Station of Ampijoroa
Ampijoroa (pronounced Ampijeroo) is the only protected example of western vegetation and its accompanying fauna easily accessible to visitors. I recommend it highly – to adventurous types with their own sleeping bags and, better still, tent. Keen naturalists who are on too tight a budget to afford Berenty will see some of the same animals (if not the precise species) in Ampijoroa – sifaka and lepilemur among others. The warden, M. Rabemazava, is hard-working and helpful, and there is a basic shelter (no beds, cement floor). This may be occupied (zoologists use Ampijoroa as a research centre) and you will anyway need to do your own cooking, so it's much safer to be self-sufficient. This may, of course, change as tourist interest in Madagascar increases, so check with the Direction des Eaux et Fôrets when you get your permit.

Ampijoroa lies about 90 km south of Majunga, to the west of the main road and the nature reserve of Andranofasika, shortly before (if coming from Majunga) the small town of the same name. I got there with Air Route Services from Tana (which dumped me at the gate to the reserve at 2.30 a.m. I crept off into the forest and had a not-at-all-bad night in my sheet sleeping bag and *Zoma* blanket, waking to the sight of a flock of flamingoes silhouetted against the pink dawn sky); A taxi-brousse from Majunga might have been better, although I had no trouble hitching a lift in a private car into Majunga.

Wild-life viewing in Ampijoroa is easy and thrilling. Right beside the warden's house and visitor's shelter is a tree that Coquerel's sifaka *Propithecus verreauxi coquereli* use as a dormitory. They are extremely handsome animals with the usual silky white fur but with chestnut-brown arms and thighs. I watched them for about an hour while they slowly woke up, stretched languidly, then spread their arms to take in the warming rays of the morning sun before starting their breakfast of leaves. Other lemurs to be seen in the forest are brown lemurs *Lemur fulvus fulvus*, *Lemur Mongoz* (if you're very lucky), and *Lepilemur edwardsi* if the warden shows you its tree. I went on a nocturnal search for mouse lemurs (*microcebus murinus*) but our torches failed to pick out the tell-tale red eyes.

The forest has some good paths and the warden may be able to guide you on an initial orientation tour. Thereafter you are free to wander happily on your own.

Maintirano
This small western port is attractive for people who want to get off the beaten track. Nothing much happens here, but there is a pleasant though basic hotel and a restaurant which turns out excellent food in a

primitive kitchen – until the owner gets bored with you! Oenone Hammersley reports: 'The first hotel we went to (Fantara) resembled a cross between army headquarters and a prison. We thought we'd arrived in Colditz – no windows, a cement floor… We moved to a very friendly and clean place, the Laizama Hotel, which overlooks the sea. There were mosquito nets and lots of gekkos in the room – both necessary to keep out the prolific insect life. The best restaurant is on the outskirts of town on the airport road – its name is Buvette et Repas Mahateatea and it looks like a garage. Eating there was always a surprise and a pleasure (we booked our meals in advance). Once we were served crab with prawn sauce, and crab salad.

'We spent much of our time sunbathing and swimming in the blood-red sea (it took us a while to find the way to the beach – across a causeway between two lagoons). It's a huge beach with pristine white sand. When not on the beach or eating, we wandered around looking at the big market (lots of fish) and the many Indian shops, all of which seemed to sell the same thing: fabrics and food.'

Maintirano is one of the places served by Air Madagascar (Twin Otter) on its Tana – Majunga run.

MORONDAVA

The Morondava area was the centre of the Sakalava kingdom. Today it most often visited for the Sakalava tombs and for the unspoilt beaches with their small fishing communities, and months of sunshine. The new road will, no doubt, increase the number of visitors to a hithertoo neglected part of the country. This is Madagascar's best area for baobabs and the birdlife is prolific (great for photographers).

Getting there and back

By Road Morondava is now served by a very good road from Antsiribe. There are regular taxi-brousses which take about 9 hours and cost around 22,000 MFG from Tana (1988).

Air   There is a service to Morondava most days of the week

Where to stay

Hotel Menabe, 7,500 FMG to 12,000 FMG (1988). Everyone recommends this hotel which has been recently decorated and is efficiently run by a helpful manager.

Grand Hotel. 5,500 FMG. Not such a bargain. Cold showers, but pleasant setting with balcony overlooking main street. Cockroach rating 7/10.

There are now (1988) three beach hotels: Hotel de la Plage (run by Moslems so no alcohol); Village Touristique (home of Carré d'As); Bougainvillea; Oasis. The latter has air-conditioning, so is the most expensive (but comfortable), the others cost 10,000 FMG to 14,000 FMG. A fifth hotel is being built near the nightclub, further down the beach.

Where to eat
In addition to the above hotels, try:
Carré d'As (popularly known as Curried Arse). Excellent Malagasy food, steak and chips and other goodies. Darts and disco!

Ranala. Very highly recommended by two different travellers for its excellent sea food in pleasant surroundings.

Excursions
Take the road to Mahabo for views of baobabs trees. There are also fine baobabs towards **Belo sur Tsiribihina** (see Addenda) – north of Morondava on a reasonable but untarred road. River Tsiribihina must be crossed by ferry.

Vezo-Sakalava funerary sculpture
The often erotic, carved wooden sculptures of the Vezo people (Sakalava, but with a specialised interest in shore fishing) are not easy to see. You will need a guide: Mr Nandrasana Farezy has been warmly recommended by John R. Jones. He charges 20,000 FMG (1988). Enquire at Centre Forestier, B.P. 117, Tel 520-96, Morondava.

Analabe reserve
This is another private nature reserve owned by the de Heaulme family. At the time of writing (1987) it is not open to tourists. However, the plan is eventually to bring it to the level of Berenty, with the area divided into three parcels: scientific study, tourism, and reserve. You should be able to find out whether Analabe may be visited from the staff at Berenty (or the Dauphin hotel in Fort Dauphin). Monsieur de Heaulme can be contacted at B.P. 37, Fort Dauphin.

The reserve lies 60 km north of Morondava, by the de Heaulme sisal plantations near the village of Beroboka sud. It contains some mangrove areas as well as marshes and lakes typical of coastal plain. Most of the animals – including lemur species – seen at Berenty may be seen here, although they are not habituated (accustomed to man).

'A noisy intruder sees nothing of this splendid [dawn] pageant. The animals, warned of his approach, either take to flight ahead of him or else stop singing until he has passed. As a result he walks in a pool of silence which travels with him as he goes, and the bush, to him, seems totally deserted except for the invisible insects which persevere with their insistent shrilling no matter what goes on around them.'
David Attenborough, *Zoo Quest to Madagascar*.

Appendices

BIBLIOGRAPHY

General – history, the country, the people

Bradt, H., editor. (1988). *Madagascar* (Exotic Lands series). Aston Publications, England. Madagascar in colour photos.

Brown, M. (1978). *Madagascar Rediscovered*, A history from early times to Independence. Damien Tunnacliffe, London. (Shoestring Press, U.S.A.) An excellent and highly readable history.

Drury, R. *Robert Drury's Journal*. Negro University Press, U.S.A. The diaries of a sailor shipwrecked on Madagascar in the 1700s.

Heseltine, N. (1971). *Madagascar*. London. A detailed and excellent over-view of the country.

Mack, J. (1986) *Madagascar: Island of the Ancestors*. British Museum, London. A scholarly and informative account of the ethnography of Madagascar, published to coincide with the exhibition at the Museum of Mankind, London, and the Natural History Museum, New York. Includes a very detailed bibliography.

A Glance at Madagascar (1973). An excellent little book, available in Madagascar, giving much useful information on the Malagasy people, their history, traditions, and beliefs. Unfortunately out of print in late 1988.

Murphy, D. (1985). *Muddling through in Madagascar*. Murray, London. A marvellously entertaining account of a journey (by foot and truck) through the highlands and south.

Nelson, H.D. et al. (1973). *Area Handbook for the Malagasy Republic*. US Government, Washington, D.C., 1973. Although dated, there is much interesting and useful background information on the country's social, political and economic problems with an extensive bibliography.

Natural history.

Readily accessible literature
Attenborough, D. (1961) *Zoo Quest to Madagascar*. Pan, London.

Caufield, C. (1985). *In the Rainforest*. Alfred Knopf, Inc. (U.S.)

Haltenorth T. and Diller, H. Trans. by Robert W Hayman. (1980) *Field Guide to the Mammals of Africa including Madagascar*. Wm.Collins & Son Ltd.

*Available from Bradt Publications.

GTM -N

Hoffmann, I. (1983). *The 'MAD' Trip*; Cact. Succ. J.1, 55-60 & 9l-95. An informal account of a botanical trip to Madagascar.

Jolly, A. (1980). *A World Like Our Own: Man and Nature in Madagascar.* Yale University Press. The outstanding book on the natural history of Madagascar with a sympathetic approach to the Malagasy people. Written in a highly readable style, this coffee table book is expensive but worth every penny.

Jolly, A. (1987). *Madagascar: A World Apart* (with photographs by F.Lanting), National Geographic Magazine 171, 148-183.

Jolly, A., Oberle, P., and Albignac, R. Editors. *Madagascar*. Pergamon Press, Oxford. This book in 'The Key Environments' series is mainly a translation of the French *Madagascar: Un Sanctuaire de la Nature*. At present it is the best general reference book on the natural history of Madagascar, although much of the information is now dated. Sections on invertebrates, amphibians, reptiles, birds, lemurs, etc, with two chapters on the vegetation and flora and good coverage of geology.

Loetschert, W. and Beese, G., Trans. by Clive King. (1983). *Collins Guide to Tropical Plants*. Wm. Collins Sons & Co. Ltd.

Oberle, P. (1981). *Madagascar: Un Sanctuaire de la Nature*. Kintana, Antananarivo and Paris. Has some good illustrations, lacking in the English version.

Specialist literature.

Faune de Madagascar, (1956). Tananarive and Paris. To date 64 volumes, birds (vol. 35), mammals (vol. 36, 44), reptiles (vols. 33, 36, 47), zoogeography (vol.13) and the remainder invertebrates. In French.

Jenkins, M.D., editor. (1987). *Madagascar: An Environmental Profile*. IUCN, Gland, Switzerland and Cambridge, U.K. Contains the most up to date descriptions of the nature reserves.

Morat, P. (1973). *Les Savanes du Sud-Ouest Madagascar*. ORSTOM, Paris. Includes a map scale 1:500 000 in which there is the 'Massif de Isalo'.

Rauh, W. (1972). *Cactus and Succulent Journal*, (US) 44. 7-16. *The Genus Pachypodium*. Discusses and compares the African and Madagascan species: a large number of photographs.

Reynolds, G.W. (1966). *The Aloes of Tropical Africa and Madagascar*. The Aloes Book Fund, Swaziland.

Richard-Vindard, G. & Battistini, R. (Editors) (1972). *Biogeography and Ecology of Madagascar*. W.Junk, The Hague. Largely in English including chapters on geology, climate, flora, erosion, rodents and lemurs. Each chapter includes an extensive bibliography.

HISTORICAL CHRONOLOGY

(Reproduced from Madagascar, Island of the Ancestors *with kind permission of the author, John Mack.)*

AD 500	Approximate date for the first significant settlement of the island.
800–900	Dates of the first identifiable village sites in the north of the island. Penetration of the interior begins in the south.
1200	Establishment of Arab settlements. First mosques built.
1500	'Discovery' of Madagascar by the Portuguese Diogo Dias. Unsuccessful attempts to establish permanent European bases on the island followed.
1650s	Emergence of Sakalava kingdoms.
Early 1700s	Eastern Madagascar increasingly used as a base by pirates.
1716	Fénérive captured by Ratsimilao. The beginnings of the Betsimisaraka confederacy.
1750	Death of Ratsimilao.
1780	The future Andrianampoinimerina declared king of Ambohimanga.
1795/6	Andrianampoinimerina established his capital at Antananarivo.
1810–28	Radama I, Merina king.
1818	First mission school opened at Tamatave.
1820	First mission school opened at Antananarivo.
1828–61	Ranavalona I, Merina queen.
1835	Publication of the Bible in Malagasy, but profession of the Christian faith declared illegal.
1836	Most Europeans and missionaries leave the island.
1861–3	Radama II, Merina king.

1861	Missionaries re-admitted. Freedom of religion proclaimed.
1863–8	Queen Rasoherina succeeds after Radama II assassinated.
1868–83	Ranavalona II, Merina queen.
1869	Baptism of Ranavalona II and her husband (the Prime Minister Rainilaiarivony). Destruction of traditional 'idols'.
1883	Coronation of Queen Ranavalona III.
1895	Establishment of full French protectorate in Madagascar becoming a colony the following year.
1897	Ranavalona III exiled first to Réunion and later Algiers. Merina monarchy abolished.
1917	Death of Ranavalona III in exile.
1938	Return of the remains of Ranavalona III for reburial in Antananarivo.
1960	Madagascar achieves full independence.

Bradt Publications

41 NORTOFT ROAD • CHALFONT ST. PETER • BUCKS SL9 0LA, ENGLAND • TEL: 02407 3478

Dear readers,

One of the nice things about publishing my own book is that I can update it regularly from letters that come in from travellers (apart from enjoying the letters themselves).

So will you help? Although I hope to continue to visit Madagascar each year, I can't get everywhere, and you - collectively - can. So if you have found changes, or errors, or new places you would like to share, PLEASE write. Don't put it off, do it NOW, or who knows what the consequence might be? ——

Also, how about sharing some of your travellers' tales? They might even find their way into the next edition!

Looking forward to hearing from you,

Happy travels,

Hilary Bradt

Hilary Bradt

PS - Keep up the good work in 1989!

INDEX OF PLACE NAMES

(For other subjects see Contents page.)

QUESTERS

The world through nature tours

MADAGASCAR, REUNION, AND MAURITIUS

24 day tours of three Indian Ocean islands, each with their own unique flora and fauna, led by expert naturalists.

Our tour of Madagascar includes Tulear, for baobabs, salt marshes and mangroves, Berenty Reserve and Perinet Reserve for their great variety of flora and fauna, and Nosy Be for snorkeling; in Reunion we visit a mountain reserve rich in ferns and orchids and containing the four species of bird unique to the island; Mauritius offers pink pigeons and parakeets, as well as the famous Pamplemousses Botanical Gardens.

With Questers you have ample time to photograph, absorb and reflect. Tour parties are small, accommodation is first class.

Call or write for a copy of our Directory of Worldwide Nature Tours.

QUESTERS
Worldwide Nature Tours
257 Park Avenue South
New York, NY 10010, USA.
Tel: (212) 673-3120

OTHER BOOKS FROM BRADT PUBLICATIONS

Africa and the Indian Ocean

Backpacker's Africa – East and Southern
By Hilary Bradt. Third edition of this popular guide covering overland travel plus climbing and hiking, from Kenya to South Africa (including Rwanda, Burundi and eastern Zaire). As in all Bradt books, this assumes the reader is interested in natural history.

Backpacker's Africa – West and Central
By David Else. Aimed particularly at the overland traveller, with information on routes, hassles, accommodation and transport.

The No Frills Guide to Sudan
The No Frills Guide to Zimbabwe and Botswana
By David Else. These simply-produced guides are constantly updated and contain hard information for the hiker/overland traveller.

The Guide to Mauritius
By Royston Ellis. A complete guide to the island for every category of traveller – businessperson, holiday maker, naturalist, with detailed background information. Published mid 1988.

South America

Backpacking and Trekking in Peru and Bolivia
By Hilary Bradt. Practical advice on all aspects of travel in those countries, with descriptions of hiking trails.

Backpacking in Chile and Argentina
By Hilary Bradt. New edition due 1988/9. More trails and advice for walkers and travellers in South America.

Backpacking in Mexico and Central America
By Hilary Bradt and Rob Rachowiecki. Volcanoes, hiking trails and national parks in the countries that offer some of the best wildlife viewing in tropical America.

Climbing and Hiking in Ecuador
By Rob Rachowiecki. Every important mountain and volcano is covered, along with hikes in the jungle and along the coast.

South American River Trips
By Tanis and Martin Jordan. A 'how to' book spiced with anecdotes by a couple who have made six trips up remote rivers in the Amazon basin.

Asia

The Trans-Siberian Rail Guide
By Robert Strauss. Everything you need to know about the six day journey from Europe to Japan or Peking. Where to buy the cheapest tickets, where to stay in the gateway countries, facts about the train and stations/points of interest en route, etc, plus anecdotes from other travellers.

In Malaysia
By Denis Walls and Stella Martin. An anecdotal and personal account of the traditions, beliefs, festivals and wildlife of the Malay Peninsula.

Europe
Guide to Czechoslovakia
By Simon Hayman. A complete guide with emphasis on budget travel and hiking in the beautiful Tatra mountains.

Backpacking in Italy
By Stefano Ardito. Walks and hikes in every region of Italy, varying from half day outings to mountain trips of several days.

This is just a selection of our travel guides. For a complete catalogue write or phone:
Bradt Publications, 41 Nortoft Rd, Chalfont St Peter, Bucks SL9 0LA. Tel: (02407) 3478

Addenda

Madagascar has been through many changes since this book was written, most notably a sharp rise in prices following the devaluations of last year. Where possible I have changed these within the text. Where FMG prices are given *without* the date, they are from 1986 and should be doubled to bring you approximately in line. Other short corrections have been made within the text.

I would like to repeat my thanks to Raniero Leto, Simon Hale, Alan Hickling, and Ted Jackson for sending the detailed material included here. I hope it will encourage other potential up-daters to know that some of this information was incorporated into the text and addenda within days of receiving it. If you buy this book in 1989 it will be as up to date as is possible in a guide book!

Page 63   **Permits** 'We were only allowed to visit Montagne d'Ambre, Isalo, Perinet and Nosy Mangabe, although we applied to visit others.' (Raniero Leto.)

Page 66   'If you only need an extension for a few weeks it is much easier to go to any police station and they will do it for you, probably in less than ten minutes.' (R.L.)

Page 67   **Permission for scientific work** The rules keep changing; phone Stephen Hobbs, the Honorary Madagascar Consul, for the latest information.

Page 68   **Aeroflot** A traveller reports that Sam Travel put up their quoted price to him at the last minute, admitting that they had so many passengers for Aeroflot they could do this. He suggests getting a quote in writing when you first book your seat. He also points out that the extra leg room in the five seats behind the door applies only to the planes from Moscow to Tana.

     Raniero Leto recommends Symphony Travel, Fulham Rd, London for Aeroflot tickets, and also points out that if you wish to have a stopover in Moscow, it is much quicker and cheaper to arrange the 48 hour visa in Tana (3 passport photos needed) and make your stop on the way home.

Page 71   **Shortages** All visitors report that there are fewer shortages these days, and most 'luxury goods' are obtainable.

Page 73	**Money** Ted Jackson found more banks accepting pounds sterling than he expected, and recommends taking money in sterling travellers cheques (I would still take a fair amount of cash in dollars for smaller towns or emergencies, and don't expect there always to be a bank. Carry enough cash).

Page 80   **Health** It has been pointed out that the water in Tana and large towns is treated, so should be OK to drink. You may anyway prefer to use water-purifying tablets or bottled water.

Some people are disturbed that Jane Wilson is so casual about Bilharzia. Although I cannot speak for Jane (who is abroad) I should point out that she *is* a doctor who studied bilharzia in Madagascar, but of course medical opinions vary.

One intrepid traveller caught jiggers. These are female sand fleas, which resemble maggots and burrow into your toes to feed on your blood while becoming vastly pregnant with eggs. Before they reach this stage they should be dug out with a sterilised needle (disinfect the wound thoroughly to prevent infection). Sand fleas, as you might guess, are found on damp sand, usually by fresh water. They attack the feet of those walking barefoot, but other parts of the body that have been in contact with the sand may also be affected.

Page 87   **Airfares** If still available at the old price, the Air Tourist Pass is a great bargain. A round trip to Nosy Be from Tana now costs £200.

Page 96   **Airport formalities** Everyone comments that these are now very much easier and quicker (half an hour arriving or leaving) but it does no harm to be prepared in case this blissful situation changes.

Page 109   **Antsirabe** Raniero Leto, a keen horseman, recommends this town as a riding centre. 'Horses are to be found near the Hotel des Thermes, the stables being near the Parc de l'Est. Always check the horses without their saddles on. If you want to do any serious riding, contact Jean-Michel Rakotondrafara, Lot 23 A 38 Est de La Gare.'

Lake Itasy This lake and its surrounding area is accessible by good road (on the way to Tsiroanomandidy) and has been recommended by a couple of travellers as being particularly beautiful.

Page 117 **Ranomafana** The rainforest here will almost certainly be designated a reserve in 1990. New scientific discoveries are being made all the time, including the finding – and tagging – of aye-aye! The access is 6 km uphill from the town 2 km beyond the village of Ambotilahy where guides are available and strongly recommended (it is easy to get lost in the forest). The 1988 rate for a guide was 3,000 FMG. A Tourist Reception Centre is being built at the entrance to the forest.

Bentioky 'There is a very comfortable Malagasy-style hotel near the petrol station. 4,000 FMG and full of character. Food great, and a local guide will take you to the tomb of a famous judge Zama Joseph; about one hour's walk.' (John Jones.)

Ampanihy There's a nice malagasy hotel for 6,000 FMG. The hotel runs rather overpriced tours to see the very impressive king's tomb of Fanilina Joseph.

There is some antagonism towards foreigners in this area. Don't take photos without permission, and better still try to interact with the local people.

Page 132 **Fort Dauphin** Julian Tennant points out that September and October are the windy months in this area. 'Never less than a force 5 gale and usually force 7 … very unpleasant and made life there pretty good hell.'

Where to Stay
A very smart new hotel, the Kaleta, has recently opened. In the middle of town, this luxury-class hotel is intended to be the centre piece for a tourist revival in the south-east of the country.

Julian Tennant recommends the newly renovated Motel Libanana (by the excellent beach of the same name) which is now owned by M. de Heaulme. 'Run by Monsieur and Madame Rivert, it is by far the best hotel at Fort Dauphin. More bungalows are being built.'

Page 140 **Moramanga** The Grand Hotel is comfortable but rather noisy. Good food at *Au Coq d'Or*, close by. Excellent fresh-water fish; clean and recommended. (Ted Jackson.)

Page 142	**Train to Tamatave** The first class fare is $10.
Page 147	**Mahavelona** 'We stayed at *Au Gentil Pecheur*, another cluster of beach chalets a few hundred metres south of Motel Hotel. It has an excellent restaurant with delicious fish. The bamboo chalets are fitted with mosquito nets and oil lamps and there is a good beach – quite strong currents, though. Single chalets 4,500 FMG, dinner 1,500 – 2,000 FMG.' (Ted Jackson.)
Page 149	**Maroansetra** Raniero Leto recommends Le Tropical restaurant. Its manager, Alain Costo, has a small boat and will take you to Nosy Mangabe for around 40,000 FMG. Mr Patrice, who runs the Hotel Coco Beach (I'm not sure if he's the same as my Mr Fidel!) owns three large boats which travel between Tamatave, Ile Sainte Marie, Manara, and Maroansetra. They sail at irregular times. The journey to Ste Marie takes 15 hours from Maroansetra and costs around 10,000 FMG. Large groups can use M.Patrice's boat to go to Nosy Mangabe for 7,000 FMG.
Page 165	**Ste Marie** *Where to stay* (updated by Raniero Leto): Lakana has rebuilt bungalows destroyed by a cyclone; now sturdier construction. The hotel has an artificially deepened swimming pool at the end of the jetty. The water otherwise is too shallow to swim in this part of the island. Prices around 10,000 FMG for a 5 person bungalow. La Crique. Much better location. Around 9,500 FMG double. Lafalafa, Ambodifototra. Expanding and developing another site as well. Double room 4,500 FMG.
Page 196	Raniero Leto spent some time in the south west, and sent the following information: **Belo sur Tsiribihina** The name means 'Where one must not dive' due to crocodiles (now depleted). Near Bekopaka there are said to be magnificent gorges and baobabs, also Vazimba cemeteries (but no first hand information available). **Miandrivazo** The hottest place in Madagascar. There is a hotel and restaurant, and a Greek man who will take tourists down the river Tsirihina to Belo – for a price. **Belo sur Mer** Recommended for its beautiful beaches.